Aloha Betrayed

T0373309

A JOHN HOPE FRANKLIN CENTER BOOK

AMERICAN ENCOUNTERS / GLOBAL INTERACTIONS

A series edited by Gilbert M. Joseph and Emily S. Rosenberg

This series aims to stimulate critical perspectives and fresh interpretive frameworks for scholarship on the history of the imposing global presence of the United States. Its primary concerns include the deployment and contestation of power, the construction and deconstruction of cultural and political borders, the fluid meanings of intercultural encounters, and the complex interplay between the global and the local. American Encounters seeks to strengthen dialogue and collaboration between historians of U.S. international relations and area studies specialists.

The series encourages scholarship based on multiarchival historical research. At the same time, it supports a recognition of the representational character of all stories about the past and promotes critical inquiry into issues of subjectivity and narrative. In the process, American Encounters strives to understand the context in which meanings related to nations, cultures, and political economy are continually produced, challenged, and reshaped.

HOOHUIAINA.

McKINLEY, Peresidena,
ika Huipuia.

aku imua o ka Aha Senate
kahi no ka Hoohui aku ia
uia i oleloia, no ka noomooia
kemaba, M. H. 1897; nolaila,
lakou na inoa malalo iho, na
e makaainana a poe noho hoi
na _____. Mokupuni o
, he poe lala no ka AHAHUI
NA WAHINE O KO HAWAII PAE-
ae i like ka manao makee me ko
kue aku nei me ka manao ikaika
o ko Hawaii Paeaina i oleloia ia
oia ma kekahi ano a loina paha.

To His Excellency WILLIAM McKINLEY, Presiden
and the Senate, of the United States of America.

GREETING:—

WHEREAS, there has been submitted to the Sena
the United States of America a Treaty for the Annex
of the Hawaiian Islands to the said United Sta
America, for consideration at its regular session in
ber, A. D. 1897; therefore,

WE, the undersigned, native Hawaiian wom
zens and residents of the District of _____ P~~
Island of _____ Hawaii _____, who are mem
WOMEN'S HAWAIIAN PATRIOTIC LEAGUE OF T
IAN ISLANDS, and other women who are in sym
the said League, earnestly protest against the
of the said Hawaiian Islands to the said Un
America in any form or shape.

o Lilia Aholo
Kakauolelo Secretary.

Mrs Kuaihelani
Pere

INOA—NAME.	AGE.	INOA—NAME.
Apua Pea	29	Mrs Kaluahine
ha	17	Miss Kaini
anamahio	14	Mrs, Kahau
pa	14	Namui,
aho	3	Miss Kali
uka	15	Miss Lili
Mrs Mele	20	Mrs Kao
Kehukai	35	Miss Kau
Hia	13	Kau
Wiliama	18	Mrs K
Kahaihamita	36	Mrs
Kaleiahua	40	Kal
Mabeka	16	Mrs

Noenoe K. Silva

Aloha Betrayed

Native Hawaiian Resistance to American Colonialism

Duke University Press   Durham & London   2004

© 2004 Duke University Press

All rights reserved

Printed in the United States of America

on acid-free paper ∞

Designed by C. H. Westmoreland

Typeset in Galliard

by Keystone Typesetting, Inc.

Library of Congress Cataloging-in-

Publication Data appear on the last

printed page of this book.

No ka poʻe i aloha i ka ʻāina

Contents

ACKNOWLEDGMENTS ix

Introduction 1

1 Early Struggles with the Foreigners 15

2 *Ka Hoku o ka Pakipika:* Emergence of the Native
Voice in Print 45

3 The Merrie Monarch: Genealogy, Cosmology, Mele,
and Performance Art as Resistance 87

4 The Antiannexation Struggle 123

5 The Queen of Hawai'i Raises Her Solemn
Note of Protest 164

APPENDIX A Text of the Objectives of *Nupepa
Kuokoa*, as Published Therein, October 1861 205

APPENDIX B Songs Composed by Queen Lili'uokalani
during Her Imprisonment 207

NOTES 209

GLOSSARY 237

BIBLIOGRAPHY 241

INDEX 253

Acknowledgments

I am grateful to all of the many spirits, minds, and hands that have contributed to this work. Among them are Deane Neubauer, chair of my dissertation committee, who helped to shape the original project. Jorge Fernandes and Jonathan Goldberg-Hiller read and commented on countless drafts. Sankaran Krishna, Anne Keala Kelly, Gabrielle Welford, Esther Figueroa, and Michael J. Shapiro also read drafts and provided many valuable suggestions. I thank Sally Engle Merry for careful reading and excellent advice. The late, dearly missed Jim Bartels generously shared his knowledge, especially of Queen Liliʻuokalani, based on his many years of dedicated research. Reshela DuPuis and Amy Kuʻuleialoha Stillman were similarly generous with their time and research. Albert J. Schütz read and proofread the entire manuscript, improving many sentences (all remaining errors are entirely my own). I benefited greatly from discussions with Kekeha Solis, Sam L. Noʻeau Warner, Kaleikoa Kāʻeo, Kerry Laiana Wong, Phyllis Turnbull, Lynette Cruz, David Keanu Sai, Kekuni Blaisdell, Lia O'Neill Keawe, kuʻualoha hoʻomanawanui, J. Kēhaulani Kauanui, Laura Lehuanani Yim, Lilikalā Kameʻeleihiwa, Meleanna Meyer, Annette Ipo Wong, Houston Wood, Jonathan Kamakawiwoʻole Osorio, Ty Kāwika Tengan, Haunai-Kay Trask, Tom Coffman, Nālani Minton, Kathy Ferguson, Neal Milner, Nevzat Soguk, J. J. Leilani Basham, Lydia Kualapai, and Gayle Brackin, as well as students and members of the activist community who listened and raised questions. I am also grateful to Brian Richardson for his intellectual and emotional as well as technical support. The love, care, and irrepressible spirits of my mother, Betty (Decker) Williams, and Myrna Minatodani contributed to this work in countless ways.

Joan Hori, curator of the Hawaiian Collection at Hamilton Library at the University of Hawai'i at Mānoa, has greatly influenced this work. She patiently made suggestions about sources, tracked down references, and gave me steady encouragement and support. Karen Peacock, Nancy Morris, and Chieko Tachinata of the University of Hawai'i at Mānoa and the librarians and archivists at Bishop Museum also assisted, especially Patrice Belcher, Linda Laurence, Janet Short, Stuart Ching, and DeSoto Brown. Marilyn Kanani Reppun of the Hawaiian Mission Children's Society Library and Barbara Dunn of the Hawaiian Historical Society each brought crucial items to my attention. I appreciate the assistance of the archivists and staff at the Hawai'i State Archives, especially Jason Achiu, Vicky Nihi, and Marlene B. D. Paahao, and that of Ed Schamel at the U.S. National Archives and Records Adminstration.

I am grateful as well to the Ford Foundation, the National Science Foundation, the Department of Political Science, and Dean Richard Dubanoski of the College of Social Sciences at the University of Hawai'i at Mānoa for substantial support. Heartfelt thanks to Ken Wissoker of Duke University Press for believing in this book and patiently and skillfully seeing it through. I also appreciate the careful and talented work of the copy editor, Jean Brady.

I am also indebted to those who kept my body and mind in one piece through the difficult times that attended the writing of this book: Kristine Gebrowsky, Clayton Chong, Michael Bridge, Carol Wood, Haunani Kauka, and Keoho Lewis, and my colleagues in the Department of Hawaiian and Indo-Pacific Languages and Literatures at the University of Hawai'i at Mānoa.

And finally, I am most deeply grateful to Dore Minatodani for all her research and tech support, and most of all for keeping our lives lit with love and humor.

Introduction

One of the most persistent and pernicious myths of Hawaiian history is that the Kanaka Maoli (Native Hawaiians) passively accepted the erosion of their culture and the loss of their nation. In 1984, in an article in the *Journal of Pacific History*, for example, Caroline Ralston claimed that the maka'āinana (ordinary people) made "no outspoken protest or resistance against the series of events which appear to have been highly detrimental to [their] well-being."[1] Haunani-Kay Trask relates a story of sharing a panel with a historian from the United States who, like Ralston, claimed that "there was no real evidence for [resistance by Kanaka Maoli]."[2] Popular historian Gavan Daws dismissed Kanaka resistance in a single paragraph, even though in the same book he continued to document it.[3] Ralph Kuykendall interpreted King Kalākaua's and Queen Emma's resistance to takeover by the United States as anti-haole racism.[4] But as Amy Ku'uleialoha Stillman has observed, "Hawaiian-language sources suggest a remarkable history of cultural resilience and resistance to assimilation."[5]

This book refutes the myth of passivity through documentation and study of the many forms of resistance by the Kanaka Maoli to political, economic, linguistic, and cultural oppression, beginning with the arrival of Captain Cook until the struggle over the "annexation," that is, the military occupation of Hawai'i by the United States in 1898. The main basis for this study is the large archive of Kanaka writing contained in the microfilmed copies of over seventy-five newspapers in the Hawaiian language produced between 1834 and 1948. In the course of my undergraduate and master's degree study programs, I could not help but notice that many of the Hawaiian newspapers are political in nature. The idea for this study originated during a course in postcolonial theory in my doctoral program, when I began to read the historiography of Hawai'i "against the grain," to use the term of Edward Said. What I read in the historiography did not concur with what I had seen in the Hawaiian-language papers: Kānaka Maoli hardly appeared in history at all.

Trask has characterized Hawaiian historiography as "the West's view of itself through the degradation of my own past."[6] The myth of nonresistance was created in part because mainstream historians have studiously avoided the wealth of material written in Hawaiian, as Nancy Morris has carefully detailed.[7] It is easier not to see a struggle if one reads accounts written by only one side, yet since the arrival of Captain Cook there have always been (at least) two sides of a struggle going on. The Europeans and Euro-Americans sought to exploit the land and subjugate the people, and the people fought back in a variety of ways. The archives in English, however, present a preponderance of material on one side of the struggle — that of the colonizers. When the Hawaiian-language materials are examined, however, it is immediately apparent that throughout the eighteenth and nineteenth centuries there was resistance to every aspect of colonialism, and that for every exertion of oppressive and colonizing power there was resistance. When viewed through a Kanaka-centered lens, it appears that from the first page of even the English-language history books the Kānaka are resisting: the killing of Cook, for example, was resistance to the attempted subjugation of the Mōʻī (ruler) of Hawaiʻi Island.

How is it that the history of struggle has been omitted to such a great extent from Hawaiian historiography? Part of the answer lies in the nature of the colonial takeover itself. As Ngugi wa Thiongʻo has explained, "the biggest weapon wielded . . . by imperialism . . . is the cultural bomb. The effect of a cultural bomb is to annihilate a people's belief in their names, in their languages, in their environment, in their heritage of struggle, in their unity, in their capacities and ultimately in themselves."[8]

Beginning in the mid-nineteenth century, the Hawaiian language was disparaged as inadequate to the task of "progress." After the political coup of 1893, the U.S.-identified oligarchy outlawed public and private schools taught in the Hawaiian language, and English became the only acceptable language for business and government. By the mid-twentieth century, the idea that English was the language of Hawai'i seemed natural, especially because, except by some persistent Kānaka, Hawai'i was no longer regarded as a separate nation with its own people having their own history and language. When historians and others composed their narratives, they "naturally" conducted their research using only the English-language sources. One of my goals in this work is to denaturalize these notions and practices, because it is still possible to obtain a doctorate in history specializing in Hawai'i and not be required to learn the Hawaiian language or use Hawaiian-language sources.

Why does it matter that this history of resistance is documented and analyzed? Why does it matter that we read what Kanaka Maoli wrote in their own language a hundred and more years ago? We might just as well ask: How do a people come to know who they are? How do a colonized people recover from the violence done to their past by the linguicide that accompanies colonialism? Although stories are passed on individually in families,[9] much is lost, especially during times of mass death due to epidemics. When the stories told at home do not match up with the texts at school, students are taught to doubt the oral versions. The epistemology of the school system is firmly Western in nature: what is written counts. When the stories can be validated, as happens when scholars read the literature in Hawaiian and make the findings available to the community, people begin to recover from the wounds caused by that disjuncture in their consciousness.

In 1998, for example, an ad hoc committee of community members, of which I was a part, approached the Bishop Museum in Honolulu with an idea to educate the public about the 1897 antiannexation petition, which during the course of this research I had located in the U.S. National Archives.[10] In response, the Bishop Museum agreed to display a reproduction of all 556 pages of the petition. Because of the publicity generated by the museum to promote the exhibit, the Kanaka Maoli community throughout the islands suddenly knew of the existence of mass opposition to annexation in 1897. I was then deluged with telephone calls every day from strangers thanking me. In the phone calls and in person, many individuals told me that they knew or suspected that their grandparents or great-grandparents had been opposed to the U.S. takeover, but that they had had no proof before this. One woman clutched her petition book to her chest and proclaimed, "Now we will never forget again." The petition and the story of the several hui that organized it changed the commemoration of the 1898 annexation in many ways. Activist David Keanu Sai coined the slogan of the commemoration: "We are who we were." The petition, inscribed with the names of everyone's kūpuna, gave people permission from their ancestors to participate in the quest for national sovereignty. More important, it affirmed for them that their kūpuna had not stood by idly, apathetically, while their nation was taken from them. Instead, contrary to every history book on the shelf, they learned that their ancestors had, as James Kaulia put it, taken up the honorable field of struggle. For people today, the petition represents the political struggle of the makaʻāinana, for although the hui were led by aliʻi (rulers) and kaukaualiʻi (aliʻi of lesser rank) it was the collective power of the makaʻāinana — 21,269 signatures — that gave it its force.

The petitions have also spurred continuing political action. They were used as documentation in a writ of mandamus to the U.S. Supreme Court (which the Court, however, dismissed), and at the Permanent Court of Arbitration at The Hague.[11] They continue to be used to educate and organize those who are reluctant to participate in discussions of Hawaiian sovereignty. The Hawaiian Civic Club of Honolulu, for example, said that the petitions inspired the middle-class Kānaka Maoli. They also accompanied indigenous-rights activists to The Hague Appeal for Peace Civil Society Conference in 1999.

But it is not just the Kanaka Maoli who can benefit from this knowledge: the untruths and half-truths of history have harmed the descendants of the colonizer along with the colonized, although in different ways. As James Baldwin wrote: "If I am not what I've been told I am, then it means that *you're* not what you thought you were *either!*"[12] If the colonizers continue to lie about history, then Baldwin says to them, "You are mad." On the other hand, he responds, if the curriculum in schools were to be changed to reflect the contributions of the colonized, "you would be liberating not only [the colonized], you'd be liberating white people who know nothing about their own history."[13]

The story of the three hui that organized the petition was not written down anywhere in English until now.[14] The contest over language was and is part of the anticolonial struggle. The hui of 1889–1898 communicated with each other in their mother tongue. It was easier that way because it was harder for the oppressor to decipher. Songs, poems, and stories with the potential for kaona, or "hidden meanings," presented even greater opportunities to express anticolonial sentiments. People made use of these forms, and they created and maintained their national solidarity through publication of these and more overtly political essays in newspapers.

There is no access to this body of thought except through the Hawaiian language. The Hawaiian newspapers have generally been mined for ethnological information, but their political content has been overlooked. As long as we read the papers solely for ethnological detail the Kanaka Maoli of the nineteenth century remain the still and silent objects of ethnology. It is only when we begin to read their political writings that the figures spring to life as speaking subjects. The most important item in my methodological toolbox, therefore, has been simply to read what the Kanaka Maoli wrote. They took great pains to write it all down, perhaps foreseeing the need to establish their presence in history.

This book, then, is simultaneously a critique of colonial historiography and, as Foucault puts it, "an insurrection of subjugated knowledges."[15] I focus on the stories, editorials, and essays, as well as the songs and poetry produced in Hawaiian and printed in the newspapers. While songs and poetry are often undervalued as historical sources, they are important for this kind of work. Vilsoni Hereniko points out that "as in other parts of Polynesia, poetry contained historical information that was not always understood by the general public, largely because it used archaic expressions, metaphors, and figures of speech."[16] Attending to such less well-understood genres of resistance writing often yields insights unavailable from other sources. Said has shown how powerful and important narratives are in both the colonial and anticolonial projects, and Michel de Certeau has also observed how stories can function as resistance.[17]

As for colonial historiography, Lawrence Levine has observed that historiography itself was for a long time conceived as "narrative storytelling about those whose power, position, and influence was palpable."[18] Within that historiography, the ordinary Kanaka Maoli were ignored as insignificant and, worse, portrayed as passive, helpless, and backward people whose colonization was at least in part their own fault (and yet, paradoxically, supposedly to their benefit as well). Following Ashis Nandy, I too "reject the model of the gullible, hopeless victim[s] of colonialism caught in the hinges of history. I see [them] as fighting [their] own battle for survival in [their] own way, sometimes consciously, sometimes by default."[19]

Foucault demonstrated that power is not simply something static held in the hands of the elite but rather is mobile throughout society and always resisted. Although Foucault did not address colonialism specifically, his work has undoubtedly opened up space to effectively contest "the tyranny of globalising discourses" so that anticolonial scholarship, including this work, can take place.[20] Presuming that a history of struggle in Hawai'i, as elsewhere, was suppressed rather than nonexistent allowed me to search it out.[21] An examination of the activities, speech, and writings of the Kanaka Maoli, cannot help but reveal that these people were not the "simple-hearted victims of colonialism [but] participants in a moral and cognitive venture against oppression."[22] Providing that revelation is what I attempt to do in this book.

My theoretical and methodological framework begins with Foucault's ideas about power and resistance. Instead of studying the institutions of power as is done in traditional history and political science, Foucault concentrated on the mechanisms of power at the end places where they are exerted.[23] He suggested that the study of the links between rationalization and power can be productive when specific rationales for "fundamental experience[s]" are examined, and he lists those experiences as "madness, illness, death, crime, sexuality, and so forth."[24] In this study I add colonialism to that list, and through an examination of the speech and other acts of the colonized I attempt to illuminate the links cited by Foucault. In "The Subject and Power" Foucault states that "in order to understand what power relations are about, perhaps we should investigate the forms of resistance."[25]

Michel de Certeau and Lawrence Levine point to the ways that subjugated peoples, while appearing to become assimilated into the dominant culture, simultaneously resist domination and retain and reproduce their traditions. Certeau notes how "the [indigenous] Indians . . . often *made of* the rituals, representations, and laws imposed on them something quite different from what their conquerors [the Spanish] had in mind . . . They were *other* within the very colonization that outwardly assimilated them; their use of the dominant social order deflected its power."[26] Levine "found that, every time [he] focused on a new form of cultural expression that seemed to function as a mechanism for deep acculturation to the larger society, [he] discovered important degrees of cultural revitalization as well."[27] In addition, Partha Chatterjee found that in the case of India's anticolonial nationalism, people created their "own domain of sovereignty within colonial society" through "dividing the world of social institutions and practices into two domains — the material and the spiritual," the latter of which he calls an "inner domain bearing the 'essential' marks of cultural identity."[28] In the following pages I show that the Kanaka Maoli were able to preserve this inner domain of cultural identity, and that the Hawaiian language often served as an area from which "the colonial intruder had to be kept out."[29] Hula (dance), moʻolelo (history, legend, story) and especially genealogy contributed to that inner domain, which was carefully guarded and preserved so that the Kanaka Maoli of today have a spiritual/cultural identity of their own on which to base their new anticolonial movement.

Chandra Mohanty, Anne McClintock, Gayatri Chakravorty Spivak, and Ruth Mabanglo have shown how valuable it is to notice the ways that women are kept out of colonial and postcolonial histories, and how important it is to search out their contributions.[30] Spivak asked: "Can the subaltern speak?," and I have had to grapple with what she meant by that question, as well as by her conclusion that they cannot, as I have attempted to represent what the Kanaka Maoli were saying at various times.[31] In nineteenth-century Hawaiʻi, as elsewhere, women's public writings were small in volume relative to men's. Like the Kanaka Maoli overall, however, women are always present if we look for them, and so I have attempted to do so. Women were active politically in the antiannexation struggle (chapter 4), but their activities remain obscure in the decades before.

In "Can the Subaltern Speak" Spivak relates a story about the kinds of covert communications that the female subaltern is sometimes forced to engage in. She tells of a young woman who participated in the armed struggle for India's independence. The young woman committed suicide but waited until she was menstruating to do so, so that her suicide could not be misinterpreted as brought on by an illegitimate pregnancy. While the young woman — the subaltern — was unable to speak overtly, her message is clear. Spivak understood her, and recounts and interprets the details of her death.[32] Kanaka women also engage in veiled communications, but of other sorts. One of the main forms of such communication was through the composition of poems and songs that were published in the newspaper (chapters 2 and 5). Other efforts were less veiled; for example Ke Kamāliʻiwahine Poʻomaikelani headed both the Board of Genealogy and the Hale Nauā for King Kalākaua (chapter 3). Women also resisted colonialism by becoming the keepers of the knowledge of hula, by sewing the national flag into quilts (chapter 4), and by memorizing and telling the moʻolelo of Hiʻiakaikapoliopele (chapter 2). Thus, although their communications are harder to discern and to decipher than those of men, they did speak. In light of my research, I would add these ideas to Spivak's question: in the situations in which the subaltern cannot speak overtly, in what ways *do* they speak? and in what ways do we listen?

In this book the Kanaka Maoli, both women and men, makaʻāinana and aliʻi, speak in a variety of ways, some of which were not understood and not *meant* to be understood by the colonizers. The word "kaona," as mentioned above, means "hidden meaning, as in Hawaiian poetry; concealed reference, as to a person, thing or place; [and] words with double meanings."[33] It is a well-known characteristic of the Hawaiian language that is generally spoken of in reference to mele but that also is common in writing and in everyday speech. An awareness of the political functions of kaona, especially the possibilities for veiled communication, helps in analyzing the words and actions of the Kanaka Maoli. If the plantation luna (foreman) and haole minister did not understand the hidden meaning in a phrase or a song, people could then, in the words of Levine, "express deeply held feelings which ordinarily could not be verbalized."[34] As Levine observed among slaves in the United States, they used "the subtleties of their song to comment on the whites around them with a freedom denied them in other forms of expression."[35] By employing kaona, the Kanaka Maoli could use everyday speech and writing to the same ends. Kaona, while useful for such individual expression of feelings, was also crucial in creating and maintaining national solidarity against the colonial maneuvers of the U.S. missionaries, the oligarchy, and the U.S. politicians. Without knowledge of the cultural codes in Hawaiian, foreigners who understood the language could still be counted on to miss the kaona. This became visible in the Kalākaua era: while the national narratives were literally put on parade, the foreigners were unable to interpret them.

Colonialism in Hawai'i, as elsewhere, is complex. It affected ali'i, kahuna (experts, healers), and maka'āinana, women and men, and residents of different islands differently. Hawai'i's people were a homogeneous group, even before European contact. Further, the strategies that ali'i used to resist subordination were markedly different from the tactics used by the maka'āinana.[36] Residents of urban Honolulu likewise experienced oppression and resisted differently from those in rural areas. In the country areas, traditional practices such as worship of the volcano akua wahine (female deity) Pele, for example, went on comparatively undetected and undisturbed. Meanwhile in urban Honolulu, where such cultural practices were subject to greater surveillance and punishment, and where printing presses were available for hire, Kanaka Maoli established their own newspapers. In times of crisis, however, such as the antiannexation struggle of 1897–1898, ali'i and maka'āinana, women and men, and urban and rural folk worked together in united resistance efforts.

Colonial historiography, moreover, does not simply rationalize the past and suppress the knowledge of the oppressed. Hawai'i is not a postcolonial but a (neo?) colonial state, and historiography is one of the most powerful discourses that justifies the continued occupation of Hawai'i by the United States today. For those of us living with the legacies and the continuing exercise of power characteristic of colonialism, it is crucial to understand power relations in order to escape or overcome their effects and, further, to understand the resistance strategies and tactics of the past in order to use them and improve on them. The reinterpretation, or placement, of mo'olelo in the oral tradition as part of a national narrative was a strategy that Kalākaua used; this book attempts to add the po'e aloha 'āina and their stories to the national narrative—in order to create national heroes from men and women formerly unknown.

Resistance and nationalism have been intertwined throughout the last two hundred years of the history of Hawai'i. Creating a nation in a form familiar to Europe and the United States was a necessary strategy of resistance to colonization because there was a chance that the nineteenth-century Mana Nui, or "Great Powers" might recognize national sovereignty. More foreign-seeming forms of government were too easily condemned as primitive and backward, as is attested to by the fate of peoples discursively represented as "tribes" rather than "nations." But as Certeau noticed in the case of the American Indians, the Kanaka

Maoli created their nation in their own ways. The monarchy overlaid a well-functioning aliʻi system, in which, in the early days, women still exercised political power. The pattern that emerges in the following chapters is one of strategic accommodation to the Western ideas of nationhood and government, combined with an insistence on the value of Kanaka cultural identity.

The history of the early accommodations to and struggles with foreigners over land, religion, and sovereignty is set out in chapter 1. Simultaneously, I have used Hawaiian-language texts as much as possible to critique the mainstream historiography of the period, roughly 1778–1860. This examination provides the background historical information for the chapters that follow.

In chapter 2, I examine the emergence of the first newspaper written, edited, and published by an association of Kānaka Maoli that is free of missionary censorship or influence. *Ka Hoku o ka Pakipika* (1861–1863) shocked the missionary establishment when those they had viewed as rather passive objects of their civilizing attentions suddenly transformed themselves into speaking subjects through this newspaper. The church establishment immediately reacted by condemning the paper in print and from the pulpit. Study of the struggle for voice in print reveals direct and indirect confrontations with the missionary establishment, as well as a growing pride in Kanaka traditions. Moʻolelo and mele that had been suppressed reemerged to inspire and to bind the lāhui Kanaka together, and cultural practices that the missionaries tried to extinguish were enacted again in print. *Ka Hoku o ka Pakipika* began a tradition of opposition newspapers in Hawaiian that lasted into the twentieth century. As Certeau says, "it is impossible to take speech and to retain it without a taking of power."[37]

Chapter 3 illustrates how King Kalākaua's cultural revival resisted a rising American-identified oligarchy who were escalating the attempted destruction of Kanaka identity and culture. Kalākaua built on the groundwork laid by *Ka Hoku o ka Pakipika*, when he directly confronted the missionaries by bringing into print the *Kumulipo*, the ancient chant of creation, and the hula and moʻolelo into public performance. These practices reinterpreted and enacted moʻolelo from the oral tradition as national narratives: the stories of figures such as Kawelo, Māui, and Kamehameha emphasized traditional leadership values and the motif of the lesser line ascending to rule. Kalākaua's cultural activities were valu-

able and increased his popularity, but his efforts were not enough. In
fact, his increased popularity most likely prompted coercive action on
the part of the missionary sons who virtually deposed him.

Chapter 4 is the story of the antiannexation struggle, starting from
Kalākaua's overthrow and extending to the U.S. military occupation in
1898. Aloha ʻāina (love of the land) was the cornerstone of resistance in
this era. It expressed the desire that makaʻāinana and aliʻi shared for self-
rule as opposed to rule by the colonial oligarchy of settlers or the military rule of the United States. At the time, self-rule necessarily took the
form of nationhood, but aloha ʻāina (which continues) encompasses
more than nationalism and is not an exact fit with the English word
"patriotism," the usual translation. Where nationalism and patriotism
tend to exalt the virtues of a people or a race, aloha ʻāina exalts the land.
It refers to the appreciation of the beauty of this land, about which both
aliʻi and makaʻāinana have composed hundreds, perhaps thousands, of
songs. Every island, every district, every valley and stream has had songs
composed lauding their beauty, but aloha ʻāina goes beyond love of
beauty as well. The Kanaka Maoli have a genealogical, familial relationship to the land. The islands were said to have been conceived and born
like human beings, of the same parents, Papahānaumoku "Papa who
gives birth to islands" and Wākea, the sky father, and Hoʻohōkūkalani,
"she who creates the stars in the heavens." The poʻe aloha ʻāina adapted
their concept of aloha ʻāina to the Euro-American concepts and structures of nationhood and nationalism as resistance to colonization, although they knew that it was those very structures that were overtaking
them. They continued to create and recreate the inner domain of spiritual and cultural identity based on their love for the land, even while
operating within the U.S. political arena.

Ke Aliʻi ʻAi Moku Liliʻuokalani was the central actor in their organizing. Chapter 5 reviews some of the genres of resistance that she used
as she attempted to rescue her nation from the United States. One of her
many battles was over how she and her people were represented in the
U.S. press. She countered those racist representations with writings of
her own and by her physical presence in society in Washington, D.C.
She also made a series of formal protests, whose impact has been minimized in mainstream historiography. Just as important, as the lāhui's
beloved aliʻi nui she communicated through mele with her people even
while imprisoned, and in the chapter I show how she worked closely

with her people, even over long distances, on their antiannexation strategies.

LANGUAGE AND TRANSLATION ISSUES

In the words of Larry Kimura, "whenever Hawaiian is translated into English, the English words used add cultural connotations to the idea conveyed, while eliminating intended connotations and meanings of the original Hawaiian."[38] Because I am basing my research on Hawaiian-language sources and yet writing this book in English, I have had to engage in a great deal of translation and interpretation. Much of that translation is unsatisfactory, however, because it is impossible to convey all of the cultural coding that English strips away, and equally impossible to avoid the Western cultural coding that English adds. In this volume I have tried to give more than one translation where it is necessary, and I have also provided a glossary to assist readers. "Pono," for example, has a multitude of meanings, including "good; appropriate; balance; well-being," and many more. Sometimes several of the meanings are intended by the author, and to choose one English word does considerable violence to the text. Further, sometimes it is not perfectly clear from the context which or how many of the possible English glosses come closest to the meaning understood by Hawaiian readers. Writers of Hawaiian, moreover, value multiplicity in meaning and thus often choose words specifically because many meanings can be derived from them. Although for ease of reading I have had to add definitions, there are fundamental limitations in doing so that need to be taken into account.

I have chosen to use several Hawaiian terms for "Hawaiian person/people" throughout, mainly the term "Kanaka Maoli." This is an old term seen frequently in the nineteenth-century Hawaiian-language newspapers. "Kanaka" means "person," and "maoli" means "real; true; original; indigenous." "Kanaka" by itself also means "Hawaiian," especially when used in contrast with "haole" when meant as "foreigner" (kanaka denotes the singular or the category, while kānaka is the plural). Kanaka Maoli was used officially at least as early as 1852,[39] and many examples of it occur in *Ka Hoku o ka Pakipika* (see chapter 3). Further, not all of the diverse Kanaka Maoli like to be called Hawaiian because that term derives from the island of Hawai'i, and it is only because

Kamehameha was from that island that the archipelago took that name. Using the term Kanaka Maoli is also beneficial because it evokes linguistic and familial relationships with other people of Oceania: for example, Maoli is cognate with Māori of Aotearoa and Māʻohi of Tahiti. It reminds us that the Hawaiian islands are centered in the Pacific (and not an appendage of the U.S. West Coast). "ʻŌiwi" is another word that I use occasionally and interchangeably with Kanaka and Kanaka Maoli.

I have not italicized Hawaiian words in the text in keeping with the recent movement to resist making the native tongue appear foreign in writing produced in and about a native land and people.[40] Readers will also notice that not all of the Hawaiian text has modern orthography (i.e., the ʻokina to mark the glottal stop and the macron to mark the long vowel). I choose to quote text as is without imposing the marks, which were not developed until the mid-twentieth century. This allows readers literate in Hawaiian to see the original spelling and perhaps glean alternative and/or additional meanings. Particularly for names of persons, I conservatively avoid using the marks, except in cases where such spelling has become standard (e.g., Kalākaua) or where the meaning of the name has been explained or is obvious.

Finally, although this book is primarily a study of resistance, two other themes emerge here. First, the Kanaka Maoli of the nineteenth century, in addition to strenuously resisting every encroachment on their lands and life ways, consciously and continuously organized and directed their energies to preserving the independence of their country. Second, throughout the nineteenth century, print media, particularly newspapers, functioned as sites for broad social communication, political organizing, and the perpetuation of the native language and culture. It has often been noted that the change from orality to literacy has eroded native forms of thought and expression, especially due to the fixing and consequent reduction in possible meanings and versions of text. Hereniko has written, for example, that "the written word has undermined the fluidity of indigenous history. Oratory allowed for debate and negotiation . . . [while] the written word fixes the truth."[41] For the Kanaka ʻŌiwi of Hawaiʻi nei, however, who observed the passing away of their relatives and friends in genocidal numbers, writing, especially newspapers, was a way of ensuring that their knowledge was passed on to future generations. It is with profound respect and gratitude for their wisdom and foresight that I have engaged in this work.

1

Early Struggles with the Foreigners

[Stories are] the method colonized people use to assert their own identity and the existence of their own history. The main battle in imperialism is over land, of course; but when it came to who owned the land, who had the right to settle and work on it, who kept it going, who won it back, and who now plans its future — these issues were reflected, contested, and even for a time, decided in narrative. — Edward Said

In this chapter I examine some of the Kanaka Maoli's early (1778–1854) struggles with the foreigners over government and land. To do so, whenever possible I use texts written by nineteenth- and early-twentieth-century Kānaka in their mother tongue. This examination provides a historical context for the chapters following, and it begins the development of several themes in the contests and resistances of the people to colonialism and imperialism. Texts written in Hawaiian allow us to see some Kanaka ways of thinking and recording the past that have previously been ignored or overlooked by historians and anthropologists unable to read Hawaiian. One of the most important recurring themes in these texts is that the Kanaka 'Ōiwi often took the tools of the colonizers and made use of them to secure their own national sovereignty and well-being. The ali'i adopted Western dress and courtly manners; they and the maka'āinana learned writing and eventually took control of the print media; and they adopted constitutionalism, codifying laws in English and American ways in order to make treaties and to be recognized as an independent nation unavailable for colonization.[1] Another important change during this period was the transformation of the meaning of "pono." In the ancient Kanaka world, pono meant that the akua, (deities) ali'i, kahuna, maka'āinana, and 'āina (land) lived in balance with each other, and that people had enough to eat and were healthy. This state of balance hinged on ali'i acting in accordance with the shared concept of pono. Later, the term was appropriated and transformed by the advent of writing and by the adoption of Western religion and government.

HISTORIOGRAPHY AND CAPTAIN COOK

The Kanaka struggles with foreigners might be said to have begun with the representative of the British drive for empire, Captain James Cook. Although the mo'olelo of Captain Cook has been exhausted in its mountains of literature in many fields of study, most of that literature relies on British accounts. Where Kanaka accounts of Cook are used at all, scholars have depended on translations, ignoring the originals written in Hawaiian. It is worthwhile, therefore, to examine the longest account of Cook written in Hawaiian, which was written by Samuel Manaiakalani Kamakau in 1866–1867 and published in a Hawaiian-language newspaper.

Gananath Obeyesekere, in *The Apotheosis of Captain Cook*, dismissed Kamakau as mimicking the beliefs of the Calvinist missionaries, categorizing his history as "one self-consciously influenced by the Evangelical charter that Kamakau himself, along with other Lahainaluna scholars, helped [Rev. Sheldon] Dibble to construct."[2] Kamakau did attend Lahainaluna school as a young adult, and he was one of the students who wrote parts of *Mooolelo Hawaii*, first published in 1838. He was a founding member of the first Hawaiian Historical Society in 1841 and went on to a career as a school teacher, legislator, and public official. But according to Thomas Thrum, Kamakau's "journalistic labors date from June, 1865," which is nearly thirty years after his student days with Rev.

Dibble.[3] Thus, as Obeyesekere himself has rightly pointed out, it is important to historicize these writings and to disaggregate them critically. During those thirty years, Kamakau became distinctly disenchanted with the Calvinist mission and converted to Catholicism. Undoubtedly, he experienced substantial intellectual development and independence of thought during that period. I am not suggesting here, however, that his account is any more valid according to the rules of haole historiography, because, as I will show, he seems to have rejected some of them, but I would suggest that his work should not be dismissed on the grounds that he had once been an enthusiastic student in the evangelical schools. How Kamakau presented the moʻolelo of Cook to his readers in 1866–1867 tells us much about how Cook was perceived within a nineteenth-century Kanaka worldview, and it is thus crucial to our understanding of the struggles over historiography, conflicting epistemologies, and ultimately, control over the land in Hawaiʻi.

The commonly cited translation of Kamakau's moʻolelo was originally done in 1961 by Mary Kawena Pukui, Lahilahi Webb, and others, drawing on work by previous authors, including Thomas Thrum. It was edited by Pukui and others and published under the title *Ruling Chiefs of Hawaiʻi*.[4] *Ruling Chiefs* is not strictly a translation of Kamakau's moʻolelo, however. The editors brought together the newspaper articles that Kamakau had written over several years and arranged them into a chronological narrative of "ruling chiefs" from Līloa through Kamehameha III. They also deleted a lot of material from Kamakau's original moʻolelo but did not mark the deletions consistently with ellipses: the reader is thus not always able to see where material has been deleted.

For example, Kamakau's translated account of the first arrival of Captain Cook starts with an ellipsis that represents seventeen pages of contextual material. This material does appear, however, in a restored version of the original narrative, *Ke Kumu Aupuni*.[5] Although *Ke Kumu Aupuni* alters Kamakau's original publication in important ways, particularly in the anachronistic imposition of diacritical marks, it presents Kamakau's narrative in a legible form without editorial reordering or deletions.

It is striking that in contrast to English-language histories Kamakau's work does not present Cook's arrival as the most important event in the narrative. Indeed, he embeds the story of Cook within the larger moʻolelo about Kamehameha I. He likewise contextualizes Kamehameha's story by recounting the moʻolelo of wars between the various aliʻi of Hawaiʻi Island, Maui, and Oʻahu. These wars were going on at the time of Kamehameha's birth and continued until well after Cook's death. Kamehameha, as is well known, became a victorious aliʻi himself, conquering nearly all of the Hawaiian islands. At the time of Cook's visits Kamehameha was a seasoned warrior but not yet a ruling aliʻi. In the December 22, 1866, installment, Kamakau narrates the moʻolelo of the battles between Kalaniʻōpuʻu, who was Kamehameha's uncle and mōʻī of Hawaiʻi Island, and Kahekili, mōʻī of Maui. The installment ends with the statement "ʻEia ka manawa kūpono no ka hiki ʻana mai o nā haole makamua ma Hawaiʻi nei'" (This was just the time of the arrival of the first white foreigners [haole] in Hawaiʻi).[6] This statement appears in quotation marks, indicating that Kamakau was quoting someone else, and, more important, that he *disagreed* with this common assertion of haole historical accounts. He goes on to tell a different history, whose sources are the ancient mele and moʻokūʻauhau (genealogies). According to those recordings of the past, which are epistemologically valid to Kamakau and other Kānaka, Cook was *not* the first white foreigner to arrive in Hawaiʻi nei. Kamakau contests at length the story that Cook and company were "nā haole makamua ma Hawaiʻi nei" (the first haole in Hawaiʻi). He first recounts many stories concerning people who traveled to Hawaiʻi from foreign lands, and the voyagers who sailed between Hawaiʻi and distant lands in the Pacific; he introduces the voyagers' stories like this: "Ma ʻaneʻi kākou e hoʻokaʻawale ai i ka moʻolelo o nā kānaka maoli o Hawaiʻi nei i holo i Kahiki, a me ko Kahiki mai i holo i Hawaiʻi nei, ʻaʻole lākou i kapa ʻia he āhole, a he haole" (Here we set out the story of the indigenous people of Hawaiʻi who sailed to Kahiki [all foreign lands] and those of Kahiki who sailed here to Hawaiʻi; they were not called āhole [a type of white fish] or haole).[7]

The stories that follow include the arrival of new aliʻi, prior to which, in Kamakau's words, "ua nele ʻo Hawaiʻi i ke aliʻi ʻole . . . ʻo nā aliʻi o Hawaiʻi, he mau aliʻi makaʻāinana, a he makaʻāinana wale nō i kekahi manawa" (Hawaiʻi was lacking because of no aliʻi . . . the aliʻi of Hawaiʻi were makaʻāinana acting as aliʻi or only makaʻāinana at times).[8] Pāʻao the kahuna brought new aliʻi from Kahiki; following him were many others who traveled back and forth to Tahiti, Sāmoa, Nuʻuhiwa, and other places. Another story, that of Kaʻulu, is an important one in the series because in the ancient mele Kaʻulu claimed to have seen the entire world, and Kamakau states that Asian and European place names are recorded in the mele. Kamakau tempers the claim, however, by saying some parts of the mele were true and some false.[9] The important point to notice here is that Kamakau and others before him knew that Kanaka Maoli had sailed on very long voyages, possibly even outside of the Pacific. Other famed travelers included Moikeha and his brother 'Olopana, who traveled between Hawai'i and Kahiki, followed by Moikeha's sons, Kila and La'amaikahiki.[10]

Among the long-distance travelers were women, who sometimes initiated the voyages. One of these was Lu'ukia, a woman born in Hawai'i. Lu'ukia, Kamakau says, was the first of her family to sail to Kahiki, where she lived with 'Olopana. When she told 'Olopana's daughter, Kaupe'a, about her handsome brother, Kauma'ili'ula, Kaupe'a desired to sail to Hawai'i to meet him. Kaupe'a then initiated a voyage, after which she met and lived with Kauma'ili'ula, became pregnant, and while pregnant sailed back to her homeland of Kuaihelani. Kauma'ili'ula later followed her and arrived on the day the child was born.[11]

Akua also appear in these travel narratives: "Ua 'ōlelo pinepine 'ia ma ka mo'olelo ka'ao a ma nā pule, a ma nā mele a ka po'e kahiko a pau, mai Kahiki mai ke akua, a mai ka lew[a] lani mai, a no ka lani mai" (It is often said in the stories and in prayers and in the songs of all the ancient people [that] the deities are from Kahiki, and from the sky, and from the heavens).[12] Among the voyagers to Hawai'i Kamakau mentions the akua Kāne, Kanaloa, Kū, and Lono, as well as Pele and her family. In the translation this part of the narrative is omitted, which means that readers of the English miss crucial information for understanding the nature of akua in the nineteenth-century Hawaiian imaginary. "Akua" here cannot actually be equivalent to what "god" signifies in the English language, because, unlike akua, gods are not physical beings that embark on journeys across oceans. The incommensurability of the two terms as highlighted in these passages could erase the debate over whether or not Cook was perceived as a god: that is, Cook may or may not have been perceived as the akua Lonoikamakahiki but this fact bears little relation to what English-language speakers of the time meant by "god." As Herb Kawainui Kāne states: "An *akua* is a being of nature, one of immense power, which may be an invisible spirit or a living person."[13] (Cook may also just have been nicknamed Lono because his ship reminded Kānaka of the mo'olelo, and because "Cook" was impossible to pronounce.)[14]

As Dipesh Chakrabarty points out, the deletion of passages works to produce and reinforce Western practices of historiography, thereby denying the reader possible glimpses into another worldview. Chakrabarty writes that "secular histories are usually produced by ignoring the signs of [divine or superhuman] presences. Such histories represent a meeting of two systems of thought, one in which the world is ultimately, that is, in the final analysis, disenchanted, and the other in which humans are not the only meaningful agents."[15] In the translation of Kamakau's work, however, the world in which humans are not the only meaningful agents, however, is hidden by this practice of deleting text that does not conform to western empiricist standards. It is accessible only in the Hawaiian language text.

Kamakau's January 19, 1867, installment begins the section on white foreigners. Even here, Cook is not the first. In the time of ʻAuanini (Kamakau did not speculate on the date), a ship of haole arrived; the captain was named Mololana, and his wife, named Māraea, was on the ship as well. Kamakau says it is not known whether they settled in the islands or sailed away again. Another ship of white foreigners arrived in the time of Wakalana, which Kamakau guesses was prior to 900 A.D. He wonders if these foreigners were the ancestors of the people in Honouliuli, Oʻahu, who have light complexions and light eyes.[16] In an ancient mele, a man named Kūkanaloa is referred to as a "kupuna haole mai Kahiki" (white foreign ancestor from Kahiki).[17] In more recent memory, in the time of Kūaliʻi, "nui nā mele inoa no Kūaliʻi e pili ana i nā haole" (there were many name songs for Kūaliʻi about the haole).[18] Kamakau dates Kūaliʻi's life from 1555 to 1730 (these dates serve only as mere guides, however, because the Kanaka system of dating was based on genealogy rather than anything analogous to the European system of years). Kamakau's final story of the arrival of haole prior to Cook is quite recent, in the time of Peleiōhōlani, whose death Kamakau gives as around 1770.[19]

It is to this substantial genealogy of travelers that Kamakau adds the story of Captain Cook, purposefully disrupting the story told by haole that Cook appeared magically and suddenly as a unique phenomenon, to the shock and amazement of the Kanaka ʻŌiwi. The narrative that Kamakau presents to us, with Cook as one in a long genealogy of travelers, is in a traditional Hawaiian vein, relying for evidence on mele from the oral tradition. His missionary teachers taught him the accepted empirical methods for writing history, and here, as with most of his other writings, he deliberately and consciously chose to use Kanaka epistemology to present the moʻolelo of Cook.

When Kamakau's text was cut up and reordered to fit the Western category of "history," the context of Cook's arrival carefully set up for the reader disappears. Just as important, and for some analyses even more so, is the fact that Kamakau's reliance on the mele and moʻokūʻauhau of the oral tradition as valid sources for his own haku moʻolelo has also become invisible. The fact that Kamakau deliberately contested haole historiographic methods is literally lost in the translation. Further, information presented in the stories of women taking leadership roles in long voyages disappears, making it possible for readers to imagine that gender relations in Kanaka past were very much like the European practice where only men were allowed to sail. Anthropologists, historians, and students in all disciplines who read only the translation of Kamakau's moʻolelo will be completely unaware of these stories of women directing and controlling their own lives, and are thus likely to derive an incomplete or even false picture of gender relations in the ancient culture.

It is important, as well, to notice that Kamakau's moʻolelo of Cook describes recurring violence, mainly on the part of Cook's men, from the very first contact. On the first day, the warrior Kapupuʻu began to take iron pieces from Cook's ship, whereupon one of Cook's men shot and killed him.[20] The aliʻi's kahuna advised against retaliating, however, emphasizing that welcoming the foreigners, despite the killing, was the pono thing to do. That night, Cook and company, rather than behaving as welcomed guests, made a display of firepower, shooting guns, cannons, and fireworks intended to frighten and intimidate the ʻŌiwi, which it surely did.

The violent episodes eventually culminated in the death of Cook at Kealakekua on Hawaiʻi Island.[21] When Cook attempted to take Mōʻī Kalaniʻōpuʻu hostage, using a technique he had developed in other places, he committed an act that was distinctly not pono and thus unacceptable to the other aliʻi and to the warriors around the mōʻī. Cook's attitude of superiority, evident in his expectation that the aliʻi would be subjugated to his authority, is clear in all the various accounts. Equally clear is the refusal of the Kānaka Hawaiʻi to be subjugated.

Cook was not the only person killed during the visit of his ship to the islands. Ralph Kuykendall's synthesis of the events does not dilute the violence perpetrated by the British visitors: "While the king was hesitating, news came that a chief crossing the bay in a canoe had been killed by a shot from one of the foreign boats. . . . Cook fired the other barrel of his gun, loaded with ball, and killed a man. . . . Lieutenant Phillips also fired and the marines on shore and the sailors in the boats began firing. . . . During the next few days there was desultory fighting, in which the Hawaiians exhibited great courage and daring in the face of gunfire, a good many of them being killed; a number of houses, behind which the native warriors sheltered themselves, were burned down by foreigners; a few of the latter indulged in reprisals for which even savages might blush."[22]

The conclusion of Kamakau's account of Cook's visit and death is another instance of reordering and deletion of text that substantially changed it. The last paragraph in the Hawaiian text is:

'O nā hua a me nā 'ano'ano o kāna mau hana i kanu ai, ua 'ōmamaka mai nō ia a ulu, a lilo i mau kumulau ho'olaha e ho'oneo ai i ka lāhui kanaka o kēia mokupuni.

1. 'O ka pala i hui pū 'ia me ke kaokao.
2. 'O ka ho'okamakama kū'ai kino.
3. 'O ke kuhi hewa he akua, a ho'omana.
4. 'O ka 'uku lele me ka makika.
5. 'O ka laha 'ana mai o nā ma'i luku.
6. 'O ka loli 'ana o ka 'ea e hanu ai.
7. 'O ka ho'onāwaliwali 'ana i nā kino.
8. 'O ka loli 'ana o nā mea ulu.
9. 'O ka loli 'ana o nā ho'omana, a hui pū me nā ho'omana pegana.
10. 'O ka loli lapa'au 'ana.
11. 'O nā kānāwai o ke aupuni.

The fruits and the seeds that his [Cook's] actions planted sprouted and grew, and became trees that spread to devastate the people of these islands.

1. Gonorrhea together with syphilis.
2. Prostitution.
3. The false idea that he was a god and worshipped.
4. Fleas and mosquitoes.
5. The spread of epidemic diseases.
6. Change in the air we breathe.

7. Weakening of our bodies.

8. Changes in plant life.

9. Change in the religions, put together with pagan religions.

10. Change in medical practice.

11. Laws in the government.[23]

In the *Ruling Chiefs* version, this paragraph is preceded by a reiteration of the ways that Cook's remains had been abused, and then the sentence, "Such is the end of a transgressor."[24] However neither the reiteration nor a corresponding sentence to "Such is the end of a transgressor" appear in the Hawaiian text. It is likely that the sentiment was taken from a statement three pages earlier, in which Kamakau faults Cook for accepting the offerings made to several akua and for eating the things consecrated to those akua. "No laila, ua hahau mai ke akua iā ia" (So the akua struck him), wrote Kamakau. The text in *Ruling Chiefs* has thus translated what Kamakau wrote as Cook's transgression against the native akua into a transgression against the Christian god. Moreover, its transposition to the end of the narrative about Cook gives it more prominence than it has in the original.

SUBSEQUENT HAOLE TRAVELERS TO HAWAIʻI NEI

Violence continued in the subsequent visits to Hawaiʻi by European and American ships, by the visitors as well as the Kanaka ʻŌiwi. Around 1794, in the Olowalu massacre, Captain Simon Metcalf and the crew of the *Eleanora* killed several hundred Kānaka in retaliation for the killing of one of Metcalf's men. Shortly thereafter, some Kānaka took revenge on the next ship to enter the harbor, which just happened to be that of Metcalf's son.[25]

Kuykendall describes Vancouver's visits as peaceful,[26] but they were marked by his attempts at colonization—he claimed the islands for Great Britain—and stained by executions of innocent men in retaliation for the attack by some warriors on the *Daedalus*. The crew of the *Daedalus*, a British naval store ship, had been attacked at Waimea, Oʻahu, and Vancouver demanded the executions even though the perpetrators could not be caught. According to Greg Dening, "it was commonly agreed, by Hawaiians and any European who enjoyed the irony, that none of the men executed were guilty." He explains that Vancouver "specially wanted the chiefs to gain a sense of empire and its reaches; he wanted them to defer to his power and remain responsible for their own."[27] Vancouver himself, then, was certainly not free of the idea of his own and Britain's inherent superiority. According to Kuykendall, he confidently interfered in the interisland wars, sure that he knew what was best for the Kanaka. Like Cook, he even believed that the flora and fauna of England were superior, and he left cattle and several kinds of fruit and vegetable plants to improve the landscape.[28] Unfortunately, these acts only served to upset the ecological balance.

Not much later, Baranov of Russia, employing the German doctor Scheffer, persuaded Kaumuali'i, mō'ī of Kaua'i, to come under "the protection of the Russian emperor."[29] With Kaumuali'i, they planned to conquer O'ahu, but Kamehameha simply ordered them to leave. Eventually, Kaumuali'i realized that Scheffer was not a good ally, and returned to a more or less peaceful relationship with Kamehameha.

MASS DEATH

As cited above, Kamakau wrote that some of the seeds that Captain Cook planted included venereal disease, prostitution, epidemics, and the weakening of the bodies of the native people, all of which were no doubt responsible for a fairly swift and devastating reduction in population. Conservative estimates of Hawai'i's population in 1778 range from 400,000 to 1,000,000; just forty-five years later that number was reduced to about 135,000.[30] The first epidemic, called ma'i 'ōku'u (crouching disease) by the Kanaka, "swept off the majority of Hawaiians." This was followed some forty years later by epidemics of measles, whooping cough, and influenza. Tuberculosis and "a steady corrosive flow of [other] infection[s]" also weakened and killed people, although not in a singular, identifiable epidemic.[31]

Kamehameha, his advisers, and the mō'ī who followed him took various actions to stop the epidemics, including placing kapu (restrictions) on the actions of foreigners[32] and constructing special temples called hale o ke akua (house of the akua) or haleopapa (house of Papa). None of these efforts succeeded, however, and mass death and depopulation ensued.

Kanaka authors in the nineteenth century offer varying analyses of the reasons for the mass deaths. In 1839, Davida Malo wrote the first Hawaiian-language account, which was translated into English by the missionary Lorrin Andrews and published in the missionary magazine intended for an American audience, the *Hawaiian Spectator*. A depressed Malo mainly blamed the aliʻi for the decrease in population, beginning with a condemnation of the savageries of the ancient times, including the "multitudes [that] were wantonly destroyed in war" and "vast many [that] were killed by robbers," as well as abortion because of women's vanity, infanticide, human sacrifices, and "indolence."[33] Throughout the article, Malo castigates the aliʻi for not taking proper care of the people, accusing them of exploiting the people for their own enrichment, and caring only for their own pleasures. He also blames the kāhuna lāʻau lapaʻau (native medical practitioners) and the people themselves for the deaths resulting from the maʻi ʻōkuʻu epidemic and the other diseases: "The great mortality that prevailed arose from the ignorance of the people at that time, their manner of living, the want of care and nursing when sick; and their ignorance of the proper use of medicine. . . . Many died with famine, many with cold, and more still from the unavoidable evil condition they were in."[34] Malo assigned blame to foreigners only in conjunction with the spread of venereal disease: "From the arrival of Capt. Cook to the present day the people have been dying with the venereal disorder." But the blame was also on the "licentiousness" of "Hawaiian females," for which, he concluded, "God is angry, and he is diminishing the people."[35]

It is clear that Malo had been rather thoroughly persuaded by the missionaries that the old ways of life were evil and savage; his conclusion was that "if a reformation of morals should take place, and the kingdom should be renewed, then it would escape destruction."[36] Noelani Arista has analyzed Malo's article this way: "While the language and imagery that Malo uses are Christian, it was Hawaiian tradition that urged Malo to condemn the actions of the chief. Only *aliʻi pono* could ensure a prosperous rule."[37] Malo had internalized the moral judgments of the missionaries, perhaps not yet aware of the mass death associated with colonialism and missionaries on the American continents. He might also have been experiencing some degree of self-hatred borne of the failure to be able to think of or do anything to stop the dying. He was an advisor to the aliʻi nui; therefore, it was his kuleana (responsibility, within his authority) to figure out how to stop it and how to save them, and he could not. Eventually, the maʻi ʻōkuʻu and the other maʻi ahulau (epidemics) took away not only the majority of makaʻāinana, but also many important aliʻi, including Kamehameha's primary advisors.[38]

Thirty years later, Samuel Kamakau, possessed of greater historical knowledge and having seen firsthand that conversion to Christianity did not stop or slow the mass death, was less apt to blame the aliʻi and the ordinary Kanaka. In 1867, Kamakau repeated and elaborated on Malo's list of evils, including war and infanticide, but he came to different conclusions. His two principal reasons for the decrease in population were the frequent epidemics and venereal disease, both brought in by foreigners.[39] Rather than interpreting the mass deaths as the results of God's anger at the lack of piety of the Kanaka, Kamakau directly blamed foreign ways. What follows is yet another passage that was deleted, without ellipsis, in *Ruling Chiefs*: " ʻO ke kumu i loaʻa mai ai kēia pōʻino a me ka hoʻoneo ʻana hoʻi i ka lāhui Hawaiʻi nei, ua maopopo, ʻo nā haole nō ka poʻe pepehi lāhui; a ʻo ka puni hanohano me ka puni waiwai, ʻo lāua nō nā hoa aloha no ka maʻi luku" (The reason for this misfortune and the decimation of the Hawaiian lāhui, it is understood, is that the haole are people who kill other peoples; and the desire for glory and riches, those are the companions of the devastating diseases).[40]

For Kamakau the situation was not pono, not because the aliʻi were not pono but because of foreigners bringing the diseases, and with them the desire to rule over and become wealthy in Hawaiʻi at the expense of the native people. Besides diseases, the haole also brought the idea of trade for money. Haole traders wanted sandalwood to sell in China, and the aliʻi desired and needed weaponry among other goods, not only for the interisland wars but to defend themselves against the haole. Many aliʻi went into debt that could only be paid with sandalwood, and so they ordered the makaʻāinana into the forests to cut all the sandalwood trees.[41] This left loʻi (irrigated terraces for taro) and other farms uncultivated and the forests out of balance. Such changes in the plant life left many people starving and weakened. Later on, the institution of taxes to be paid in cash also caused people to be alienated from their ancestral lands, which undoubtedly contributed to the weakening of their bodies, not to mention their spirits.[42]

Regardless of how they attempted to explain the mass deaths, the authors, the aliʻi, and the makaʻāinana grieved over the enormous loss of life and worried about the fate of the lāhui — on a scale that we today can barely imagine. In reference to similar catastrophes that befell the Yup'ik people, Harold Napoleon wrote that "the cataclysm of mass death changed the persona, the lifeview, the world view of the Yup'ik people." He further described the survivors in this way: "Their medicines and their medicine men and women had proven useless. Everything they had believed in had failed. Their ancient world had collapsed . . . from their inability to understand and dispel the disease, guilt was born into them. They had witnessed mass death — evil — in unimaginable and unacceptable terms."[43] An anonymous Kanaka student at Lahainaluna wrote in similar terms in 1834: "Hookahi no hewa nui, o ka make ia ka Okuu nei" (There was only one great wrong [in the past], that being death, the 'Ōku'u epidemic).[44]

Napoleon writes that in the trauma, confusion, and fear, the Yup'ik "survivors readily followed the white missionaries and school teachers . . . who told them their old beliefs were evil."[45] Their behavior afterward is nearly identical to the symptoms of post-traumatic stress disorder, which Napoleon calls "an infection of the soul."[46] A. W. Crosby calls the behavior "anomie," which leads to self-destructive coping mechanisms, such as addictions to narcotics and alcohol.[47] As Napoleon says: "No people anywhere will voluntarily discard their culture, beliefs, customs, and traditions unless they are under a great deal of stress, physically, psychologically, or spiritually."[48] Davida Malo's blaming of the ali'i and the traditional culture may also be reexamined in light of a statement by Napoleon: "The case can be made that many of the survivors of the Great Death suffered from posttraumatic stress disorder, and that it was in this condition that they surrendered and allowed their old cultures to pass away."[49] Like the Yup'ik, the Kanaka 'Ōiwi Hawai'i were forever changed by the horrific experience of mass death.

'AI NOA

The 'ai kapu (eating taboos) was a system of rules that specified that men do all the cooking, that men and women eat separately, and that certain foods, especially the kino lau (many physical forms) of certain male gods, be kapu to women. The system was established by the ancient mo'olelo of Wākea, who wanted to sleep with his daughter, Ho'ohōkūkalani, without his mate, Papahānaumoku, finding out. Thus a system of kapu, including the eating kapu, was put into place by Wākea and his male kahuna that kept women out of the men's eating house and kept men and women apart for a few nights each month. This system remained in effect, especially among the ali'i 'ai moku, the ruling chiefs, until the death of Kamehameha.

In May 1819, Kamehameha died after a long and illustrious life. He named his son, Liholiho, as his successor, but bequeathed the war akua, Kūkā'ilimoku, to Liholiho's cousin, Kekuaokalani. Kamehameha himself had inherited Kūkā'ilimoku when Kalani'ōpu'u died, leaving the reign to his son, Kiwala'ō. Many generations before, Līloa had bequeathed Kūkā'ilimoku to his son, 'Umi, of a lesser genealogy, while giving the aupuni (government) to his more genealogically legitimate, but less pono son, Hakau.[50] Kamehameha had been grooming Liholiho since childhood to take over his rule, but it is possible that he observed that the young man might falter, and so in effect arranged for Kekuaokalani as a backup. If Liholiho ruled in a pono way, Kekuaokalani would be loyal and all would be well. If not, then Kekuaokalani, if he took care of the akua and thus behaved in pono ways, would take over the rule.

Kamehameha did not predict the most momentous of the events that would follow his death. As part of the mourning practices, the 'ai kapu was suspended and a temporary period of 'ai noa (free eating) was established. "Ua make akula nō ka mea nāna e mālama ke akua, a ua pono nō ko kākou 'ai noa 'ana" (The one who cares for the akua has died, and [thus] our free eating is pono).[51] This was a limited 'ai noa, however, which was restricted to the aloali'i—those surrounding the ali'i nui. At this time, Liholiho was sent with Kekuaokalani north to Kawaihae because Kailua, where the mō'ī had died, was considered defiled by the death. About a week later, Ka'ahumanu sent for Liholiho; Kekuaokalani advised him not to return to Kailua because "ke lohe mai nei kākou, ke 'ai noa maila 'o Kailua" (we hear that Kailua is free eating).[52] When a second messenger was sent Liholiho agreed to go, but Kekuaokalani refused and advised Liholiho not to agree to the free eating. The following day, Ka'ahumanu announced that Liholiho was the new mō'ī, to be called Kamehameha II, while also announcing that she herself would share his rule and would have the title kuhina nui.[53]

That evening the ali'i wahine Keōpūolani fed her younger son, Kauikeaouli, in a symbolic gesture of free eating. Liholiho returned to

Kawaihae and began drinking alcohol. According to Kameʻeleihiwa, he "attempted to perform the very sacred and rigorous ʻAha ritual through which the *mana* [power, authority] of the war *Akua* Kū could be secured by the *Mōʻī.* . . . Because of the general drunkenness, merrymaking, and disorderly behavior, Liholiho's ʻAha ritual was a failure."[54] Samuel Kamakau's account of this event is slightly different: he wrote that Liholiho successfully consecrated the heiau (place of worship, shrine) at Honokōhau through the ʻaha ritual; however, the new mōʻī could not decide either to command an end to the free eating, which would be problematic, because Kaʻahumanu had claimed joint rule, or to join his mother and proclaim the permanent ʻai noa. He continued to drink. In both versions, Liholiho is caught between his powerful coruler and mother, Kaʻahumanu, and his cousin in possession of the war akua, Kekuaokalani. He finally succumbed to Kaʻahumanu's and his birth mother's pressure, and proclaimed the ʻai noa.

Kekuaokalani, believing himself to be pono and taking care of Kūkāʻilimoku as had Kamehameha and ʻUmi before him, declared war to restore the ʻai kapu. He died in the battle at Kuamoʻo, outside of Kailua, Kona. In the words of Kameʻeleihiwa, "Kekuaokalani's defeat meant more than the demise of the *ʻai kapu*, it was also a death blow for the sanctity of tradition."[55] Now it was clear to everyone that the old akua had little or no mana.[56]

Many theories have been advanced about the reasons Kamehameha's wāhine broke the ʻai kapu, but, as Kameʻeleihiwa wrote, "we will never know why Kaʻahumanu insisted that Liholiho, and indeed the entire *Lāhui*, should agree to the breaking of the *ʻai kapu*."[57] Some historians have suggested that Kaʻahumanu was seeking political power, but she had achieved that without establishing ʻai noa. Kaʻahumanu had claimed the title of kuhina nui, which gave her the power to rule jointly with the mōʻī *before* the permanent breaking of the ʻai kapu.[58] Moreover, the other aliʻi had not objected to Kaʻahumanu assuming this new office.

Kameʻeleihiwa explains that historians have tended to ignore the significance of the mass death to the institution of the ʻai noa: "Epidemic disease and massive death were signs of loss of *pono*, but Kamehameha — who ruled at the time — was the epitome of a *pono Aliʻi.* . . . Yet, despite his *pono*, the people continued to die at a horrendous rate . . . for all his efforts he could not give them life." Kameʻeleihiwa posits that Kaʻahumanu and the others observed that the foreigners broke the ʻai kapu constantly, yet did not die in the epidemics. Perhaps Ka'ahumanu and the other ali'i nui "thought the 'ainoa was the white man's secret to life." Furthermore, when the kāhuna and the maka'āinana saw that Kūkā'ilimoku no longer had mana, the kāhuna nui, Hewahewa, ordered the burning of the temple images, and the maka'āinana "went on a furious rampage."[59] Kame'eleihiwa concludes that the people had lost faith in the 'ai kapu because the akua had failed to protect them.

THE MISSIONARIES

"Darkness covered the earth and gross darkness the people" begins the memoir of Hiram Bingham, of the first company of missionaries to Hawai'i, a story in which that company appear as the bringers of light.[60] Many stories have been told of the "pioneering" missionaries, of their bravery and altruism or, conversely, of their drive to power and ho'oma-kauli'i 'āina (lust for land).[61] In attempting objectivity and fairness, mainstream historians have been critical in their portrayal of the severely puritanical Congregationalists, yet have rationalized or helped to justify their actions by essentializing the Kanaka Maoli as backward savages and intellectually lazy beings whose way of life was decaying and who themselves were disappearing as a result of their own degraded ways.[62] Because there are so many stories told in so many different ways, there is no reason to present here a new history of the arrival and early activities of the missionaries; instead I will summarize the stories, highlighting some of the struggles over how pono was to be defined. I will also briefly review what is often described as the missionaries' greatest accomplishment: the introduction of literacy and the establishment of the print media in Hawai'i nei.

It has been written many times that a young Kanaka 'Ōiwi named 'Ōpūkaha'ia inspired the U.S. missionaries to come to Hawai'i. Along with an even younger man named Hopu, 'Ōpūkaha'ia and other Kanaka youths signed on as hands on the whaling and merchant ships that passed through Hawai'i nei. 'Ōpūkaha'ia learned English, first aboard a ship then in a series of schools in New England. He converted to Christianity in 1815 after meeting up with the zealous evangelicals of the growing U.S. mission movement.[63] Through their contact with these young men, along with their desire to travel to foreign lands and save heathen souls, the missionaries found Hawai'i appealing. William Hutchison explains that the Americans felt "special obligations toward foreign missions" — obligations that were linked to the ideas of manifest destiny, biblical commands to preach all over the world, and "a fitful concern about the Indians." But their obligation was as much to their home churches as to the people of those foreign lands; as Hutchison states, "the missionaries were considered important to the renovation of their own churches and society," and he adds that the movement "dispatch[ed] some two thousand missionaries over a sixty-year period." When the movement grew to "huge proportions and great public notice" the missionaries cast themselves as "couriers" of an entire, favored people.[64]

At the time that 'Ōpūkaha'ia, Hopu, and the others lived in New England, the American Board of Commissioners for Foreign Missions was attempting to convert various American Indian peoples. Hutchison quotes their objectives as "'civilizing and christianizing' in that order" and as assimilationist in vision.[65] A major site for the civilizing and assimilating of Indians was the Foreign Mission School at Cornwall, which the board established for the purpose of training various natives to proselytize among their own people. 'Ōpūkaha'ia (known in English there as Henry Obookiah) converted with enthusiasm, and became such a star pupil at the Cornwall School that Hutchison likens him to a celebrity among the missionaries.[66] Bingham quotes 'Ōpūkaha'ia as requesting that missionaries be sent to Hawai'i.[67]

Unfortunately, 'Ōpūkaha'ia's experience at the Cornwall School ended the way of an inordinate number of other native students—he became sick and died.[68] By that time, however, he had already sparked evangelical desires for Hawai'i as a destination as a heathen nation for missionaries to civilize and convert. In late 1819, the first company set sail for Hawai'i, including seven couples and three "Hawaiian helpers from Cornwall School": Thomas Hopu, William Kanui, and John Honoli'i.[69] They also brought home the unconverted George Humehume, son of Kaumuali'i, the aforementioned mō'ī of Kaua'i.

Although the missionaries believed that God had prepared the way for them because the 'ai kapu had ended just months before their arrival, they did not find the conversion of the Kanaka 'Ōiwi to happen as readily as that of 'Ōpūkaha'ia. Their project thus challenged them and kept many of them in Hawai'i for the rest of their lives, and many have descendants who continue to live in Hawai'i today (where they are among the wealthiest and most powerful people). The missionaries had little trouble obtaining permission to stay, even with the "obvious reluctance and an unflattering lack of enthusiasm" on the part of the aliʻi, who did not take to their proselytizing right away.[70] Kamakau reports that some aliʻi around Keōpūolani, after their first meeting with Hopu, during which he attempted to proselytize, nicknamed him "Māʻoi" (intrusive).[71]

But eventually it was Keōpūolani, the ruling aliʻi wahine who had ended the ʻai kapu, who first converted and who greatly influenced the conversion of other powerful aliʻi. She was the highest-ranking aliʻi in the archipelago, as well the birth mother of the mōʻī and of the other two children in line for rule of the islands. The others among that powerful group of women who effected such major changes were Kaʻahumanu, the kuhina nui, who became the most feared and revered of the queens, and Kapiʻolani. All were favored wāhine of Kamehameha and all converted early to the new religion.

These women, along with the other aliʻi, were interested in learning the palapala (reading and writing). The aliʻi already knew some of the power of writing; Kamakau gives a rather lengthy list of Kānaka, women and men, who prior to the arrival of the missionaries had learned to read and write English.[72] Missionaries now offered to "reduce the [Hawaiian] language to writing" and teach the aliʻi to read and write in their own language.[73] From the aliʻi point of view, they were thus acquiring the technology that would allow them new ways to communicate with each other. From the missionary point of view, however, the Kanaka ʻŌiwi were perceived to lack alphabetic writing, which was a proof of their uncivilized nature. The establishment of the writing system, and the subsequent printing of tracts and books were thus an integral part of the "civilizing" process. Walter Mignolo, writing about the Spanish colonization of the New World, states: "During the process of colonization . . . the book was conceived . . . as a text in which truth could be discerned from falsehood, the law imposed over chaos. The book, furthermore, also played a very important role in the reverse process of sign transmission: from the metropolis to the colonial periphery. Printed books facilitated the dissemination and reproduction of knowledge and . . . contributed to the colonization of languages."[74]

Accordingly, the first company brought with them both a professionally trained printer, Elisha Loomis, and a printing press. In about two years they had developed an alphabet for Hawaiian and began to print primers for use in mission schools. Aliʻi first sent their assistants to the schools to learn, and then, according to Lorrin Andrews, "schools were formed for their particular benefit."[75] First hundreds then thousands of aliʻi and makaʻāinana were enrolled in mission schools learning the palapala. Schütz writes that "by the mid-1830s, letter writing had apparently become routine."[76] The first reading materials were religious tracts and elementary-level school texts such as a speller and an arithmetic text.

The reduction of the language to writing was meant to, and did, facilitate the process of conversion to Christianity. It was in the production of the religious texts in Hawaiian that the word "pono" must first have been used to translate such Christian concepts as "righteousness," which previously had no referent in the minds of the Hawaiians. Whereas pono had been used previously to describe the ideal behavior of aliʻi and other concepts such as balance, completeness, and material well-being, it now took on the foreign connotation of conforming to Christian morality. Rightness meant something different in the two worlds, but the missionaries were able, in barely questioned translation, to appropriate this powerful term—an appropriation that would have radical consequences. From one mission primer, for example, students copied the following sentence: "E pa-la-pa-la-ia na i-noa o ka poe po-no ma-lo-ko o ka bu-ke o ke o-la" (The names of the righteous [pono people] will be written inside the book of life).[77] Here we can see that the Christian god is imagined as having a book, and that the inscription of one's name in the book guaranteed life. In the colonial imagination, the possession of books was a mark of superiority, even for deities, and thus one that the native akua distinctly lacked.

But translating the term pono into Christian righteousness was a trying task for the missionaries. Most Kānaka did not enter as quietly into that foreign and restricted lifestyle as some histories would have us believe. Bingham's memoirs are brimming with complaints about the struggle with the indolent, pleasure-seeking Kanaka. Indeed, his chapter about the second year of the mission starts this way: "While some of the people who sat in darkness were beginning to turn their eyes to the light . . . others, with greater enthusiasm, were wasting their time in learning, practising, or witnessing the *hula*."[78]

Kamehameha's children with Keōpūolani were destined to carry on as rulers over the islands, and so with Kaʻahumanu were the most important to convert first. Liholiho (Mōʻī Kamehameha II) and Kauikeaouli (later to become Mōʻī Kamehameha III), along with Nāhiʻenaʻena, their sister, all resisted the demands of the missionaries in various ways and at various times. Liholiho famously said to Bingham: "'Elima oʻu makahiki i koe, a laila, huli au i kanaka maikaʻi'"[79] or (In five years, I will turn and forsake sin; Bingham's own, loose translation.)[80] Kauikeaouli and Nāhiʻenaʻena grew up under the influence of the missionary William Richards but also understood that they were meant to live together and produce more sacred children. Marjorie Sinclair has documented their years of struggle, torment, and rebellion against the missionaries in her biography of Nāhiʻenaʻena.[81]

The aliʻi nui couple Boki and Liliha, along with other aliʻi nui, also actively opposed Kaʻahumanu and the missionaries. One example of Liliha's rebellion is described as follows: "In 1831, Chief Paki joined with his cousin, Kuini [Queen] Liliha, in an attempt to take over Oahu (*Pahikaua*). *Pahikaua* (literally, war knife, or sword) was the name given to the attempt made by followers of Liliha to retaliate against Kaahumanu for the threat made by [her] against Liliha if she continued to live in her independent fashion. . . . Kaahumanu was missionizing throughout the islands, proclaiming the new taboos against murder, adultery, Hawaiian religious practices, hula, chant, ʻawa, and distilleries."[82] The opposition to Kaʻahumanu failed, however. And by 1831 Liholiho had died on a journey to England, leaving the adolescent Kauikeaouli to reign as Kamehameha III and the powerful Kaʻahumanu as the virtual ruler of the kingdom. The missionaries then established Lahainaluna Seminary to train Kanaka men for the ministry. Many of the most influential advisers to the ruling aliʻi attended the seminary, which also gave rise in 1834 to the first newspaper published in Hawaiian. The newspaper, called *Ka Lama Hawaii*, or as Bingham translates it, the "Hawaiian luminary," was the first in a series of periodicals planned by the mission to "supply the means of useful knowledge in the arts and sciences, history, morals, and religion; to point out existing evils, their character, seat, extent and consequences."[83] In other words, as Mignolo points out, it would act as the conduit for the colonial culture.

Students wrote articles for the last page of the four-page paper, and they also learned the publishing process, including printing press operation. The same year that *Ka Lama Hawaii* was established it was followed by *Ke Kumu Hawaii*, which was published at the Honolulu mission for the mission schools. At *Ke Kumu Hawaii*, more Kānaka learned the operation of the press, although the paper folded after it became too expensive to publish. *Ke Kumu* was soon followed by *Ka Nonanona*, which was controlled by the mission but also worked in cooperation with Kamehameha III's government to provide news to the general public, thus significantly broadening both scope and readership. The mōʻi and his advisers soon grasped the usefulness of such an instrument. The government sponsored two newspapers, *Ka Hae Hawaii* (1856–1861) in Hawaiian and the *Polynesian* (1840–1841; 1844–1864) in English. While the main purpose of these papers was to communicate laws and government policies, the missionaries in charge of publication also used them to proselytize, to civilize, and to promote ideas such as farming for profit rather than subsistence. Kanaka ʻŌiwi worked in various capacities at all of these newspapers, and increasingly many submitted for publication writings such as moʻolelo, moʻokūʻauhau, mele, and their opinions on religion, politics, and other matters. The print media thus acted as a major agent in the colonizing activities, especially of the Protestant mission, but also acted to cohere the "imagined community" that was the nation, which was coming into being at the same time.[84]

EARLY STRUGGLES OVER SOVEREIGNTY

Like many countries in the Pacific and around the world in the early nineteenth century, Hawaiʻi was at times the target of colonial aggression. In 1839, after the death of Kaʻahumanu's successor Kīnaʻu, Miriam Kekauluohi was appointed kuhina nui. Prior to 1839, French priests of the Roman Catholic Church had arrived and attempted to establish a mission. This move was vigorously opposed by the anti-Catholic Calvinists, however, who by this time had become advisers to the mōʻī and the kuhina nui. Needless to say, the priests were sent away in fairly short order. In July 1839, the *Artemise*, a French warship commanded by Captain Cyrille Laplace, arrived in Honolulu to make several demands, including that French priests be allowed to establish a mission, that a land grant be made for such a mission, and that the government pay $20,000 as guaranty for the other demands. If these demands were not met, Captain Laplace was to make war on Hawaiʻi. In the absence of the mōʻī, Kekauluohi agreed to all of the demands, including payment of the cash.[85]

This incident impressed on Kamehameha III and his advisers that Hawaiʻi was vulnerable to the "Great Powers," as they were known. In 1841, Sir George Simpson, former commander of Fort Vancouver where many Kānaka had emigrated to work, arrived at Hawaiʻi. According to Kamakau, "He saw how men of his country had taken advantage of the gentle Hawaiian race . . . and he offered to act as ambassador to the queen of England to obtain from her . . . official recognition of King Kamehameha III as an independent ruler over an independent country."[86] Former missionary William Richards and the mōʻī's other advisers agreed that this was a necessity, because those nations not recognized and accepted into the family of nations were vulnerable to colonization. The Hawaiian kingdom had already taken some steps toward conforming to the European conventions of statehood, including the creation, in 1840, of a constitution and the enactment of laws of recognizably European type; the assessment and defining of the territory of the islands; and the agreement of the people of the archipelago that they were one nation. All that was lacking was recognition of the nation by the members of the exclusive club of European nations and the United States. Kamehameha III's declaration that the kingdom was Christian meant that Hawaiʻi had also met that unwritten requirement for membership. The mōʻī thus sent Simpson on one vessel, plus one of his closest and most trusted advisors, the aliʻi Timoteo Haʻalilio, together with William Richards on another ship, to journey to the United States, England, and France to obtain recognition of Hawaiʻi's independence.

While they were gone, Richard Charleton, the British consul in Hawaiʻi, became involved in a dispute with aliʻi over a house lot. Lord George Paulet, commanding a British warship, demanded that Charleton be given the land. This demand was accompanied by others disrespectful of Hawaiʻi's sovereignty, and by threats of war. The mōʻī's response was to inform Paulet that Sir George Simpson was on his way to settle matters with Queen Victoria, and that Paulet's demands were "contravening the laws established for the benefit of all."[87] Then, under protest, the mōʻī provisionally ceded the sovereignty of Hawaiʻi to Paulet until Queen Victoria could be apprised of the conflict. The British government promptly disavowed Paulet's act, and dispatched Admiral Richard Thomas to Hawaiʻi. On his arrival Thomas reprimanded Paulet and restored Hawaiʻi's sovereignty. The date was July 31, 1843, which was celebrated for the following fifty years as Lā Hoʻihoʻi Ea, or Restoration Day.

Haʻalilio and Richards went first to the United States, where they obtained a verbal agreement from President John Tyler to respect Hawaiʻi's independence. They then proceeded to Europe, where for several months they negotiated with the officials of Great Britain and France, and where they received distressing letters about Paulet's threat to their nation. On November 28, 1843, they obtained the signatures of officials of both Great Britain and France on a joint proclamation recognizing Hawaiʻi as an independent nation and a member of the family of nations. November 28 was officially celebrated thereafter as Lā Kūʻokoʻa, or Independence Day. Haʻalilio and Richards returned to the United States to continue their work, and then finally departed for home in December 1844. Ke Aliʻi Timoteo Haʻalilio died on the ship just days into the journey home.[88]

It was on the first Lā Hoʻihoʻi Ea, July 31, 1843, that Kamehameha III announced, "Ua mau ke ea o ka ʻāina i ka pono" (roughly, "The sovereignty of the land has been continued because it is pono"), which became the mōʻī's motto. It later became the motto of the kingdom, and then (strangely or perversely) was appropriated as the motto of the State of Hawaiʻi, where it is usually translated as "The life of the land is perpetuated in righteousness." "Ea," which can mean "life" or "breath" as well as "sovereignty," in its original context was clearly meant to signify sovereignty. The word pono, as I have shown, has a multiplicity of meanings, and had been appropriated by missionaries as well as government officials to translate the Christian concept of righteousness. In the mōʻī's phrasing, it likely corresponds more closely to "justice" and, more broadly, what is good or beneficial for the people. Simultaneously, it is an assertion that the mōʻī's government was the appropriate and correct one.[89] Translation of pono into "righteousness" or even "justice" is an example of the reduction of an understood multiplicity of meanings in the Hawaiian language to a single meaning in English, with a different set of connotations altogether.

It was in response to foreign aggression, and also to missionary claims that the Kanaka ʻŌiwi were savage and uncivilized, that the mōʻī and the aliʻi nui changed their ways of government by adopting a constitution on which European and American types of laws could be based and by adhering to international norms of nation-statehood. These moves were made with the goal of preserving sovereignty—that is, to avoid being taken over by one imperial power or another.[90] Further, and

less obviously, it was to try to refute the charges of savagery and back-
wardness that were continuously thrust at them.

The constitution and laws in Hawai'i, while European in form, also
reflected Kanaka Maoli ideas of what was pono in government. This is
seen especially in the inclusion of women in government in the early
years. Ali'i wahine (female ali'i) had always been part of government,
and for some years they continued to be. The office of kuhina nui was
most often held by women, the first and most powerful of whom was
Ka'ahumanu, who claimed status as coruler with Liholiho. Thereafter,
the office passed to Kīna'u, then to Kekauluohi (under whom the first
constitution was finished and passed),[91] then briefly to the male Keoni
Ana, then to Victoria Kamāmalu Ka'ahumanu, and, after her death,
briefly to her father, after which it was abolished.[92] The first Hale 'Aha
'Ōlelo Ali'i, or House of Nobles (excluding the mō'ī), consisted of five
women along with ten men.[93] Ali'i wahine also served as island gover-
nors, among them Kuini Liliha on O'ahu, Kekauonohi on Kaua'i, and
Ruth Ke'elikōlani on Hawai'i Island.[94]

The introduction of foreign concepts in government and law
met with substantial resistance. Kamakau wrote that "the reason why
[foreign-style laws] were passed was because the old chiefs were dead,
those who had refused absolutely to approve the new laws except in the
matter of protection from crime and keeping the peace among the people."[95] Maka'āinana in particular opposed the presence of powerful foreigners in the government and foreigners' ability to own land. A well-
known example of published protest is "Na Palapala Hoopii O Na
Makaainana" (Petitions of the maka'āinana), first printed in July 1845
in *Ka Elele*, the Hawaiian-language mission newspaper. The following
month it was translated into English and published in the missionary
magazine the *Friend*, under the title "A Petition to Your Gracious Majesty, Kamehameha III, and to all Your Chiefs in Council Assembled."[96]
The overriding concern of the maka'āinana was "the independence of
[the] kingdom," and toward preserving that independence, the petition
asked the mō'ī to "dismiss foreign officers . . . appointed to be Hawaiian
officers," to disallow foreigners' ability to become naturalized subjects,
and to prevent any further land being sold to foreigners. A note at the
end reads: "It is said that over 1600 names were subscribed to this
petition." The maka'āinana wrote that the ali'i, rather than foreigners,
should serve as officers under the mō'ī: "e like me ka noho ana o ko lakou

poe makua malalo iho o kou makuakane o Kamehameha I" (as their fathers were under your father, Kamehameha I).[97] The ali'i answered the petition, represented by Keoni Ana (John Young Jr.) and "Jeone Ii" (John Papa 'I'i). They reassured the maka'āinana first that "aole loa e pono ke kuai aku i kekahi aina i ka haole o ka aina e" (it is by no means proper to sell land to aliens), but that it was pono for certain loyal foreigners to be able to purchase land "i kuewa ole ai lakou" (so that they not be homeless), but also that those foreigners not be allowed to sell the land to any other foreigner.[98] Despite such confusing reassurances, the sale of land became the next big project for the ali'i who in strange coalition with the forces seeking to commodify and colonize the land, sought to preserve sovereignty and to deal with the tragic and devastating problem of depopulation.

COLONIAL CAPITALISM AND THE STRUGGLE OVER LAND TENURE

In precolonial, precapitalist times — what anthropologist Marion Kelly calls Hawaiian times — the people took care of the land in what they conceived of as a reciprocal relationship, and they managed and governed themselves in what is usually described as the ali'i system. Nineteenth-century foreign observers, such as W. D. Alexander, described the political-economic relationships and the land tenure system as bearing "a remarkable resemblance to the feudal system that prevailed in Europe during the Middle Ages."[99] Such a characterization, however, represents the ali'i as lords, as landowners and oppressors of an unfortunate serfdom. As Kame'eleihiwa has noted, this is an inadequate description because the Hawaiian system was stratified but interdependent, and the ali'i, kahuna, and maka'āinana regarded themselves as related much more closely and affectionately than did feudal landlords and serfs.[100] Kame'eleihiwa described the relationships among akua, ali'i, and maka'āinana this way: "*Ali'i Nui* were the protectors of the *maka'āinana*, sheltering them from terrible unseen forces. . . . Should a famine arise, the *Ali'i Nui* was held at fault and deposed. . . . Should an *Ali'i Nui* be stingy and cruel to the commoners . . . he or she would cease to be *pono*, lose favor with the *Akua* and be struck down, usually by the people. . . . A reciprocal relationship was maintained: the *Ali'i Nui* kept the *'Āina* fertile and the *Akua* appeased; the *maka'āinana* fed and clothed the *Ali'i Nui*."[101]

Land tenure was the central feature of this system of political and social relationships based on obligations as well as bonds of affection. When a new island or district ruler, an ali'i 'ai moku, came into office, he or she would appoint konohiki, who were also ali'i, as administrators over the large district areas called kalana and ahupua'a. The konohiki would, in turn, appoint lesser konohiki over the smaller areas within each district. The maka'āinana farmed and fished within their district, and also gathered firewood and anything else they needed from anywhere within their kalana or ahupua'a. Certain days of each month were devoted to farming areas set aside for the support of the konohiki and the ali'i 'ai moku. Ali'i and maka'āinana went on fishing expeditions, both together and separately, and shared the catch.[102] Besides labor in farming and fishing, maka'āinana gave 'auhau (tribute) to all the konohiki up to and including the ali'i 'ai moku. The konohiki also gave 'auhau to the konohiki and ali'i 'ai moku above. Prior to the cash economy, 'auhau was conceived as "tribute" to the ali'i and, if not excessive, it apparently was not usually resented by the maka'āinana. In *Ka Lama Hawaii* in 1834, an anonymous student wrote an article, titled "No ka Pono Kahiko a Me ka Pono Hou" or (Concerning the ancient pono and the new pono) in which he explained that the 'auhau had been well understood and fair but now was becoming "huikau," or confused. He wrote: "Eia ka mea lilo i kela auhau. O ke kanaka aiahupuaa, he nui kana mea e lilo i kela auhau, a o ke kanaka aiili, uuku iho kana mea e lilo, o ke kanaka aikihapai, uuku loa kana mea e haawi aku. O ka poe kuewa, aole a lakou mea lilo aku. I keia manawa, ua huikau, aole akaka" (Here is what was given for that 'auhau. The person who ruled an ahupua'a had much to give for that 'auhau, and the person who ruled an 'ili [a smaller district within an ahupua'a] had a little less to give, and the person who just farmed a garden had very little to give. Wanderers did not give anything. Now, it is all mixed up, it is not clear).[103]

The kuleana "authority" that allowed certain ali'i to "kū i ka moku," or rule a district or island and receive 'auhau, included the obligation to manage the land and ocean resources wisely—to set kapu (roughly, here, meaning temporary restrictions) and kānāwai (rules) in consultation with other ali'i and kāhuna. Everybody had specific kuleana to mālama 'āina, or care for the land: according to Kame'eleihiwa, "in practical terms, the *maka'āinana* fed and clothed the *Ali'i Nui*, who provided the organization required to produce enough food to sustain an ever-increasing population."[104] The ali'i status with its accompanying kuleana was determined genealogically, but the 'āina, akua, 'aumakua, kahuna, and maka'āinana were also conceived of as belonging to the same family as the ali'i. Joseph Poepoe explains in "Moolelo Hawaii Kahiko" that in mo'olelo (i.e., metaphorically) Wākea is the oldest son, the ali'i (who is simultaneously akua); his next youngest brother is the kahuna; and the youngest is the maka'āinana, or kauā (servant).[105] Similarly, Haumea, goddess of childbirth and government, is portrayed as akua, ali'i, and kahuna all at once. Kamakau, as shown earlier, provides an example of a time that maka'āinana had to serve as ali'i.[106] Furthermore, genealogy alone was not enough to determine who would "kū i ka moku"; an ali'i 'ai moku who wanted to obtain and retain that position had to be a good land and ocean resource manager, a good leader, and good caretaker of the akua, 'aumakua, 'āina, and maka'āinana. If he or she fulfilled his or her duties, the bonds with the maka'āinana were those of affection as well as obligation.

Osorio argues that the māhele, the change of land tenure to private property, "was a foreign solution to the problem of managing lands increasingly emptied of people" because of the epidemics and low birthrates.[107] In the system described above, the ali'i 'ai moku, now the mō'ī of the entire archipelago, had interests in all lands; the appointed konohiki had interests in all lands under their control; and the maka'āinana had interests in the lands that they worked. The maka'āinana, furthermore, had rights to fish and to gather within their ahupua'a or kalana. In 1846, not long after the petition of protest by the maka'āinana, the government created a Board of Commissioners to Quiet Land Titles. The board translated the ancient system into the foreign language of private property thus: "If the King should allow to the landlords [i.e., konohiki] one-third, to the tenants one-third, and retain one-third himself, 'he would injure no one unless himself.'"[108] In a great simplification of the actual process, we may say that starting from such a conception the board conceived a plan in which the konohiki (consisting of all ali'i under the mō'ī) would pay commutation fees to extinguish the mō'ī's interest in their lands and eventually receive a fee-simple title. In the following year, the mō'ī and all the ali'i agreed that all remaining lands would be subject to a three-way division (with the exception of the mōʻī, who would retain all his private lands): one-third would go to the government, one-third to the aliʻi (konohiki), and "the remaining third to the Tenants." The konohiki lands, including the mōʻī's, were subject to claims by the makaʻāinana, and all lands were "subject to the rights of the Tenants."[109]

Over the next few years, konohiki and makaʻāinana had to present claims in order to receive their land grants and fee-simple titles. The claimant usually had to pay to have the land surveyed before the claim could be filed, and sometimes he or she had to pay commutation fees. The notices of rules about how to file claims and the deadlines to do so were published in newspapers and announced in churches. According to Osorio, in the end "the Mōʻī possessed more than one million acres of the kingdom's 4.2 million acres, 251 konohiki and Aliʻi Nui owned or possessed about a million and a half acres, and the 80,000 Makaʻāinana had managed to secure about 28,000 acres among them."[110] Keanu Sai, however, has noted more recently that makaʻāinana were allowed to file claims after the official deadlines, and that claims are being filed even to this day. Further, the government lands were offered to the makaʻāinana at low prices, at first fifty cents per acre, then later one dollar per acre. The mōʻī and the aliʻi nui thus attempted to protect the rights and interests of the makaʻāinana by enacting and enforcing laws that they believed would preserve the state of pono. In 1850, the legislature passed a bill that allowed foreigners to purchase land in fee-simple terms. Although representatives of the makaʻāinana objected to the bill, they deferred to the aliʻi nui of the House of Nobles.[111]

The aliʻi, including the mōʻī, took the advice of the new kāhuna[112] — missionaries and business advisors from England and America — that such a transformation of land management would act to restore the population, would inspire the makaʻāinana to work hard for material rewards in the capitalist economy being put into place, and would ease commercial treaty making with other members of the family of nations. In the process, makaʻāinana were reconceived as hoaʻāina, which then was translated as "tenant(s)";[113] konohiki became "landlords"; and traditional obligations and bonds were replaced by laws. Osorio notes that "from the Makaʻāinana point of view, then, the law was systematically rending all traditional ties to the chiefs."[114] Even the word "ʻauhau" was co-opted into the new system as "taxes."[115] While the specific "rights of Tenants" were protected under the new law, makaʻāinana and konohiki became more vulnerable to losing their means of making a living and were only able to exercise gathering rights as specified in the law.[116] In Osorio's words, they "could be divested of their property through sale and through other less scrupulous means without the weight of tradition, custom, konohiki, or Mōʻī to intercede on their behalf."[117] What the mōʻī and aliʻi nui thought would be the "pono hou," or new pono, the "malu" (protection; safety) brought by the missionaries, actually put the makaʻāinana in an even more precarious situation.[118] And, in the end, the new pono failed to stop the epidemics and low birthrate.

The main beneficiaries of the māhele were the haole advisers and some aliʻi nui. Kameʻeleihiwa has documented the large acquisitions of land by those advisors who were the architects of both the māhele and the subsequent body of private property law in Hawaiʻi. Even G. P. Judd, who had initially opposed the sale of land to foreigners, owned great tracts of the most valued lands on Maui and Oʻahu.[119]

THE LEGACY OF KAUIKEAOULI

From his childhood as the young mōʻī Kamehameha III until his death in 1854, Kauikeaouli led Hawaiʻi through the multiple challenges to his nation's sovereignty and to his people's dignity. With his council of aliʻi nui, which included women, along with his haole advisers, he transformed Hawaiʻi into a nation-state recognized by the would-be colonizing nations, and in doing so he preserved his nation's independence. The Kingdom of Hawaiʻi adopted what it needed from the European and American systems, while preserving as much as possible its own traditions. It was a constant struggle, however, for Kauikeaouli and all of his people to accommodate and adapt to the demands of the larger countries to conduct business and international politics in their foreign styles, while maintaining pride in the ways of his father. Understanding the reciprocal relationships necessary for a state of pono while responding to the demands, advice, and, too often, the insults of the new kāhuna could easily have been an impossible task. But Kauikeaouli left the nation with a fairly workable constitution and with its status as a member of the family of nations as protected as it could be from the desires of the colonizers who were dividing the world among themselves.

The reign of Kauikeaouli was the last in which women held political power publicly as members of the House of Nobles. The 1840 House of Nobles included five ali'i wahine, but in 1848 there were four, by 1851 it was down to two, and the final woman was appointed in 1855, the year following Kauikeaouli's death.[120] The increasingly hegemonic European and American styles of governance and patriarchal social codes eroded the ancient Kanaka modes of governance that accorded ali'i nui places on the council based on their genealogy and talent, regardless of whether they were male or female.

Kauikeaouli supported schools that created nearly universal literacy in the mother tongue but also instituted English-language schools so that his people could become bilingual. In the same way, after many years of resistance, he accommodated the missionary demand for conversion of all to their brand of Christianity. At his death, the ali'i and maka'āinana who were left had to struggle to continue to control the land under the less-than-ideal circumstances created by the māhele, to resist the more rapacious aspects of plantation capitalism that resulted, and to fight the discursive war that represented themselves and their ancestors as savage beings inferior to the haole.

2

Ka Hoku o ka Pakipika

EMERGENCE OF THE NATIVE VOICE IN PRINT

The Puritans were a daring lot, but they had a mean streak.

— Ishmael Reed

By 1860 the Hawaiian kingdom was on its second Western-style constitution, and although the aliʻi were firmly in charge of the throne a
colonial two-tiered structure was developing across the main institutions of the land, with the Europeans and Americans on the top tier and
the Kanaka Maoli at the bottom. Following the Māhele, Europeans and
Euro-Americans began purchasing large tracts of land. At the same time
many makaʻāinana became alienated from their traditional lands by
these political and economic processes. The aliʻi nui considered West-
erners to be knowledgeable in the workings of government and so the
aliʻi often appointed them to positions of power within the kingdom. In
the judicial system most judges were haole, especially at the top levels,
while most of those judged were Kanaka Maoli. Land agents for the
government were often haole; their applicants (or supplicants) were
Kanaka Maoli. The churches were controlled by haole, because the
Euro-American ministers were reluctant to give up control over even

small village parishes. Finally, schools were divided into two types, select and common: "Select schools, besides being, as the term implied, of better quality than the common schools, had various special objectives: to qualify their students for positions above the level of the common laborer, to teach them the English language, to supply teachers for the public schools, to train girls to be good housewives and mothers. . . . English was the medium of instruction and a tuition fee was charged."[1]

Common schools were conducted in Hawaiian, and rather than "qualify their students for positions above the level of the common laborer" they were part of the project of transforming Kanaka Maoli into common laborers. Because of their language and their access to cash, most haole were able to send their children to select schools while most Kānaka Maoli had to be content with common schools. At the same time, on the developing plantations the owners and luna were haole, while the field laborers were Kanaka Maoli or Asian immigrants.

In this chapter I describe the newspaper *Ka Hoku o ka Pakipika* as one site of Kanaka Maoli resistance to the rising colonial capitalism that the U.S. Calvinist missionaries supported and in which they participated and that the aliʻi nui both opposed and facilitated in different ways. The battle over whether or not, or how severely, Kanaka Maoli were to be subjugated was largely a discursive one, fought with paper and ink through weekly newspapers. In order to more fully understand the role of these newspapers, I offer here a review of the political, economic, and ideological context(s) in which they appeared.

POLITICS, THE ECONOMY, AND THE MŌʻĪ

In King Kamehameha III's later years, after two decades of resistance, the missionaries were allowed to become a relatively uncontested moral force that enjoyed influence over the government.[2] They had engineered the māhele and the political structure of the newly formed kingdom, and they had moved into positions of power in the cabinet and privy council. But Kamehameha IV (Alexander Liholiho) and his brother Ke Kamāliʻi Lota Kapuāiwa, a member of the House of Nobles and minister of the interior (who would reign later as Kamehameha V), constituted a new force in politics that did not accept or appreciate that the Calvinist missionaries' ideas alone should reign. Kamehameha IV had in fact removed Richard Armstrong from his cabinet by reducing his title from minister of public instruction to president of the Board of Education.[3] Now, although the missionaries were gaining power in the economic arena, they were also experiencing some losses in the political arena because of the resistance of these two aliʻi nui to instituting American ways.

From the start of the reign of Kamehameha IV the planters were exerting pressure on the mōʻī to assist them with their two most pressing difficulties: selling their sugar duty-free in the United States and ensuring a supply of cheap labor. Both of these pressures presented threats to Hawaiian sovereignty: first, because one obvious way of guaranteeing the duty-free market was to be annexed to the United States and, second, because the proposed solutions included government support for pressuring Kanaka subsistence farmers to become impoverished wage laborers, and the importation of immigrant labor to fill the "need," which would overwhelm the declining population of Kanaka Maoli. The situation thus made the kingdom more vulnerable to the colonizing powers.[4] Edward Beechert notes that "the question of sovereignty and the welfare of the sugar industry were never separate questions in the political maneuvering of the nineteenth century."[5] Planters exerted power in the government—in the cabinet as well as the House of Nobles and House of Representatives—toward the increase of the sugar economy, while the aliʻi nui, including the mōʻī, tried to accommodate them without sacrificing the sovereignty of the kingdom. It was during this period that discussion of a reciprocity treaty with the United States as a substitute for annexation was revived.

In 1861, the Civil War in the United States began. Kamehameha IV declared Hawaiʻi's neutrality, most likely against the wishes of the missionaries, who were mainly New Englanders and abolitionists. Missionary sons (born in Hawaiʻi and thus subjects of the kingdom) Samuel Armstrong and Nathaniel Emerson, for example, interrupted their studies at Williams College to accept commissions and fight in the Union Army. The mōʻī, however, had to attend to the continued independence of the country, which required neutrality lest the nation be held hostage by warships from one side or the other.[6] The U.S. Civil War was, moreover, a boon to the Hawaiʻi sugar planters, who gained new markets when sugar production in the U.S. South ceased because of the war.

During this time a series of tragic events gripped Kamehameha IV's life and eventually caused his death. The first was his shooting of his secretary, Henry A. Neilson. Ralph Kuykendall writes that "the king's mind had been poisoned against Neilson by some means — idle or malicious gossip . . . the queen's name was somehow involved." Kamehameha IV then "sought out Neilson, and shot him with a pistol at close range."[7] The young mōʻī apparently never recovered from his grief and remorse for his act; and Neilson died of his injuries two and a half years later. Around this time Kamehameha IV asked the Episcopal (Anglican) Church to establish a mission in Honolulu, another move that no doubt angered the U.S. Calvinists. In fact, the American Board of Comissioners for Foreign Missions protested the king's request directly to the archbishop of Canterbury, but to no avail. The first important act of the Anglican mission was the baptism of Albert, Prince of Hawaiʻi, the only child of Kamehameha IV and Queen Emma. Unfortunately, the four-year-old prince, heir to the throne and the bearer of the hopes of the nation, died a few days after this baptism. Kuykendall quotes one of the newspapers as saying, "The death of no other person could have been so severe a blow to the King and his people."[8] Kamehameha IV himself died of grief and despair just one year later.

THE RISE OF THE PLANTATION ECONOMY

Despite the resistance of the various mōʻī to domination by the missionaries, they were persuaded that a capitalist economy would benefit the country and that they must conform to a European/American political-economic system. Although Kamehameha III originally intended to create a system that would ensure pono for his people by instituting the māhele, the change instead led to foreigners being allowed to buy large tracts of land on which they built sugar plantations. Noel Kent explains that sugar plantation economies are large-scale production enterprises, and in the mid-nineteenth century they were located in colonies or other areas with populations vulnerable to exploitation, including the Caribbean, the U.S. South, and Hawaiʻi nei. Kent adds, further, that "sugar societies thus generally came to be characterized by a series of interlinked phenomena: a heavy concentration of political and economic power in the hands of those in control of the plantation apparatus, a sharply stratified class structure with a strong racial and/or cultural component, and a concentration on one export to the metropolitan areas of North America and Europe." The hands in control, says Kent, were those of a diverse group of businessmen, including some former whalers, but many were also missionaries and their sons.[9]

Missionaries had been active agents in the māhele and in the subsequent alienation of the Kanaka Maoli from the land in several ways. When Robert Wyllie, minister of foreign affairs, sent out a survey to determine the state of the people and the land in 1846 and again in 1858, he sent it to "all Christian Missionaries, Planters and Graziers upon the Islands." Wyllie's survey asked for census information, but also asked for the following information:

- Daily wages paid to laborers computed in cash, not including provisions.
- How the moral and physical labor of the natives is affected by excessive unpaid labor exacted of them.
- What are the best means of abolishing that indolence and indifference and introducing habits of general industry continuously pursued.
- Have the natives any means for buying land or cattle, that is, can they pay for them.
- Best means of preserving and improving the native race and rendering them industrious, moral and happy.
- If capitalists should apply their capital to any considerable extent to the purposes of agriculture, could they depend upon a sufficiency of native labor, and at what wages per day.[10]

Wyllie further asked not whether, but "how far the native chiefs oppress the natives," and not whether, but "what moral or improving effect upon native females . . . has their marriage to white men." He wondered, "Would it be practicable and beneficial to introduce the English language entirely?"[11] Missionaries were the primary information gatherers for this enterprise, and thus directly linked to the māhele and to the acquisition of land by foreign capitalists. An undergirding of white supremacist thinking is clearly discernible in the questions. For Wyllie and his missionaries and planters, "natives" are presumed to be indifferent and indolent; "chiefs" oppress the people; and "native females" must experience a range of "moral or improving effect[s]" from marriage to white men. This survey is strikingly similar to one described by Benedict Anderson: "Note also alongside the condescending cruelty, a cosmic optimism: The Indian is ultimately redeemable — by impregnation with white, 'civilized' semen, and the acquisition of private property, *like everyone else.*"[12]

In agreeing to gather this information, the missionaries in effect became government agents and were thus complicit in the establishment of colonial capitalism. This kind of demographic surveillance is precisely the type that Foucault notes arose in the nineteenth century as one of many new techniques of power: "[T]he emergence of demography, the evaluation of the relationship between resources and inhabitants," Foucault states, contributed to the development of what he calls "biopower," without which capitalism could not have flourished. Further, capitalism would not even have been possible, he adds, "without the controlled insertion of bodies into the machinery of production and the adjustment of the phenomena of population to economic processes."[13]

Missionaries and their children and grandchildren became a large part of the bourgeois class of planters. Many were able to buy large enough tracts of land for plantations because of their privileged positions and/or contacts in the government. Edward Bailey, for example, arrived in Hawai'i in 1837 to join the mission, but left it in 1850 to start a sugar plantation. He "conducted the earliest manufacture of sugar at Wailuku . . . [and] also had an active part in starting the Haiku Sugar Company."[14] Richard Armstrong, the same missionary who became minister of public instruction, attempted to start a sugar operation at Wailuku as early as 1840. Other missionaries, including William P. Alexander, assisted in the project by surveying the land: "Measures are in progress towards sugar works at Wailuku. In reference to it, I am requested to survey all the King's land north of Wailuku River."[15] Alexander himself, along with his son James, started a plantation in 1862, and his other son Samuel became a partner in the large sugar concern Alexander & Baldwin, which, along with Castle & Cooke, are members of the "Big Five" companies that controlled Hawai'i's economy for many decades.

Sometimes the line between mission work and establishing plantations became indistinguishable. In Alexander's report of his mission activities for 1860, he stated: "We have hundreds of acres of fertile soil that might easily be irrigated by our perennial streams that burst forth from our mountain glens, yet we produce almost nothing but kalo: whereas we ought to produce and export a thousand tons of sugar

annually."[16] Kalo (taro) was the staple of the Kanaka subsistence economy. It is still a staple food for Kanaka Maoli today, though it is scarce
and expensive as a result of the change to a cash economy based on
sugar, pineapple, and tourism.

It was missionaries who facilitated the start of the first plantation at
Kōloa, Kaua'i, in the face of protests from both island governor Ka-
ikio'ewa and the maka'āinana living there. Plantation owners procured a
fifty-year lease of the entire ahupua'a of Kōloa, and in the words of
Arthur Alexander, "the whole-hearted endorsement of their enterprise
by the American missionaries undoubtedly helped the partners in obtaining their lease, for it was not easily obtained." Alexander further adds
that when "the jealousy of the petty chiefs, in seeing their lands thus
alienated, proved, for some time, a great obstacle to their success,"[17]
missionaries intervened to resolve the troubles in favor of the plantation
developers.

We can see, then, that the missionaries commanded a powerful
influence over government officials and worked as government agents
in the era of developing plantations. They and others, using their positions of influence and their capital, bought land previously farmed by
maka'āinana for subsistence and turned that land into plantations for the
production of the cash crop sugar.

MISSIONARY PLANTERS AND THE DISCOURSES
OF WORK AND CIVILIZATION

The planters' concern over the indolence of the "natives," as described
above in Wyllie's survey, is related to missionary discourse of an earlier
time that persisted into this era and well on into the twentieth century.
Max Weber's study of the links between Calvinist ideology and the
development of capitalism is most illuminating here, even though he did
not address the imposition of capitalism in the colonial situation. Ideo-
logically, for the puritanical missionaries, work was of the utmost importance. As Weber characterizes the Calvinists: "Waste of time is . . . the
first and in principle the deadliest of sins." Even "contemplation is . . .
valueless, or even directly reprehensible if it is at the expense of one's
daily work." Further, "Unwillingness to work . . . is symptomatic of the
lack of grace."[18] This discourse fits seamlessly into the planters' designs:

the planters wanted workers willing to labor for long hours with little pay. When the Kānaka Maoli refused to do so, they were called lazy and extortionate.[19]

Examples of this discourse are found in the Hawaiian Evangelical Association attempts from 1857 to 1859 to legally ban hula. It might be assumed that the missionaries objected to hula on the grounds that it threatened the Christianizing of the people or that it was licentious and therefore evil. But the discourse throughout the move for the ban reveals that the association was more worried about labor than about religion, or, at the very least, that the two were inextricably intertwined. In 1857, for example, the *Pacific Commercial Advertiser* published an editorial in support of the ban. The editor wrote that "natives care little for anything else than witnessing [hula] by day and night. They are in fact becoming a nuisance, fostering indolence and vice among a race which heaven knows is running itself out fast enough, even when held in check with all the restraints which civilization, morality and industry can hold out."[20]

The Hawaiian Evangelical Association contended that hula "interfere[s] materially with the prosperity of the schools," which was also a concern relating to labor. Students in the common schools were expected "to pay their own way by the sweat of the brow . . . in digging taro or planting potatoes."[21] In addition to contributing to the material prosperity of the schools, this practice was no doubt part of training students for a life of labor in the fields. And it was the labor of the makaʻāinana that enriched the missionary planter.

Weber also shows how the Calvinist commitment to work in a "calling" led its practitioners to wealth in capitalist economies. It was not against the Calvinist code to accumulate wealth, except where such wealth might lead to "the consequence of idleness and the temptations of the flesh."[22] The Calvinists's asceticism led them to limit their consumption of luxuries while continuously working and saving, of which Weber says, "the inevitable practical result is obvious: accumulation of capital through ascetic compulsion to save."[23]

In Hawaiʻi, the missionaries turned these values into immense profits through the plantation economy. Their ideology necessarily included a firm conviction of their own superiority, and thus they saw little contradiction in becoming the owners of the land and overseers of the production while the people they had come to save labored and lived in poverty. Weber observes that "this thankfulness for one's own perfection by the grace of God penetrated the attitude toward life of the Puritan middle class, and played its part in developing that formalistic, hard, correct character which was peculiar to the men of that heroic age of capitalism."[24] The values that resulted in such economic power contributed to the missionary planters' ability to convert that economic power into social and political power as well.

The same discourse of work justified the subjugation and conversion of Kanaka Maoli into laborers. Samuel N. Castle, for example, said that he advocated the sugar plantations not for his own profit but "to benefit workless Hawaiians."[25] Labor would help elevate the savage to civilization. This notion is similar to certain rationalizations of slavery in the United States that claimed, for example, that "negroes were changed from barbarians to a degree of civilization under the coercive power of slavery."[26] In fact, the defense of slavery often depended on this very same discourse, as Winthrop Jordan so carefully details. Jordan quotes Representative William Loughton Smith of South Carolina's insistence on the necessity of slavery at the U.S. Constitutional Convention in 1787: "It is well known that they [the slaves] are an indolent people, improvident, averse to labor: when emancipated, they will either starve or plunder."[27]

Tightly woven with the discourse of work were the discourses of race and civilization. By 1861, Euro-Americans in the United States had developed a particularly racialized worldview. Anthropologist Lee D. Baker demonstrates how "the institutionalization of slavery and scientific ideas of racial inferiority were critical steps in the evolution of the formation of a racialized worldview." He explains that scientists "fused their aesthetic judgments and ethnocentrism to form an elaborate system to classify the races into a rigid, hierarchical system," which was then used in North America "to [buoy] existing power relationships, political goals, and economic interests, which in turn institutionalized racial inferiority." Scientific studies were used to "explain that Negroes and Indians were savages not worthy of citizenship or freedom."[28]

Related to this was the discourse of civilizing the savages. For the Calvinist mission, to "civilize" the Kanaka Maoli was to lift them up to enlightenment from what the missionaries often called their "degraded" status. The missionaries were charged with raising "an entire people 'to an elevated state of Christian Civilization.'"[29] That the Kanaka Maoli were part of an uncivilized race was the primary assumption of the first and each succeeding company of missionaries. It justified the appointment of missionaries, the bearers of civilization, to their positions of power. Later, after eighty years of missionization, the same discourse was deployed to justify the U.S. political takeover of Hawaiʻi: the uncivilized were said to be incapable of self-government.

Furthermore, by 1861 the discourse of civilization was already a long tradition on the American continent. According to Baker, Spanish explorers represented the indigenous peoples of the New World as savages, and the English elite then borrowed this discourse to impose it on the "wild" Irish. Baker goes on to say that "the same traits used to depict the Irish as savage in the seventeenth century were used to classify African Americans and Native Americans as savages during the following three centuries."[30] The discursive hierarchy of savagery, barbarism, and civilization was used to rationalize colonial policies that enslaved Africans and displaced and destroyed the indigenous peoples.

This discourse was reinforced in the eighteenth and nineteenth century by scientific studies that asserted the natural inferiority of certain uncivilized races. In Baker's view, in the United States the idea of "race" is inextricably linked not only to the imagined "scientific" hierarchy of peoples but also to missionary ideology. It has its antecedents "not in the science of race but in the theology of heathenism, the saved, and the damned."[31] Thomas Gossett adds to this theme by stating that slavery itself was justified as "a means of converting the heathen."[32]

The discourse of civilization also contributed to the disempowering of Kanaka women, especially in the political arena. Through the imposition of Euro-American constitutions, laws, and churches, women's public voices and previous paths to power became increasingly limited. It was through discourse that women's relegation to the private sphere, as in Europe and the United States, became hegemonic.

NEWSPAPERS AS SITES OF DISCURSIVE STRUGGLE

In this struggle among the mōʻī, other aliʻi nui, the makaʻāinana, missionaries, and planters of various types, newspapers would become the main battleground for competing discourses. For forty years the mission controlled the power of the printed word in Hawaiʻi. The missionaries used this power not just to save souls but to assist in the progress of plantation/colonial capitalism, to control public education, to mold government into Western forms and to control it, and to domesticate Kanaka women. Then, in 1861, to the shock and outrage of the missionary establishment, a group of Kānaka Maoli, makaʻāinana, and aliʻi together, transformed themselves into speaking subjects proud of their Kanaka ways of life and traditions and unafraid to rebel. Their medium was a Hawaiian-language newspaper called *Ka Hoku o ka Pakipika* (The star of the Pacific). This paper began a long tradition of nationalist, anticolonial resistance through the print media.

Although precise circulation statistics are not available, it is certain that the newspapers were widely read. According to Helen Chapin, "Without a doubt, the Hawaiian language newspapers had the largest readership of any papers in the Islands. Among these, by far the largest number were opposition papers."[33] Chapin notes further that "a vigorous Hawaiian nationalist press emerged in the 1860s. . . . It quickly gained and held the largest circulation and the majority of readers until the century's end."[34] Schools conducted in Hawaiian in 1861 numbered around 266, with a student population of over 8,000. By this time, literacy in Hawaiian was "almost universal,"[35] and as I show below, this large, literate population of Kanaka Maoli desired reading material of all types.

Prior to and at the time of the emergence of *Ka Hoku o ka Pakipika*, the mission published evangelical and school newspapers, as well as indirectly controlled the government newspapers. Missionary son Henry Whitney owned a nominally independent English-language newspaper, the *Pacific Commercial Advertiser*. In 1856, Whitney started a paper called the *Hoku Loa o Hawaii*, which actually was a single page included in the four-page *Advertiser*.[36] Reader and newspaperman Kānepuʻu complained that the subscription price for readers of both languages was the same, $6 per year, even though the English readers got three-fourths of "na olelo oloko, ono ke moni aku" (the language inside that was delicious to swallow).[37] After a time Whitney suspended the paper, and when he resumed it the Hawaiian-language page was gone.

Then, in 1859, the mission started a monthly paper called *Ka Hoku Loa* (The distant star) (not to be confused with *Hoku Loa a Hawaii*; see the accompanying table). The editor of *Ka Hoku Loa* was Henry Parker, son of missionaries and pastor of Kawaiahaʻo Church. Desirous of any news in Hawaiian, Kānepuʻu and others petitioned Parker to publish it

TABLE 1. Hawaiian newspapers, 1856–1864.

NAME	TYPE	LANGUAGE	EDITOR	DATES
Ka Hoku o ka Pakipika	resistance	Hawaiian	J. W. H. Kauwahi, David Kalākaua	Sept. 1861 to May 1863
Nupepa Kuokoa	establishment	Hawaiian	Henry Whitney	Oct. 1861 to Dec. 1927
Hoku Loa o Hawaii	establishment	Hawaiian	Henry Whitney	July to Sept. 1856
Ka Hoku Loa	Calvinist mission	Hawaiian	Henry Parker	July 1859 to Dec. 1864
Ka Hae Hawaii	government	Hawaiian	R. Armstrong, J. Fuller	Mar. 1856 to Dec. 1861
Polynesian	government	English	A. Fornander	1840 to 1841; 1844 to 1864
Pacific Commercial Advertiser	establishment	English	Henry Whitney	1856 to present

Note: Classification generally follows that by Helen Geracimos Chapin in "Newspapers of Hawai'i, 1834–1903" (*Hawaiian Journal of History* 18 [1984]:47–86) and *Shaping History* (Honolulu: University of Hawai'i Press, 1996), except I have substituted the category "resistance" for her term "opposition." "Establishment" means the paper represents dominant and prevailing interests.

weekly, but Parker left to accept a teaching post at Lahainaluna seminary before any such change could take place.

At this same time a government paper was being published in Hawaiian, *Ka Hae Hawaii*, under the editorship of J. Fuller. Readers petitioned this paper as well to increase its size to include foreign and island news, mele, legends, and letters, but the proposed size and content increases were never implemented.

KA HOKU LOA

Both *Ka Hae Hawaii* and *Ka Hoku Loa* served colonizing functions. Both reinforced the missionary dictate that labor equaled salvation, participated in the attempted domestication of Kanaka women, and asserted that every aspect of Western culture was superior to native culture, especially religion. *Ka Hoku Loa* was associated with the Hawaiian Evangelical Association, the semiautonomous administrative board for the mainly Calvinist U.S. missions in Hawai'i. The missions had previously been administered by the American Board of Commissioners for Foreign Missions. The Hawaiian Evangelical Association had been formed in 1854 as part of a policy change "to make the American missionaries and their families permanent members of the Hawaiian body politic."[38] The reasons for starting *Ka Hoku Loa* were expressed in its first issue, as follows: "Ua ulu nui ka hewa ma kela wahi ma keia wahi, iwaena o na mea he nui; kakaikahi nae ka poe i ku e kinai i ka hewa, a e kokua i ka pono. . . . E papa aku ana ia me ka wiwo ole i na hewa i hanaia ma na wahi kiekie, a me na hana kolohe i hoopukaia iwaena o ka lehulehu, a e hoike aku ana me ka makau ole, ka hopena weliweli o ka lahuikanaka, a me ke aupuni i makau ole i ke Akua" (Sin has increased everywhere, among many people, and few are those who have stood up to extinguish sin and assist righteousness. . . . [This paper] will forbid, bravely, the sins committed in high places and the naughty behavior among the people, and will show without fear the terrible end of a people and a government who have no fear of God).[39] It is thus clear that the missionaries considered their own morals and mission to allow them to stand in judgment on even the mō'ī. The king may run the government, but the missionaries, in their own minds inherently superior, were to judge and instruct.

Each issue of *Ka Hoku Loa* contained various reports of the Hawaiian Evangelical Association or other related missionary associations, which served as the primary site for their "civilizing" discourse. An issue in 1861, for example, contained an editorial explaining that 383 church members had been expelled in Hawai'i in the previous year. The editorial gives six reasons for the expulsions, the first of which was "o ka hana ole i ka hana maoli, kekahi hewa no ia" (not doing real work, which is a sin). The editorial elaborated by explaining that some "kanaka" go from island to island, making friends, staying with different people, "a hala ka makahiki paha i ka noho wale ana" (until a year passes of just sitting/living). It further asserted that "mai loko mai o ka noho molowa ana i ulu ai ka moekolohe, ka ona, ka piliwaiwai, a me na hewa e ae he nui wale" (out of laziness grows adultery, drunkenness, gambling, and a great many other sins). Other reasons for expulsion included not going to church; drinking; "na hana haumia" (defiling/impure actions); not keeping the marriage laws; and not keeping the Sabbath, on which one was not to "sit around" or go visiting: "i hookahi wale no huakai hele i ka Sabati, oia hoi ka huakai hele i ka hale o ke Akua" (there should be just one journey on the Sabbath, the journey to the house of God). Another reason stated was "ka hoomana kii" (idol worship), which included Kanaka Maoli medical practices, because such activity included prayer to the ancient akua; of specific concern was prayer to the female akua Hiʻiaka and Kapo.[40] The church paper thus reinforced the discourse of civilization and salvation through the Protestant virtues of work and asceticism, which conveniently justified turning Kanaka into plantation laborers.

In October 1861, *Ka Hoku Loa* published a full-page condemnation of Kanaka Maoli medicine, calling it idolatry, falsehood, and murder. People also wrote letters reporting that they had seen lapaʻau "medicine" being practiced, and they urged others to instruct their families to give it up.[41] The editors also published stories such as "Lapaau ana" (Healing), a short retelling of the story from the Bible in which a woman is healed by merely touching Jesus's robe.[42] Kanaka Maoli were still suffering from epidemics and the spread of Hansen's disease (leprosy) was just beginning, thus all types of medicine were needed during these crises. But medicine was another site of struggle, as the missionaries sought to persuade the native people that their centuries-old knowledge was inferior to European scientific knowledge.[43]

Ka Hoku Loa also attacked Kanaka moʻolelo. In November 1861, missionary John Emerson (father of Nathaniel and Joseph), wrote that people are afraid of "na akua lapuwale" (worthless gods) because "ua hai na kanaka kahiko i na kamalii i na kaao, i na mele, a me na moolelo piha i na mea lapuwale e puiwa ai" (the old Hawaiians told the children the legends, the songs, and the stories/histories that were full of worthless things to frighten [or startle] them). His main point was that moʻolelo should not be published in the newspapers: "Ina i makemake na kanaka naaupo e hai i na mea lapuwale i na keiki a lakou e puiwa ai, no lakou ia; aka aole pono ke paiia ma na Nupepa [*sic*]" (If ignorant/uncivilized people wish to tell worthless things to their children to frighten them, that is their own business; but it is not right that they be published in the Newspapers). Emerson used the valley of Kaliuwaʻa (now known in English as Sacred Falls, and now closed because of a deadly rockslide) as a specific example of ongoing practices. Nearly everyone, he wrote, "kanaka naaupo" (ignorant/uncivilized Kanaka) as well as "hoahanau" (church members), take offerings there because they are afraid "o huhu mai lakou [na akua], a hoolele mai i na pohaku maluna o ko lakou mau poo" (lest they [the gods] become angry and throw rocks down upon their heads).[44]

In his writings cited above Emerson uses the word naʻaupō. This word, and its opposite, naʻauao, are notable for the implications in their translation. Naʻau means thoughts or feelings (one's interior self), a metaphorical extension of the physical meanings, "intestines, bowels, guts." Ao and pō are adjectives; ao means light, daylight; pō means darkness, night. To be naʻauao is to be enlightened, educated, wise, and civilized. Although the word civilized is not given in Pukui and Elbert's *Hawaiian Dictionary* as a gloss for naʻauao, the word uncivilized does appear as equivalent for its opposite, naʻaupō, along with "ignorant" and "unenlightened."[45] An underlying assumption in this discourse is that haole ways of life are naʻauao and Kanaka ways are naʻaupō; Emerson's task as missionary was to fight all that was naʻaupō and replace it with ways that were naʻauao.

KA HAE HAWAII

Ka Hae Hawaii (The Hawaiian flag) was founded in 1856 as a publication of the Department of Public Instruction. J. Fuller was named as editor, but the paper was controlled behind the scenes by Richard Armstrong, the missionary serving as minister of public instruction.[46] Its purpose was "e kokua mai ma na mea e holo mua i keia aupuni" (to assist progress in this nation). "Progress" meant Euro-American protestant culture, as indicated in this sentence from the same statement of purpose: "Mai ka wa ia Lono a me Kamehameha nui, ua holo mua ia kakou; aole nae i pau ka hemahema a me ka naaupo" (From the time of Lono [Captain Cook] and Kamehameha the Great, we have progressed; but incompetence/lack of skill [hemahema] and savagery/ignorance are not over).[47] The paper hoped to assist progress by supporting farming, and to a lesser degree, trade and the schools. The government paid Fuller's salary, so the price of *Ka Hae Hawaii* was only $1 per year, "no ka pepa, a me ka inika a me ka pai ana" (for the paper, the ink, and the printing).[48]

A letter from Kamehameha IV endorsed the newspaper: "I ike na keiki o ka aina, i ka Hae Hawaii, e komo ana iloko o kela hale keia hale, e paipai ana i ka palaualelo e hana, e kahea aku ana i ka naaupo e naauao, a e hoohuli ana mai ka hewa 'ku a i ka pono" (So that the children of the land will see *Ka Hae Hawaii*, entering into every house, encouraging the lazy to work, calling the ignorant/uncivilized to learning/civilization, and converting from sin to righteousness.)[49]

Ka Hae Hawaii instructed its readers, these "children of the land," just as it would children, although the readership was mainly adult and literate. The paper contained basic descriptions of foreign countries and peoples written in a fashion similar to children's encyclopedia articles. Along with the basic information, however, were discussions written in judgmental and critical terms. For example, an article on Persia describes the people as follows: "Aole i akamai i na hana, he ike iki no nae kekahi poe i ka palapala, aole nae i naauao loa" (Not skilled in work, some are somewhat literate, but not well educated/very civilized). As for the leaders, "E noho hookano wale mai ana no na 'lii, a me ka poe waiwai, aole imi i na mea e pono ai ka aina," (The rulers/royalty and the rich live arrogantly, they do not seek for things that will benefit the land).[50]

In a short article on Africa, *Ka Hae Hawaii* published this description of women soldiers: "He puali koa wahine ko ka Moi o Dahomei, ma Aperika, he 3,000 lakou. He mau wahine ano hihiu a ino loa, me he mau Leopadi ke ano i ke kaua ana. Ua aahu ia lakou i na lole wawae, he palule a me ka papale koa, a o ko lakou mea kaua, he pu me na pahi nui. He akamai ko lakou i ka hana paikau, a ma ke kaua maoli he ikaika loa no, me he poe Daimonio la ka hana ana" (The King of Dahomey, in Africa, has women soldiers, 3,000 of them. These are rather wild and very evil women, like Leopards when they fight. They are dressed in pants, shirt, and soldier's hat, and their weapons are guns and large knives. They have skill in marching, and in true battle they are very strong, they are like Demons in their actions).[51] Racism against dark-skinned people is evident here in the comparison of the women to animals and demons. Further, the depiction of the strong Dahomey women is meant to contrast to the picture of proper behavior for women and girls prescribed in the paper. One such article starts with a list of the faults of Kanaka women: "Nui ka hemahema o na wahine Hawaii. . . . [Nana] au i ka wahine, he pelapela ke kino, aole kuonoono ka lauoho, a me kahi lole aole maemae. Pela no hoi ka hale, he pelapela, huikau kela mea keia mea o ka hale" (Hawaiian women have many failings. . . . [When] I look at the woman, her body is dirty, her hair is not well-kept, and the dress, not clean. It is the same with the house, it is dirty, and everything in the house is mixed up). The anonymous author continues with recommendations, and further fault-finding: "O ka ka wahine hana ia, o ka malama i ka hale, a maemae. Eia nae paha ka hewa nui, o *ka noho wale o na wahine*; aole hana ma ka lima, moe wale no i ka moena. . . . Aole pela na wahine o na aina naauao, i ao pono ia" (The woman's work is to care for the house until it is clean. This is perhaps the greatest fault, *it is women just sitting*; not working with the hands, just lying on the mat. . . . Women in civilized countries, who are well-taught, are not like that). According to the article, housework has other benefits, as well: "Ua maemae hoi ke kino a me ka hale o ia wahine naauao, a makemake loa kana kane ia ia. Aole lilo ka manao o ke kane i ka wahine e, no ka mea, he wahine maikai kana" (The body and the house of the civilized woman is clean, and her husband likes her a lot. The mind of the husband is not on other women because he has a good woman).[52]

Related to the admonitions to conform to Euro-American gender behavior were condemnations of well-known aikāne (friend, male lover of male ali'i nui), in articles such as "Ka wa ia Kaomi" (The era of Kaomi, 1833–1834).[53] Kaomi was a male lover of Kauikeaouli (Kamehameha III) despised by the missionary establishment. According to the article in *Ka Hae* he was half Tahitian and half Hawaiian; he was literate and had served as a Christian minister in Queen Ka'ahumanu's court. He eventually left preaching, however, and when Ka'ahumanu died Kaomi became close to the young Kauikeaouli. According to historian Kamakau, "He became a favorite of the king . . . because he knew . . . the art of healing . . . [and] had learned . . . how to diagnose a disease by feeling the body of a patient and could prescribe the proper medicine to cure it."[54]

Many missionary-inspired laws were openly transgressed while Kaomi was an intimate of the king: Kamakau states that "fighting, murdering, adultery, prostitution, plural marriage, disregard of the marriage law, drunkenness and the distilling of liquor went on all over Oahu."[55] According to the newspaper story, "o ka haunaele nui oia mau makahiki, no Kaomi ia, oia ke alii o ka haunaele ana" (all the disturbances of those years related to Kaomi, he was the king of disturbance). Among the disturbances, "ua puhiia ka okolehao, ua hulaia na hula a puni ka aina"

('Ōkolehao [a liquor] was brewed, hula was danced all around the land), the effect of which was that "Ua haaleleia hoi ka mahiai, a nahe-lehele a wi loa na aina, a lilo na makaainana mamuli o na lealea a na hulumanu, a oki loa ka aina a pau i ka pololi a me ka ilihune" (Farming was abandoned, until the lands were overgrown and famine-struck, and the people were lost because of the entertainments of the court favorites, all of the land was devastated by hunger and poverty).[56] In the story, Ka-omi was in the end abandoned by the young king, deserted to wander, ill and destitute, until he died. The story is meant to be a lesson in Calvinist morality, and to reinforce the discourse of salvation and civilization through labor.

In *Ka Hae* readers would assist in the civilizing/educational process by reporting on fellow Kānaka Maoli who practiced traditional cus-toms. Here is an excerpt from one of these letters: "O ka lawe ana o kekahi poe i na iwi kupapau i ka lua o Pele, i mea e hoomana ai ia Pele, i akua no lakou. O ka hana mau keia a kekahi poe e noho nei ma kai o Puna" (Some folks [take] bones to the crater of Pele, in order to conse-crate Pele as a god for them. This is the persistent activity of some people living near the coast of Puna). The letter writer, K. W. Kawaiahao, describes the people's search for the proper "kaula Pele" (Pele prophet/ seer) who would join them on the journey to the crater, ensuring that they were taking the proper offerings: "kahi moa keokeo, he wahi luau no hoi; he puaa paahiwa no hoi" (a white chicken, a bit of young taro leaf, of course, and a completely black pig as well). Kawaiahao also describes their journey, in what order they walked, and that the kāula chanted before the bones were put into the crater at the spot designated. He then ended: "Kainoa paha ua pau ka pouli ma Hawaii nei, eia no ka ke hele pu nei me ke aupuni o Kristo. Auwe! . . . E hoi hou anei kakou i na hana o ka pouli?" (I thought the darkness was ended in Hawai'i; but here it is traveling along with the government of Christ. Auē! Shall we return to the ways of darkness?).[57]

Such letters to *Ka Hae, Ka Hoku Loa*, and later to *Nupepa Kuokoa* seem ambiguous in their intent, however, because while they called for authorities to enforce laws or church rules against such practices, they simultaneously recorded the details of the practices, even sometimes including the text of the necessary prayers.

Ka Hae ran both short and long mo'olelo, one of which was classi-cal Hawaiian while others, like "He mooolelo no Kalaipahoa," characterized the ancient practices as evil, and congratulated the people on abandoning them.[58] *Ka Hae* ran the first written version of the classical Hawaiian legend, *He Moolelo no Kamapuaa* (A story of Kamapua‘a), about the pig god Kamapua‘a, who is a sort of trickster. His home is the valley of Kaliuwa‘a, the place of offerings lamented by John Emerson. The story, written by G. W. Kahiolo, ran for fourteen weeks and included many chants.[59] The twentieth-century translators of this text said of Kamapua‘a: "He was racy, but not without a certain charm; he was earthy and crude, but it was all part of his appeal. He was Kamapuaa, a destructive hog demigod of ancient Hawaii about whom many tales were told. . . . Women are his great delight and he is always chasing them."[60] But Joseph Emerson (son of John, the missionary, and brother of orientalist and Pele chronicler, Nathaniel) wrote that "the legend requires sixteen hours to repeat, and is perhaps one of the best commentaries on the ineffable depths of impurity in which some heathen delight to wallow. In general, the more vile, obscene, and hateful the god, the more ready were the deluded people to render him worship."[61] It may have been this very mo‘olelo of Kamapua‘a that prompted John Emerson to remonstrate against mo‘olelo in *Ka Hoku Loa*.

Despite its occasional willingness to publish traditional mo‘olelo, *Ka Hae Hawaii* primarily engaged in civilizing discourse by urging Kānaka Maoli to work, by denigrating them and other native peoples, and by attempting to domesticate Kanaka women.

KA ‘AHAHUI HO‘OPUKA NŪPEPA KŪIKAWĀ O HONOLULU

Out of frustration with *Ka Hoku Loa* and *Ka Hae Hawaii*, and a need to talk back to the colonizing forces, especially the Calvinists, a hui of Kanaka men formed an association to publish a newspaper for their own political opinions, as well as their own traditions. J. H. Kānepu‘u, who had previously exhorted *Ka Hae* and the other papers to expand their Hawaiian-language content, proposed to his friend G. W. Mila (Mills) that they establish a paper that would be "e pili ole i ka aoao hookahi wale no, aka i nupepa e pili ana i na aoao a pau. Aoao Kalavina, Katolika, Moremona, poe makemake i na kaao, poe makemake i na mele maikai, poe makemake i na Nuhou o na aina e, a pela aku" (not affiliated with one denomination, but a newspaper concerning all the denominations. Calvinist, Catholic, Mormon, people who want stories, people who want good mele, people who want news from abroad and so forth).[62] Out of this proposal the special newspaper publishing association was born, the ʻAhahui Hoʻopuka Nūpepa Kūikawā o Honolulu, which initially consisted of 22 members.

It is important to note here that in addition to their wish to provide traditional Hawaiian orature[63] (at this time and through this medium transforming into literature), as well as the freedom to publish antimissionary and pro-Kanaka opinions, Kānepuʻu and his hui desired "news from abroad," which they felt was being withheld by the government and church newspapers. This was a primary lack that the association wished to address in *Ka Hoku o ka Pakipika*.

The pilot issue of *Ka Hoku o ka Pakipika* immediately contested the foreign, puritanical standards for publishable content. This first issue contained a mele in the Hawaiian language, titled "He Mele Aloha no ka Naauao," (A song of affection for education/civilization).[64] Two weeks later, *Ka Hae Hawaii* printed a letter in which the author wrote: "Malaila ua heluhelu au i na olelo pelapela, lapuwale, he mea hoohaumia i ka naau o ke kanaka. Hilahila wale kekahi mau olelo i hoolahaia ma ia pepa, he mau olelo i paa i na manao wela o ke kuko, e hoao ana i na kuko ino a pau o ke kanaka" ([In *Ka Hoku o ka Pakipika*] I read obscene, worthless words, something to contaminate/defile the minds of people. Some of the words published in that paper were very shameful, they were words held in the burning thoughts of desire, tempting all the evil desires of people).[65]

The author of the letter, who signed it "Puni Maʻemaʻe" (Chastity/purity lover),[66] went on to worry that *Ka Hoku* would continue to publish such "mele pelapela, haumia haku ia e kanaka moekolohe no ko [*sic*] lakou mau wahine hookamakama!" (obscene, indecent songs composed by adulterers for their prostitutes!). Puni Maʻemaʻe charged that such obscenity would lead to the death of the Hawaiian youth, and, further, that a newspaper has mana: "He mana nui kona no ka pono, ka malamalama, ame ke ola o keia lahui; a i ole ia, he mana kona no ka ino, ka pouli, a me ka make o ka lahui Hawaii" (It has great power for righteousness, enlightenment, and the life of this lāhui; or it has power for evil, darkness, and the death of the Hawaiian lāhui). In writing these statements Puni Maʻemaʻe protested against the publication of the paper, "ma ka inoa o keia lahui nawaliwali e hooikaika nei e lanakila ma luna o ko lakou mau kuko ino" (in the name of this weak people struggling to win over their evil desires), and he compared the mele to a tomb, which may be polished bright and shiny but still contains death.[67]

This letter was reprinted in the first numbered issue of *Ka Hoku o ka Pakipika*, along with a reply signed "Puni Nūpepa" (Newspaper lover). Puni Nūpepa wrote that the mele does not contain evil, adulterous, or obscene words that would kill the Hawaiian people:

> Owau no kekahi i ike, he mele kahiko keia i hakuia no ka naauao, e ke kumu a me na haumana, a ua hana ia no hoi keia ma na la hoike, i ko makou wa e noho haumana ana na J. W. Kaiwi, e noho mai la i ke kai anuanu o Fatuhiva . . . Wahi a Punimaemae, ua hanaia ia mele no ke ano hookamakama wale no . . . he aha hoi o J. W. Kaiwi, ka mea nana i ao mai, a nana no ka hapanui o na olelo iloko oia mele?
>
> (I am one who knows, this is an old song composed for education/ civilization, by a teacher and students, and it was done for the examination days, when we were students of J. W. Kaiwi who is now living in the cold seas of Fatuhiva . . . According to Chastity/Purity Lover, this song was made only for prostitution . . . What then is J. W. Kaiwi, the one who taught, and the one who composed most of the words of this song?)[68]

What then was J. W. Kaiwi? He was a Kanaka Maoli convert to Christianity who served as a missionary to the Marquesas Islands (Fatuhiva is an island of the Marquesas group). The Kanaka missionary had chosen to express his love for education/civilization using metaphors common in his own language, which Puni Maʻemaʻe and other missionaries then translated into their language and concluded were obscene.

Puni Nūpepa argued that no newspaper is perfect, and even the Bible is not free of words such as "adultery." He then challenged Puni Maʻemaʻe further: "Ina he haole oe e Punimaemae, e hoohalike kaua i ka hale kupapau, aole nae aʻu i ike he hale kupapau ulaula kekahi, koʻu ike he hale kupapau keokeo" (If you are haole, let us compare our tombs, I have never seen a brown tomb, what I have seen is a white tomb).[69] Puni Nūpepa thus dared Puni Maʻemaʻe to reveal himself as haole, and implied that if death were resulting from anyone's actions, it was from the haole, not from the Kanaka. Puni Nūpepa objected as well to the characterization "lahui nawaliwali" (a weak people) by recalling the bloody battles of Kamehameha I, clearly implying that a Kanaka would not make such a characterization.

The Kanaka Maoli knew that Puni Maʻemaʻe was haole because of the way he reacted to the mele. Puni Maʻemaʻe knew enough Hawaiian to write a letter, and he knew enough about Hawaiian songs to know that they are replete with metaphor and figurative language, but he was unable to understand what they meant. More important, he was unable to understand that the language concerning lovemaking was a metaphor. Because of that inability, he was excluded from the communications going on among the Kanaka Maoli in the publication of the mele, and it enraged him. The use of such metaphorical language in mele and also in moʻolelo allowed the Kanaka Maoli to communicate while escaping the surveillance of the missionaries, in ways that have parallels to the African slaves in the United States.[70] The reaction from the missionary quarter was to attempt to silence those communications.

The editors of *Ka Hoku o ka Pakipika* confronted these missionary "speech police." On November 7, a long editorial charged that when similar mele were published in *Ka Hae Hawaii* they were not considered shameful or obscene, and the author gave an example. He went on to say, "Aole nae paha hoi e hihi, o kau mea no i lealea ai, i ka puka ana nae paha mai ka Ilikeokeo ae, a i na [*sic*] no paha na ka iliulaula, olelo no oe, paa iho la ka waha" (Perhaps you do not wish to get into an argument about this: that the thing that you enjoy when it is published from the Whiteskin, if published by a brownskin, you say, the mouth should stay shut).[71] This author obviously asserted that the issue was not one of obscenity after all, but that the charge of obscenity was being made in order to silence the Kanaka Maoli.

Some Kānaka responded in provocative ways, as in this letter that begins in strikingly sexual language, as if purposely to further anger Puni Maʻemaʻe:

> E ka Hoku o ka Pakipika. — Aloha oe:
> E ae mai oe iaʻu e hooipo aku me oe, "kuu aikane punana a ke onaona," no keia wahi kumu manao i manao ai au e hoike akea aku i kekahi mea i hana ia ma ke Kulanakauhale Alii.
> (To the Star of the Pacific. — Greetings:
> Allow me to make love with you, "my aikane, nest of fragrance," concerning a topic that I thought to make public about something that has happened in the Royal City.)[72]

It is important to remember that to the Puritan missionary sensibility, any nonclinical or nonlegal mention of sex in print would be considered obscene and taboo and was sure to provoke repressive action. In Hawaiian, however, such descriptive language is normal and thus not considered obscene. Further, sex itself was not shameful; it was openly discussed and even taught to children by grandparents until well into the twentieth century.[73] Along with "hooipo" (make love), the use in the letter of the word aikāne is possibly inflammatory because although it is defined in the contemporary dictionary simply as "friend" (generally of the same sex), in a ruling chief's court, aikāne held special places as close companions to the ruling chief. Those relationships were often homosexual, such as Kaomi's relationship to Kamehameha III.[74] If the relationship was sexual it was described as "moe aikāne," or, to sleep with an aikāne. The word ai by itself means to have sexual relations, and the word kāne means man or male. But here the seemingly explicit (and possibly homo-) sexual language is a metaphor for something else: the communication of the letter writer's thoughts to the newspaper.

This difference in reading and use of language in the original mele and the letter points to one of the inadequacies of translation — that is, that the translation of words alone cannot adequately convey meaning because of the many aspects of the two cultures that are not shared.[75] Puni Maʻemaʻe could understand enough of the mele to form an opinion about its content, but he was not immersed enough in Hawaiian culture to understand the metaphor. The language of romantic, probably physical, love used as metaphor in both situations was not at all obscene and was perfectly acceptable to the native speakers of Hawaiian, but it was outrageous to the puritanical church people. It is also possible, however, that *anything* the Kanaka Maoli published at the time might have caused the same reaction. The simple act of claiming the power of print for themselves was enough to outrage the missionaries, who considered themselves the teachers and parents of the Kanaka, whom they thought of as childlike and in constant need of surveillance, supervision, and instruction.

THE HAOLE DESIRE FOR CONTROL

The invitation to love quoted above was actually simply an introduction to a letter by Kānepuʻu that described briefly how the paper came to be published. According to this letter, Henry Whitney wanted to control the publication of the paper. Kānepuʻu and others had arranged to rent the government printing press for their new paper, but then Henry Whitney offered a bid for a contract to rent them his press. Because Whitney's quoted charges kept rising, Mila, Kānepuʻu, and most of the original members voted to remain with the government press. Another letter writer confirmed that the problem was that Henry Whitney wanted to control the paper, rather than just print it: "E noi mai ana e hookuu aku ka Ahahui, ia ia na lilo a pau a me ke poho a me ka puka, a nana ponoi ka Nupepa, a e lilo ka Ahahui i mea ole . . . oia na ano nui oia palapala hoike a H. M. Wini" ([His bid] was asking that the [Newspaper] Association dissolve, that the expenses, the losses and the profits, and the Newspaper itself would be his [Whitney's] own, and the Association would become naught . . . those were the major points of H. M. Whitney's bid).[76]

This was unacceptable to the majority of members of the association because it would mean the loss of Kanaka Maoli control of the content of the paper. The author of the letter, J. W. Kalaiolele, wrote that the organization then split, and "ke halawai nei ka *aoao hina wale aku* ma ka aoao o Wini . . . A o ka poe i koe; ke kupaa mau nei lakou me ka luliluli ole a hiki i ke ko ana" (the *side that fell so readily* to Whitney's side is meeting . . . and the people remaining; they are persisting with unshakable resolve until [the newspaper project] is fulfilled).[77] In other words, some members of the association decided to follow Whitney, who then established *Nupepa Kuokoa* as a rival to *Ka Hoku o ka Pakipika* under Whitney's ownership and editorial control, while the remaining members of the association stayed faithful to their cause.

The conflict over the paper was sometimes framed as missionary desire to control it, which is related both to the charges of obscenity and to Whitney's desire to control the content of the paper. An unsigned editorial in the September 26 issue of *Ka Hoku o ka Pakipika* begins:

I ke kui ana aku o ka lono e pai ana kekahi Nupepa *ku i ka wa* ma ka olelo maoli — i Nupepa i kokua ole ia e ke Aupuni, aole hoi ma ka aoao hookahi kana hana — i Nupepa hoi kahi e hiki ai ke kamakamailio no na mea e pili ana i ke Aupuni, na aoao hoomana, ka mahiai ana, a me ka noho ana o kanaka, a kahi hoi i hiki ai i na kanaka maoli ke hoike pono aku i ko lakou mau manao . . . ua hoeuia ka manao kue o kekahi, a ke [w]alo aku nei mawaena o keia mau Mokupuni ka pihe o ka uwa kumu ole o ka poe nana i kukulu i keia manao kue. . . . Ua nui na hana ino i hanaia i mea e

poino ai keia Nupepa iloko o kona wa opiopio; o kekahi poe e ku ana ma
na kuahu halepule, ua kapa mai lakou i keia Nupepa he "puahiohio,"
nana e make nui ai i keia lahui.

(When the news went out that a *special* Newspaper would be published
in the native language — a Newspaper not sponsored by the government,
nor by any denomination — and a Newspaper where people could dis-
cuss the Government, the churches, farming, and people's lives, and a
place where Kanaka Maoli could fully express their opinions — opposition to this was stirred up, and the shouts of the people forming this
baseless opposition are resounding all around the Islands. Many bad
things have been done to harm this Newspaper in its young days; some
people standing at the church pulpits have called this Newspaper a whirl-
wind [of worthless talk]/something to misinform people/sway people
off the right path, one to bring mass death to this nation/people.)[78]

The reference here to "mass death to this nation/people" is not literal
but rather a reference to the part of the evangelist Christian discourse
that says that puritanical morality guarantees everlasting life, and that
swerving off that path means death. We can begin to see here that Puni
Ma'ema'e was not alone in his opinions but instead was part of the larger
church community. This account charged that there was a group of
people determined to put the newspaper down, and that some of them
were ministers of certain churches. The editorial goes on to say that, "Ua
oleloia hoi, ua lilo ka hoole ana o keia Nupepa i kekahi rula o ka ekalesia"
(It has been said that refusal of this Newspaper has become a rule of the
church), following which is "No ke aha la hoi i kue mai ai keia poe i ko
kakou pono, e na kanaka Hawaii? No ke aha i hoolilo ia ai na kuahu o na
halepule i kahi e hoakea ai i ka Nupepa a Wini (he haole) e pai ia ana?
Kainoa ua kukulu ia na hale pule no ka hoomana ana i ke Akua, aole o ka
hoolaha ana o na mea kuai o keia ao nei" (Why have these people
opposed what is to our benefit, Hawaiian people? Why have the alters of
the churches become a place to publicize Whitney's [a haole] Newspaper that is being published? We thought the churches were built to
worship God, not to advertise the sale goods of this world). The letter
writer then swiftly proposes an answer: "Ua hopohopo paha ko lakou
manao e loaa auanei ia kakou ka noonoo ano okoa i ko lakou mea i
oleloia mai" (Perhaps they are worried that we will acquire thinking
which differs from what [we] have been told by them).[79]

An editorial on October 3 identifies the problem as paternalism on the part of the missionaries, asserting that perhaps they were attempting to relegate the Kanaka Maoli to an infantile status:

He kanaha makahiki i hala mai ka hoomaka ana mai o keia lahuikanaka e aoia, a e ike i ka palapala a me na mea naauao o keia noho ana, mamuli o ke ao ana a na misionari Amerika; . . . ua kanaka makua na keiki . . . nolaila ke kukulu ana . . . i Nupepa no lakou iho . . . ua pau ka noho ana malalo o na makua oia na Kumu, a ua oo hoi, ua paa ka manao e hoona-auao i na makamaka. Aka ke keakea mai nei na makua, me he mea la e olelo ana, aole oukou i hiki i na makahiki e oo ai, na makou ia hana, a ma ia ano, ke hoohuli ia nei i kekahi mau keiki [*sic*].

(Forty years have passed since this people began to be taught to know reading and writing, and the naʻauao things of this life, under the in-struction of the American missionaries; . . . [Now] the children have become adults . . . therefore the establishment of their own Newspaper . . . living under parents, that is the Teachers [missionaries], is over, we have matured, our minds are made up to educate our peers. However, the parents are opposing us, as if saying, you have not reached the years of maturity, it is we who will do this work, and in so doing they are making us into children.)[80]

It would thus be much more to the liking of the missionary community that Whitney control any new, so-called independent, newspaper, espe-cially because as the son of missionaries of the "pioneer company" (the first company of the American Board of Commissioners for Foreign Missions) Whitney was one of their own.[81]

Agents attempting to sell subscriptions and deliver *Ka Hoku o ka Pakipika* reported being obstructed by missionaries, as in the following example:

Ke hoike aku nei au i ka mea hou i puka mai iaʻu, mai kuu Makua o ka olelo hoopomaikai, oia o Mr. Rev. W. P. Alexander. Penei:

"O ka Hoku o ka Pakipika, no ka aoao lealea ia, no ka Diabolo la, e imi oe e kinai ia pepa." Pela mai nei kela iaʻu, ma kona Leter [*sic*]. . . . Ua kauoha ia mai nei au e hooikaika e paipai i na kanaka i ka lawe i ka "Nupepa Kuokoa."

(I hereby tell you what has come to me from my father of the blessed Word, Mr. Rev. W. P. Alexander, viz.:

"The *Star of the Pacific*, it is on the side of pleasure; it is for the Devil; seek you to destroy this paper." So he said to me in his letter. . . . I have been commanded to exert myself in urging the people to take the *Nupepa Kuokoa*.[82]

The *Polynesian*, a Honolulu English-language paper, went on to report that "the Rev. Pastor at Koolaupoko had been catechising and exhorting some of his church members not to take the new native journal, alleging that it was a wicked and bad paper." According to this report nearly all the ministers joined in the condemnation: "We have only heard of two names who have not lent themselves to this unprovoked persecution of a native enterprise."[83]

The *Polynesian* was edited by Abraham Fornander, who at this time took over the government press in a lease agreement, thereby freeing his own paper from government control. Fornander's editorial of November 23 also presents the controversy as Kānaka Maoli desiring control over their own paper versus the missionary desire to have it controlled by haole. Here are some excerpts from his editorial: "The greatest opposition . . . comes from the Protestant Missionaries, who . . . use every endeavor to crush the *Hoku* and stop its circulation . . . The editors of the *Hoku* are defending themselves valiantly, and the contest has led to some very plain talking as regards the limits of clerical interference with the political and economical relations of the people. . . . the spirit of the conflict seems to be one of mental emancipation . . . The truth is, that there is a mental revolution going on among the native population, which the Missionaries are equally incompetent to comprehend, to master or to avert."[84]

We can see here that there was not a simple divide in which all haole were opposed to *Ka Hoku*, and all Kanaka Maoli were for it. *Ka Hoku*, in fact, selected a haole editor, Mila (G. W. Mills), as someone to translate articles from English for the paper, but it was understood that "e hana ana nae ua haole nei, mamuli o ka mea i ae ia aku e ka Ahahui kanaka Hawaii" (this haole would do what was agreed to by the organization of Hawaiians).[85] In other words, although Mills was an editor, general editorial and publishing control was in the hands of the Kanaka Maoli association, and the luna nui (editor-in-chief) was Kanaka Maoli J. W. H. Kauwahi. Furthermore, it was stated, "Ua kokua nui no na haole i keia Nupepa, ua haneri a oi ae ko lakou nui, no ko lakou aloha i neia hana a kanaka Hawaii" (many haole have assisted this Newspaper, there are a hundred or more of them, because of their love or kind feelings for this project of the Hawaiians).[86] Abraham Fornander surely was one of them.

FIGHTING FOR THE RIGHT
TO SPEAK AND TO BE KANAKA

For the next year and a half or so, the pages of *Ka Hoku o ka Pakipika* would fill with editorials that talked back to the missionary discourse that disparaged Kanaka culture and worked to disempower Kanaka politically, as well as alienate them from their lands, domesticate Kanaka women, and change both men and women into impoverished plantation laborers. Kānaka also accomplished this through the publication of traditional moʻolelo and mele that celebrated their indigenous language and culture.

Resistance to the discourse of salvation through labor appeared in the pages of *Ka Hoku o ka Pakipika* both symbolically and in castigation of unethical activity by missionary planters. The symbolic was expressed, for example, in the one song that appeared in the paper in English, called "Oh, Come, Come Away." Here are the first three lines:

Oh come, come away, from labor now reposing,
From busy care awhile forbear,
Oh, come, come away.[87]

Edward Bailey, the planter on Maui, was chastised in *Ka Hoku o ka Pakipika* for abusing his power as a former missionary. According to the story in the paper, his cattle ran into a Kanaka neighbor's yard, destroying some property. When Bailey was confronted by the neighbor and asked to pay for the damage, he retaliated with a peculiarly chilling death threat to the Kanaka farmer. Bailey reportedly told the farmer that he had written down the names of the publishers of *Ka Hoku o ka Pakipika* and sent the paper to God. Coincidentally, two of them died shortly thereafter. Bailey also suggested that because the farmer had been seen with the evil newspaper, he could add his name to the death list.[88] The editors of *Ka Hoku o ka Pakipika* asked (and answered): "Aole anei oia ka mea i kauohaia ai e ka Haku mai hoahu i ko oukou waiwai ma ka honua? No ka puni waiwai ia manao i ulu mai ai; a ua makemakeia e ike na mea a pau i ke ano o ka poe a lakou i hilinai ai" (Are they not the ones commanded by the Lord not to accumulate wealth on the earth? It is because of love of wealth that this has arisen; and it is desired that everyone should know the character of the people that they trust).[89] *Ka Hoku o ka Pakipika*, like *Ka Hae Hawaii*, advocated farming as a way of life and a means of livelihood but, as the example above demonstrates, the editors resented and resisted the authority of the missionaries who had become plantation owners and were attempting to subjugate Kanaka Maoli by intimidation. *Ka Hoku o ka Pakipika* provided an effective means of talking back to the haole planters.

The Kanaka Maoli also fought the racist discourse that depicted them as savages or barbarians, — that is, as uncivilized. The writers and editors of *Ka Hoku o ka Pakipika* demonstrated that Kanaka Maoli had mastered the technology of the haole (the printing press and the palapala), and then went further to show off their skills in both traditional literature and modern political writing. They countered the hierarchical racism by refusing to grant it any validity and by valuing their own language and culture to a high degree. Their language about themselves reveals pride in their heritage: "kanaka" was not yet an epithet to be ashamed of.

In other words, to some extent, Kanaka Maoli agreed that they had become civilized. For them, however, agreeing to become civilized had more to do with retaining their independence as a sovereign nation than with acceptance of the racial or cultural hierarchy. Sally Merry shows how Hawai'i's continued independence hinged on proving itself as a member of the exclusive club of civilized nations.[90] The peoples who could not show themselves to be "civilized" were being taken over by the Mana Nui "Great Powers" all over the world, including in the Pacific. For many Kānaka Maoli, to be na'auao meant to be literate and educated in business, law, and/or politics, but it did not mean that traditional arts and customs should be condemned to a dark, soulless past.

Ka Hoku o ka Pakipika asserted this Kanaka brand of being na'auao through publication of written versions of the ancient mo'olelo, many of which appeared on its pages in print for the first time. On the front page of the September 26, 1861, issue was the first installment of the "Mooolelo no Kawelo" (Story of Kawelo), a tale from the ancient oral

Ka Hoku o ka Pakipika's first regular issue. The front page consists entirely of the "Mooolelo no Kawelo." (Courtesy of the Hawaiian Historical Society) tradition that includes chants and prayers to the old gods. Kawelo is a supernatural youth raised in a family of aliʻi ʻai moku. The important tension in the story surrounds the issue of who of several cousins in the family will grow up to "ku i ka moku" (literally, "stand upon the island"), that is, who will become the single ruling aliʻi of the island of Kauaʻi. Kawelo must develop skills and strategies to take the contest from his physically larger cousins and uncles, who might also have a clearer genealogical right to rule. The boy is favored from birth; his grandparents choose him to hānai (raise). As a youth he travels to Oʻahu with his grandparents and learns farming there, while his older cousins learn "mokomoko" (boxing or wrestling). On Oʻahu Kawelo also takes a sweetheart and begins to train in hula. He then goes on to learn "ke kaua" (battle). His girlfriend, Kanewahineikiaoha, and her father go with him to learn as well.[91] After Kawelo masters ke kaua, he decides to learn fishing, which leads to his adventure with Uhumākaʻi-kaʻi, a supernatural fish who drags Kawelo and his fishing teacher to Kauaʻi and back.

It is through prayer to the native akua that Kawelo ultimately kills the fish. It is also through pule (prayer) combined with training in his various disciplines that Kawelo gains mana, so that, later in the story, when one of his uncles, Aikanaka, dispossesses Kawelo's parents of their land, Kawelo is ready to do battle and win. The power of prayer to the ancient akua is an important recurring theme in this and other moʻolelo published in *Ka Hoku o ka Pakipika*. When messengers are sent by Kawelo's distressed parents, for example, those messengers are delayed and troubled throughout their journey because they failed to pray before eating. Before proceeding to Kauaʻi to make war on Aikanaka, Kawelo stops to build a heiau, then "hoouluulu iho la o Kawelo i na akua ona, o Kaneikapualena a me Kulaniehu" (Kawelo appealed to his gods),[92] who are forms of the major gods Kāne and Kū.

Kawelo's wahine plays a crucial role as a messenger in the war preparations, and she accompanies him to Kauaʻi as well. In the descriptions of the armies, women and children are said to have participated: "o na koa . . . elua lau kanaka, aole nae i helu ia na wahine a me na keiki" (as for the soldiers . . . there were eight hundred of them, but women and children were not counted).[93] In this story, women are reported to travel alone, learn the arts of war, and participate in war. These are reported as unremarkable small details of the story, not as unusual events.

Perhaps the most important legend to appear in *Ka Hoku o ka Paki-pika* is "He Mooolelo no Hiiakaikapoliopele" (The legend of Hiʻiaka-ikapoliopele), the grand epic of the coming of age of Hiʻiakaikapolio-pele, the youngest sister of Pele, the volcano goddess. Unlike "Mooolelo no Kawelo," this story of Hiʻiaka is very long and was serialized weekly from December 26, 1861, through July 17, 1862. It is signed by the author, M. J. Kapihenui of Kailua, Koʻolaupoko, Oʻahu. This was the first publication of the epic (up to a dozen others have been published since in the Hawaiian language), and it is the uncredited source for most of Nathaniel B. Emerson's book *Pele and Hiiaka: A Myth from Hawaii*.[94] While Emerson has been credited with saving this knowledge from disappearance,[95] the Kanaka Maoli themselves realized that moʻolelo could be preserved by publication, and they chose to do so themselves fifty years prior to and independent of Emerson's researches and pub-lications. In fact, Kānepuʻu predicted that future generations would want these stories, and that the knowledge of them would disappear along with the people if it were not consciously preserved. He worried that not every bit of the Hiʻiaka story and its chants was appearing in print if the editors were cutting out parts for brevity's sake. If they left something out, he asked, "pehea la anei e loaa ai na koena i na hanauna hope o kakou, ke makemake lakou e nana[?] . . . e hele ana kakou i ka nalowale, e hele ana o Kau ka makuahine o M. G. [*sic*] Kapihenui i ka nalowale. E makemake ana ka hanauna Hawaii o na la A.D. 1870, a me A.D. 1880, a me A.D. 1890, a me A.D. 1990" (How will the generations after us obtain the remainder [which is being left out], when they wish to see it? We will be gone[;] Kau, the mother of [author] M. G. Ka-pihenui will be gone. Generations of Hawaiians in 1870, and 1880, and 1890, and 1990 will want this).[96]

The story that generations of Hawaiians want concerns the most important deities of hula. The moʻolelo begins with a scene in which Pele admires the young beauty Hōpoe dancing hula on the island of Hawaiʻi at a place called Hāʻena, the easternmost point in the archi-pelago. Pele asks her sisters to reciprocate, but only Hiʻiakaikapoliopele does. She composes and chants an oli (chant) in tribute to the beautiful Hōpoe and her "hula lea." The word leʻa is a modifier that means "pleas-ing, delightful," but has a definite sexual connotation because it also means "sexual gratification, orgasm."[97] Such poetry consciously makes use of double meanings of these kinds of words. Hiʻiaka is clearly en-

tranced with Hōpoe in a way that might easily be interpreted as romantic and/or sexual. After her chant, Hi'iaka goes off with Hōpoe to dance
hula and surf, an event that is sometimes interpreted as the birth of
hula.[98] Hi'iaka's sisters go off to fish, and Pele goes into a sleeping/
dreaming state in which her spirit follows the sound of a hula drum to
the island of Kaua'i. Pele's spirit appears as a beautiful young woman as
she approaches the house from which the sound of the hula drum ema-
nates. Inside she sees a young (male) ali'i, Lohi'au, playing the pahu,
the hula drum. This house is located at another place also called Hā'ena,
but now on the northwest side of Kaua'i, one of the westernmost islands
in the archipelago. Now it is Pele's turn to be entranced; she falls in love
with Lohi'au. This is a parallel structure characteristic of Hawaiian literature: Hi'iaka is entranced with Hōpoe performing hula at Hā'ena on
Hawai'i; Pele is entranced with Lohi'au performing hula at Hā'ena on
Kaua'i. Hula is a major recurring element throughout the mo'olelo, as is
envinced by its richness in hula-associated oli, mele, and pule, and hula
is central to the narrative.

The main story is about Hi'iaka's travels to fetch Lohi'au for Pele
after Pele has to return to the volcano because she cannot remain in a
spirit state indefinitely. Thus Hi'iaka must leave her own new-found
love to fetch that of her older sister's. Before Hi'iaka's journey, Pele
imposes the following kauoha (command): "Mai moe olua, mai honi,
mai iniki, mai lalau aku, a lalau mai, o make olua ia'u" (do not sleep
together, do not kiss, do not pinch, do not reach for each other/have a
sexual affair, lest I kill you two). The work "iniki" is translated as "pinch"
but it also has many romantic/sexual connotations in song. Likewise
"lalau" might be either "lalau," to go astray, to have sexual affairs, or
"lālau," to seize, take hold of, grasp, reach out for.[99] These ambiguities
are, of course, both common and intentional in Hawaiian, and they
constitute a literary device that provides pleasure to the knowledgeable
reader.[100] Hi'iaka then imposes kauoha of her own; she wishes to protect Hōpoe from Pele's volcanic rages that destroy the landscape and
anything on it: "o kuu moku lehua nei la, mai ai oe ma laila . . . o kuu
aikane, mai ai oe," (my lehua grove, do not consume by fire there . . . my
aikāne [Hōpoe], do not consume by fire). Pele agrees to those kauoha,
and Hi'iaka sets off on her journey.

Hi'iaka travels largely on foot, with her young female companions,
Pā'ūopala'e and Wahine'ōma'o. Women's lives are the main concern of

the legend, first in Pele's community, then in Hi'iaka's heroic epic, a coming-of-age tale in which she explores and exercises her powers as a goddess to heal and to kill. According to John Charlot, "Pele, her sisters, and their friends establish a community dominated by strong-willed women, in which men most often play a tangential and even comic role (the name of the principal love interest, Lohi'au, translates as 'slow')." He further observes that "the passions of women for each other — both loving and hating, constructive and disruptive — are often the main motivations of the action. Those passions can be sexual, a clear reflection of the bisexuality common in classical Hawaiian life."[101]

Hi'iaka's epic, like Kawelo's, is full of prayers of various sorts to the indigenous akua as well as mele, oli, hula, and details of native medicinal remedies — all of which were forbidden to Kānaka Maoli in 1861. An outstanding example of prayer to native akua occurs when Hi'iaka and Wahine'ōma'o arrive on Kaua'i and meet with a man named Malaehaakoa and his wife Wailuanuiahoano, who worship Pele. Hi'iaka and Malaehaakoa chant to each other as the women approach, and the lame Malaehaakoa is miraculously able to walk and cut firewood shortly thereafter. He prepares food for the women, and "ia Wahineomao i ai [sic], alaila, hoomaka o Malaehaakoa e hula me kana wahine, me Wailuanuiahoano, hapai ae laua i keia mele loihi loa, penei. (He hula Pele keia)" (while Wahine'ōma'o ate, then, Malaehaakoa began to hula with his wife, Wailuanuiahoano, they took up this very long mele [This is a Pele hula]).

The couple then sing and dance the Pele hula, the words of which are printed as part of the story. The mele as printed is 234 lines long and there are many references to Pele as "akua" or "akua nui," (great or important deity).[102] Malaehaakoa also refers to Pele and Hi'iaka together as his akua: Hi'iaka asks, "Hana oe i kou hale a maikai no wai?" (You have made your house nice, for whom?), and Malaehaakoa replies, "No o'u mau akua" (For my akua). Hi'iaka asks again: "No wai?" (For whom?) And Malaehaakoa says, "No Pele, no Hiiakaikapoliopele" (For Pele, for Hi'iakaikapoliopele).

An example of the use of native medicine, banned at the time of publication, is when Hi'iaka revives Lohi'au, who has killed himself because Pele disappeared and he did not know how to find her. When Hi'iaka brings Lohi'au back to life she must say the correct prayers, and the prayers must be uttered correctly or Lohi'au will not live. The prayers are printed in *Ka Hoku* as part of the moʻolelo, and the details of Hiʻiaka's healing methods are also given.

Hiʻiaka, Wahineʻōmaʻo, and the revived Lohiʻau travel back to Pele's land, having other adventures along the way. Before she arrives home Hiʻiaka knows that Pele has broken the kauoha and has consumed the lehua grove and Hōpoe in one of her volcanic rages. Near the end, Hiʻiaka takes revenge on Pele for her destruction of Hōpoe by making love to Lohiʻau in Pele's view. There then ensues a great battle, during which many hulihia are chanted. "Hulihia" means "overturned; a complete change, overthrow; turned upside down,"[103] and as one might imagine, these chants describe the violence of volcanic eruptions and related phenomena such as earthquakes and thunderstorms. Kapihenui ends the legend there.

Almost all actions in the epic are taken by women, and their "power is specifically female."[104] Along the way, Hiʻiaka defeats many moʻo, which are spirits that threaten the well-being of humans. She also heals many humans of various illnesses. All of the moʻolelo published in *Ka Hoku*, and especially "Hiiakaikapoliopele," thus forcefully resisted the missionary discourse that disparaged Kanaka medicine and presented the ancient culture in a way that reminded the readers that theirs was not an inherently inferior language or way of life. The moʻolelo and the mele and pule contained within are obviously highly valuable works of art. The ancient religion, complete with the text of prayers, is described in positive ways in all of these stories, as it is in other articles in the paper. The editors published these works knowing that they would be condemned by some of the most powerful people in Hawaiʻi, but they also knew that they had the support of quite a few aliʻi nui, most notably that of Prince Kalākaua, who even edited the paper for some time. *Ka Hoku o ka Pakipika* also provided a venue for women to publish. Although Kanaka Maoli were already largely accommodating the injunction against women participating in the public sphere, women published mele in *Ka Hoku*, including love songs, kanikau (chants of mourning), and traditional mele. In these ways, *Ka Hoku o ka Pakipika* encouraged ordinary Kanaka to be proud of their language and their culture.

NUPEPA KUOKOA

The newspaper that Henry Whitney established to compete with *Ka Hoku o ka Pakipika* was yet another site for the colonizing discourses. Helen Chapin quotes him as writing in the *Advertiser*: "Though inferior in every respect to their European and American brethren, they [Kanaka Maoli] are not to be wholly despised. . . . They are destined to be laborers in developing the capital of the country."[105]

Whitney's idea was that the Kanaka Maoli should learn to live more like the haole in order for colonial capitalism to develop. *Nupepa Kuokoa* (Independent newspaper) would provide crucial assistance for this colonizing project. Its objectives were published in Hawaiian in the Hawaiian Evangelical Association's *Ka Hoku Loa*, and a slightly different version was published in *Kuokoa* itself. An excerpt from *Ka Hoku Loa* reads as follows:

A eia na mea e paiia ma keia pepa.

Akahi. — O na Nu hou mai na aina e mai, na mea e ao aku, a e hooluolu i na kanaka.

Elua. — E hoolaha na *manao haole* [*sic*], ko lakou noho ana, maa ana, oihana, a me na hooikaika ana; i mea e hooponopono, hoonui, a kaikai i na manao o kanaka; i like auanei na kanaka me na haole. . . .

Elima. — E ku paa no keia pepa ma ka aoao o ka *Oiaio a me ka pono*; aka, aole ia e kokua i ka paio ana o kela aoao haipule keia aoao haipule. . . .

Ehiku. — E hoike hoi keia pepa i na Nu hou no keia pae aina. E imi no e hoomakaukau i na mea heluhelu i kela hebedoma keia hebedoma, e hooala mai, a e hooakea i na manao o kanaka, a e kokua i ko Hawaii poe e noonoo, a manao, a hana, a noho elike me na haole.

(Here are the things to be published in this paper.

One. — News from abroad, things to be taught, and to please people.

Two. — To publicize *haole opinions/ideas/beliefs*, their way of life, customs, trades/professions, and endeavors, in order to correct, increase, and lead the thoughts of Hawaiian people, so that the Kanaka will be like the haole. . . .

Five. — This paper will be steadfast on the side of *Truth and righteousness*; but it will not support the struggle of [amongst] all the religious denominations. . . .

Seven. — This paper will also tell News of these islands. It will seek to prepare the readers each week, to awaken [them], and to broaden the minds of people, and to assist Hawai'i's people to think, feel, act, and live like haole people.)[106]

Here I have translated the word kanaka as "people," but it is important to recall that Whitney is addressing Kanaka Maoli not the foreign population, who were not thought to need the same kind of educating. *Kuokoa*'s purpose, then, is clearly directly at odds with *Ka Hoku o ka Pakipika*: *Ka Hoku* is identified strongly as Kanaka, with a clear mission to value Kanaka identity, traditions, and thought, whereas *Kuokoa*'s stated aim is to replace Kanaka identity, traditions, and the like with foreign (haole) ways and thoughts.[107]

In keeping with this idea, *Nupepa Kuokoa* published various mo'o-lelo, mostly of European rather than Hawaiian origin. Three major fairy tales were translated into Hawaiian from the German, from the seventh edition of *Kinder- und Hausmärchen* by the Brothers Grimm (1857).[108] These fairy tales, especially "Twelve Brothers," portray European life and fantasies in which women are silent and submissive. *Kuokoa* also ran a few classical Hawaiian mo'olelo such as "He Moolelo No Umi, Kekahi Alii Kaulana o Ko Hawaii Nei Pae Aina" (A history of 'Umi, one of the famous chiefs of the Hawaiian Islands) by Simeon Keliikaapuni.[109] However, relatively few Hawaiian texts were published in *Kuokoa* compared to the European and U.S. histories and stories.

Continuing the work of the defunct government paper *Ka Hae Hawaii*, *Nupepa Kuokoa* published reports that old traditions and practices were continuing, as in this example: "'Pau Ole Ke Kuhihewa' [Superstition Continues]. Christian moralizing follows words from Kimo [James Dawson] that old Hawaiian religion and 'superstition' is still practiced. Some Hawaiians are reported to be feeding a mo'o kupua [ancestral lizard] [*sic*] residing in a fish pond."[110] *Kuokoa* also worked directly with the mission in publishing articles such as "He Mau Mea Hoonaauao i Keia Lahui Hawaii" (Some things to educate/civilize this Hawaiian people). This article was described as "he papa hoike i na mea a ke Akua i papa mai ai, aole e pono ke mare pu" (a list showing the people that God has forbidden, [who] should not be married together) and includes a listing of thirty people whom a man may not marry, starting with his own grandmother and including his sister and the "wahine a ke kaikaina o kona makuakane" (the wife of the younger brother of his father) and so on. A corresponding list—those whom a woman may not marry—was also included in the article.[111]

Nupepa Kuokoa published a few mele, some of them traditional. Readers of *Ka Hoku o ka Pakipika* considered *Kuokoa*'s printing of any traditional mele to be supremely hypocritical because the publication of mele was the first reason cited for newspaper readers to condemn *Ka Hoku* and take *Kuokoa* instead. A letter from S. K. Kuapuʻu to *Ka Hoku o ka Pakipika* is headlined "Maemae! Maemae!!" (Purity/cleanliness! chastity!!), and it states that Kuapuʻu enjoys *Nupepa Kuokoa*, but it should be considered as a different kind of paper, just as there are different kinds of birds. Some birds eat clean food and some eat unclean food (carrion). The birds that eat clean food know to stay away from the carrion, and so should it be with newspapers; if those condemning *Ka Hoku o ka Pakipika* consider mele to be unclean, they should keep to their cleanliness, states Kuapuʻu, "o aha? O maemae ole hoi paha auanei ka nupepa maemae, ina aole hooko ia keia, ke olelo nei au, maemae ole! maemae ole!! Kainoa hoi i hewa hoi ka *Hoku o ka Pakipika* i ke komo o na mele o na kanikau, a he aha ka hoi ka mea o ka owili pu ana aku ia ope hookahi, ke pilau la hoi kela ia mea" (or what? Or perhaps the clean newspaper will become unclean, if this is not done [keeping mele out], I am saying, unclean! unclean!! I thought it was wrong for the *Hoku o ka Pakipika* to include mele and kanikau, and so what is the reason for the twisting together [of these contradictions] into a single bundle[;] [your paper] is being contaminated by this thing).[112]

CONCLUSION

With the exception of *Ka Hoku o ka Pakipika* all of the Hawaiian-language newspapers in this period were related to or controlled by U.S. missionaries: *Ka Hoku Loa* was the paper of the missionary organization; *Ka Hae Hawaii* was created and produced under the supervision of missionary Richard Armstrong; and the independent newspaper *Nupepa Kuokoa* was owned and operated by missionary son Henry Whitney and received the endorsement of the Hawaiian Evangelical Association. *Ka Hae Hawaii*, *Ka Hoku Loa*, and *Nupepa Kuokoa* were thus all part of the colonizing process to attempt repression of traditional Hawaiian cultural forms, especially to convert the Kanaka Maoli into hard workers. They represented, respectively, the government under missionary influence, the Calvinist mission, and the wealthy business class made up of missionary sons like Henry Whitney. All three papers were replete with discourses of work and industry, woven together with the discourses of purity, salvation, and civilization.

Ka Hoku o ka Pakipika was a rebellious voice claiming to represent all the Kanaka Maoli, even those of the despised religions of Catholicism and Mormonism. It fought the Calvinists both overtly and covertly and in both plain and veiled language. For the first time in print its authors and editors dared to profess pride in their traditions and culture. As Fornander said, there was a "mental revolution" going on, a revolution meant to cast off the yoke of Puritan control over every aspect of Kanaka lives; a revolution where ink flowed rather than blood and that took place largely in the reflection and recreation of the oral tradition. The mental revolution also meant overt resistance to the domestication of Kanaka men by contesting the representations made of them as weak, lazy, and uneducated and to the domestication of Kanaka women by presenting moʻolelo and mele in which women in traditional society wielded power and lived adventurous lives. It provided space for Kanaka Maoli writers to write their own history, as well. S. N. Haleʻole, for example, wrote several historical pieces in addition to many legends.

Traditional practices such as hula and lāʻau lapaʻau, along with the ancient religion, had been the objects of repressive laws. *Ka Hoku o ka Pakipika* reproduced these traditional practices in print form so that they could be communicated among the Kanaka Maoli of the time and preserved for the benefit of future generations. This was in direct opposition to the project of "civilization," and it thus laid the groundwork for the movement that developed some years later under Kalākaua, "Hawaiʻi for Hawaiians," which provided a foundation for the cultural renaissance of that era (see chapter 3). The information thus preserved is also crucial to the reconstruction today of Kanaka Maoli identity as a distinct people and separate nation.

Ka Hoku o ka Pakipika provided space for women to contest the attempted domestication being discursively carried out by the other papers and in church and school. As women lost places from which to launch resistance or counterhegemonic strategies, they increasingly relied on tactics such as the literary ones given in *Ka Hoku o ka Pakipika*.[113]

The ancient legends in this newspaper reinforced Kanaka women's knowledge of their powerful female ancestors and deities. Tales and legends are informative, as Certeau says, because "they are deployed, like games, in a space outside of and isolated from daily competition, that of the past, the marvelous, the original. In that space can thus be revealed, dressed as gods or heroes, the models of good or bad ruses that can be used every day."[114] The representation of women in the Hi'iaka epic is quite different from the picture of womanhood that Armstrong was trying to convey in *Ka Hae Hawaii*. Pele is demanding, jealous, angry, unpredictable, and vengeful. Further, the other women in the epic engage in meaningful and pleasurable activities: they fight off evils, outsmart rapists, chant and dance hula, surf, practice medicine and religion (one and the same at times), and have loves and profound relationships, especially with each other. They are not cooking, cleaning house, or worrying about husbands. They are not domesticated; rather, they are adventurous. Indeed, the legend instructs a different moral code: Hi'iaka loves men while remaining entirely independent of them. She punishes a man for hitting his wife, as well. Wifely submission to husbands was not part of the Kanaka moral code in the mo'olelo.

In addition to its literary work, *Ka Hoku o ka Pakipika* provided translations of foreign news stories because such news was essential to preserving sovereignty. The sovereignty of the Kingdom of Hawai'i had already been seriously threatened by France, Britain, and, more covertly, by the United States. The Kanaka Maoli knew that much of their fate depended on the actions of these Mana Nui "Great Powers." Then, as now, Kanaka needed to be informed of world events in order to conduct their political and economic lives wisely. The withholding of foreign news from the general populace was another infantilizing strategy of the missionary establishment, and *Ka Hoku o ka Pakipika* strove to provide the news from abroad necessary for an informed and politically involved citizenry in a sovereign nation.

As Chapin describes, *Ka Hoku o ka Pakipika* was the first of a long series of Kanaka Maoli nationalist newspapers. For the first time, Kanaka Maoli in rural areas and on neighbor islands were connected to the center of anticolonial nationalist thought on a weekly basis. The Kanaka nationalists had learned from the government and mission presses how to produce and distribute a newspaper. The Hawaiian language thus became a threat to the ongoing colonial project; it had the potential to become a "language of power," as Benedict Anderson puts it.[115] The language of the almost universally literate makaʻāinana class bound them together as a nation. For the colonizers, the communication among this comparatively large "imagined community" was dangerous in part because many of them could not understand Hawaiian. The administrative language was often English and interpreters were used when necessary in government or business. Armstrong "strongly supported the use of English in Hawaiʻi's school system . . . and by 1854, government-run English schools were effectively competing with the Hawaiian medium schools."[116] As the century proceeded, demands for government and other business to be conducted in English became more frequent and strident. *Ka Hoku o ka Pakipika* thus played a crucial part in the formation of anticolonial nationalism among the Kanaka Maoli. It became a model for the nationalist Hawaiian-language press for the next century and, just as important, it provided space for anti-hegemonic voices at a time when U.S. hegemony in Hawaiʻi was still in question.

In its recitations of traditional mele, moʻolelo, and moʻokūʻauhau, *Ka Hoku o ka Pakipika* reflected and communicated a specifically Kanaka national identity. This national identity was based in the ancient cosmology and the realm of the sacred that the haole did not share. This is similar to the anticolonial nationalism that Partha Chatterjee describes in colonial India. Chatterjee says that anticolonial nationalism in India "divid[es] the world of social institutions and practices into two domains — the material and the spiritual. The material is the domain of the 'outside', of the economy and of statecraft, of science and technology. . . . In this domain, then, Western superiority had to be acknowledged and its accomplishments carefully studied and replicated. The spiritual, on the other hand is an 'inner' domain bearing the 'essential' marks of cultural identity. . . . Nationalism declares the domain of the spiritual its sovereign territory and refuses to allow the colonial power to intervene in that domain."[117]

Ka Hoku o ka Pakipika reinscribes and reinvokes the ancient cosmology as its sovereign territory, so to speak. Many Kānaka Maoli did not experience the conflict between the ancient beliefs and their Christianity that the missionaries expected or wanted them to experience. Some Kānaka Maoli reconciled conflicts by comparing people and events in the ancient tradition with the ones described in the Bible.[118] As kuʻualoha hoʻomanawanui jokingly says, "the Hawaiians had four hundred thousand gods. One more was no big deal."[119] Through *Ka Hoku o ka Pakipika*, the Kanaka Maoli were able to create a new kind of sacred space in which the ancient gods and traditions lived again. One reason the resistance took place in a sacred space rather than a political one is that it *could*. While the economic system was driven by aliʻi colluding with colonial capitalist power, and while political sovereignty existed at the mercy of great states with warships, rifles, and cannons, the Kanaka Maoli were a people small in number and unable to raise up a great navy. They could, nevertheless, retain a sovereign identity as a lāhui, through preservation of their language, stories, songs, dance, and cosmologies. They did and do have themselves, a collective identity, rooted in an ancient, sacred past.

Ka Hoku o ka Pakipika may not have been radically antihegemonic in that it did not urge its readers to establish a more self-determining or self-governing Kanaka society by taking up arms and ousting the mahaʻoi foreigners who were controlling their lives. Its editors understood well the dangers that a small nation faced in the imperial century, and so they focused on the possible: a strengthening of pride in heritage, the preservation of valuable traditional knowledge, and the provision of a space to contest the more grievous acts of the colonizers. *Ka Hoku o ka Pakipika* laid the foundation of cultural resistance that its most famous editor, David Kalākaua, built on when he reigned from 1874 to 1891.

3

The Merrie Monarch

GENEALOGY, COSMOLOGY, MELE, AND

PERFORMANCE ART AS RESISTANCE

The foundation of the Hale Nauā is from the beginning of the
world and the revival of the Order was selected and the base
levelled [*sic*], the outer and inner pillars erected, the beams and
scantling attached, the rafters bound with cord, the roof plated
and thatched, the erection of the Iku Hai's mansion completed in
the month of Welo (September), on the night of Kane, in the
reign of His Majesty Kalakaua I., the 825th generation from
Lailai, or 24,750 years from the Wohi Kumulipo (the beginning), and Kapomanomano (the producing agent), equivalent to
40,000,000,000,024,750 years from the commencement of the
world and 24,750 years from Lailai, the first woman, dating to the
date of the present calendar, the 24th of September, A.D. 1886.

— Preamble to the Constitution of the Hale Nauā

In the early 1860s the print media emerged as one of the primary weapons for Kānaka Maoli engaged in nationalist resistance to the colonial maneuvers of the U.S. missionaries. Newspapers from that time on served to consolidate the lāhui, allowing people to communicate with each other from Hawai'i Island to Ni'ihau. As Benedict Anderson has observed, the print media in the vernacular contributed to the imagining of the nation among people who did not know each other personally but now shared a large community.[1] The lāhui was also created in the collective imagination by Kanaka Maoli grouping themselves as alike, sharing a language and culture, albeit with regional variations, and in opposition to the haole. That opposition was not simply an othering based on differences in color and language, but an attempt to fend off U.S. and various European colonial advances. Hawai'i, the nation or the lāhui, did not exist as a singular entity before the arrival of foreigners; it was, rather, Hawai'i, Maui, O'ahu, and so on. Moreover, newspapers and literacy introduced the Kanaka Maoli to similar anticolonial struggles around the world.

In this chapter I will examine some of the resistance strategies and tactics that King Kalākaua devised in reenacting and revitalizing the traditional culture. In the previous half century since the arrival of the Puritan missionaries, Kanaka traditions had suffered serious erosion: hula had been banned by church edict, as had the native healing practices called lapa'au. Any vestiges of the ancient religion were fervently condemned. To counteract these, Kalākaua expanded on the work of *Ka Hoku o ka Pakipika*, in which the ancient religion and dance were (re)presented in literary forms. During his reign, he brought the ancient traditions forward even further, off the page and into public performance. The old religion, dance, mo'olelo, mele, and mo'okū'auhau were like the iwikuamo'o (spine) for the lāhui; without their own traditions they could not stand up to the colonial onslaught. Alexander Liholiho and Emma had rebelled against the U.S. missionaries by inviting the Anglicans to establish a church in Hawai'i. This act has often been analyzed as both Anglophilism and anti-Americanism, because Hawai'i's sovereignty struggle of the nineteenth century has often been cast as a struggle between the United States and Britain.[2] But Ralph Kuykendall also says that "the Episcopal Church, while supplying a religious need, was also expected to serve as a safeguard of the Hawaiian monarchy."[3] Lota Kapuāiwa (Kamehameha V) allowed, and most likely encouraged, the semiprivate performances of hula at funerals and engi-neered the weakening of the legal ban on hula, changing the proposed ban to a licensing requirement.[4] Kalākaua, following in his footsteps, went much further: he defied the missionaries' rules by, among other activities, arranging for public performance of the hula and publishing the genealogical prayer, the *Kumulipo*.

The revitalization of these ancient ways armored people against the pernicious effects of the constant denigration of Kanaka culture by the U.S. missionaries and their descendants and allowed them to know themselves as a strong people with a proud history. This knowledge directly contradicted, and thus effectively contested, the discourse that represented them as backward savages incapable of self-government. The *Kumulipo*, which connected the reigning monarch to the creation of the universe, assured the people that the nation was in the proper hands. The enactment of the moʻolelo through dance and various exhibitions was revolutionary in that it overturned and forever ended the mission-ary prohibition against such activities. Just as important, the public performances played a crucial role in the development of Hawaiʻi's national narratives.[5] For Kalākaua and the lāhui these performances worked simultaneously as official narratives of the nation and as under-ground narratives that the haole community did not understand. In that way they functioned to constitute the nation as the lāhui Kanaka Maoli, excluding those they were resisting.

In the historiography of Hawaiʻi, King Kalākaua, who reigned from 1874 to 1891, may be the most reviled and ridiculed of the mon-archs. He was caught by the demands for profit and economic well-being on one hand, and the necessity of retaining the sovereignty of the Kanaka Maoli on the other. He acceded to the haole clamor for the reciprocity treaty, which bound Hawaiʻi tightly to the United States and represented a significant loss of sovereignty in its prohibition against the Hawaiian government leasing to any other nation any land in the king-dom.[6] He made other unpopular decisions, some of which involved miring the nation in a large debt. His closest associates were often people that the puritanical establishment despised: an opportunistic man from the United States with grandiose ideas, Walter Murray Gib-son; the suspect Italian, Celso Caesar Moreno; and the shrewd capital-ist, Claus Spreckels, who maneuvered the entire ahupuaʻa of Wailuku, Maui, out of the kingdom's hands. It was also Kalākaua's misfortune that the sons of the first missionaries came fully of age during his reign. Unlike their parents, the sons had no constraining influence such as the American Board of Commissioners for Foreign Missions to deter them from overthrowing the government.

The missionary sons, by exhibiting the same arrogant attitudes of superiority as their fathers and making use of the same discourses of civilization and savagery, determined to establish full colonial rule over the Kanaka Maoli. Some Kānaka Maoli, who later became heroes in the antiannexation struggle, assisted the sons for a short time. For example, Joseph Nāwahī and G. W. Pilipo, who disagreed particularly with the loss of sovereignty incurred with the reciprocity treaty and who were concerned about the large national debt, temporarily assisted Lorrin Thurston and the others who sought to overthrow Kalākaua. This allegiance, however, lasted only until it became clear that Thurston and company would never consider the Kānaka as equals, and were holding meetings of the leaders of their political party to which the Kānaka were not invited.[7]

During Kalākaua's time Western hegemony meant, in part, that the people consented to the structure of government in the form of a nation-state. As Jonathan Osorio says, they came to believe in their nation as a reality, while the haole settlers and their children did not: "The *haole*, even those born in the Islands, had their own 'native' countries whose existence and viability was more real to them than was the Kingdom."[8] Both Kalākaua and Queen Emma used the slogan "Hawai'i for Hawaiians" as an emblem of nationalism that also resisted haole rule. This resistance to colonial second-class status for their people has been interpreted as racism,[9] but while racism works at subjugating another class or race of people, the slogan was part of a larger effort by the Kanaka Maoli to forestall their own subjugation.

The enactments of tradition that Kalākaua undertook that strengthened the identity of Kanaka Maoli as a people proud of their past and of their achievements made him more popular, and his legacy of national pride has persisted to this day. Kalākaua is particularly revered by practitioners of hula and traditional religion, who call him the Merrie Monarch. For example, Jennie Wilson (née Kini Kapahukulaokamāmalu McColgan), a dancer in Kalākaua's court and hula performer at the Chicago World's Fair in 1893, attributed all contemporary knowledge of hula to Kalākaua's revival efforts, and Elizabeth Tatar has written that

Ka Mōʻī Kalākaua. (Courtesy of Hawaiʻi State Archives)

"King Kalākaua . . . was, perhaps, the monarch who was the most insistent about 'perpetuating and preserving' traditional Hawaiian music and dance."[10]

Kalākaua was not from the Kamehameha line, and that fact contributed to much of the cultural renaissance that he fostered. Adrienne Kaeppler says that Kalākaua "was interested in demonstrating his high rank and status according to Hawaiian tradition."[11] Rule over the nation had remained the exclusive domain of Kamehameha I and his descendants from the formation of the kingdom until the death of William Lunalilo. When Kalākaua was elected after Lunalilo's death, it was against the wishes and beliefs of many Kānaka Maoli, who thought that Queen Emma had a greater claim to the throne because she was a descendant of Kamehameha I's younger brother, Keliʻimaikaʻi, and was the widow of Alexander Liholiho (Kamehameha IV). Kalākaua was descended from another aliʻi nui, Keaweaheulu, Kamehameha I's cousin and close adviser.[12] Before the deciding vote in the legislature, there were public arguments over the genealogical claims of both Emma and

Kalākaua, each side trying to minimize the claim of the other. When Kalākaua's election was announced, a group of "Emmaites" rioted, attacking only Kanaka Maoli legislators.[13]

The legitimacy of Kalākaua's presence on the throne was contested from time to time throughout his reign and continued even after his death. Sanford B. Dole's biographer wrote of Queen Emma's death: "The old Hawaii of wise, far-seeing *alii* had passed. The ruler of Hawaii in 1885 [Kalākaua] was one to whom his princely heritage . . . meant little or nothing except as exploited by . . . [the] glitter of crown and throne."[14] But, according to George Kanahele, "[Kalākaua] believed strongly that the political survival of his kingdom depended upon the cultural and spiritual revitalization of the Hawaiian people."[15] Although some acts of Kalākaua such as the public performance of hula at his coronation and publication of the *Kumulipo* have been interpreted in the past as political maneuvers to retain power against threats from other ali'i nui, those identical acts functioned as resistance to cultural destruction and loss of sovereignty for the lāhui. Osorio says that "these [acts] were highly assertive of the glory and vitality of Hawaiian traditions and affirmed the cultural distinctions between Native and foreigner."[16] They constituted, as did their literary forms, a core of identity for Kanaka Maoli, grounded in the realm of the sacred.

In this context, the *Kumulipo* can be read as a political text — that is, as a narrative of the lāhui from the beginning of time. Kalākaua brought it forward during his reign in order to legitimize his right to rule, but it functioned doubly to legitimize the existence of the nation itself. The nation's sovereignty was unstable in ways that were parallel to Kalākaua's own instability on the throne. His activities were aimed at constituting and strengthening the nation through reenacting the traditional cosmology, which could not help but strengthen his position. He attempted to use tradition as resistance to colonization in many ways, including establishing the Papa Kū'auhau o Nā Ali'i Hawai'i (board of genealogy) and the Hale Nauā to document traditional knowledge; arranging for the public performance of hula at the Poni Mō'ī (coronation); and arranging hula and dramatic performances of national narratives at the jubilee, his fiftieth birthday celebration.

GENEALOGY AND COSMOLOGY

In Kanaka Maoli tradition, the right to rule was primarily legitimated by moʻokūʻauhau. In her study of the *Kumulipo*, Martha Beckwith notes that "position in old Hawaii, both social and political, depended in the first instance upon rank, and rank upon blood descent—hence the importance of genealogy as proof of high ancestry."[17] According to Samuel Kamakau, power could also accrue to a (male) aliʻi because of his skill at war: "Sometimes the hereditary chief lost his land, and the kingdom was taken by force and snatched away by a warrior, and the name of 'chief' was given to him because of his prowess." Even in this case, however, in order for the aliʻi to retain power, "he then attached himself to the chiefly genealogies, even though his father may have been of no great rank (*noanoa*), and his mother a chiefess."[18]

According to Kameʻeleihiwa, the premier scholar of Kanaka genealogy: "The genealogies *are* the Hawaiian concept of time, and they order the space around us. Through them we learn of the exploits and identities of our ancestors. . . . Even though the great genealogies are of the *Aliʻi Nui* and not of the commoners, these *Aliʻi Nui* are the collective ancestors, and their *moʻolelo* . . . are histories of all Hawaiians, too." Kameʻeleihiwa goes on to explain how the stories of the ancestors' courage inspired people of the nineteenth century, and continue to do so today, and how they served as models for behavior, then and now. She notes that "genealogies anchor Hawaiians to our place in the universe and give us the comforting illusion of continued existence." This was especially important in Kalākaua's time, when depopulation was a serious threat, and foreigners "cruelly predicted the complete demise of the Hawaiian race as inevitable."[19]

In Kanaka genealogies and cosmologies, both male and female forces are always present.[20] Dualisms are abundant, and pono is created and maintained by the balance of complementary forces. For example, Wākea, the sky father, does not himself create islands, but rather mates with Papahānaumoku, the earth mother, and she gives birth to the islands. Women's names are always included in the moʻokūʻauhau, from which their mana, just as powerful as men's, is derived. This cosmology provided the traditional and spiritual basis for Kanaka women to accept and exercise political and other kinds of power. However, because by this time the overt exercise of women's power in the political arena had been seriously eroded due to the demands to conform to Western styles of governance, Kalākaua avoided placing women in positions analogous to Western political office and instead relied on aliʻi wahine as advisers and appointed them to positions with less overt titles yet still with profound political implications.[21]

KA PAPA KŪʻAUHAU O NĀ ALIʻI

In 1880, the Papa Kūʻauhau Aliʻi o Nā Aliʻi Hawaiʻi (Board of genealogy of Hawaiian chiefs) was established by an act of the legislature that was initiated by Kalākaua. Kalākaua appointed Ke Kamāliʻi Poʻomaikelani, an older sister of Mōʻīwahine Kapiʻolani, as president of the board. Poʻomaikelani prepared a report of the board that was published in 1884 in both Hawaiian and English. According to the English version, "The principal duties of the Board shall be, viz.: 1. — To gather, revise, correct and record the Genealogy of Hawaiian Chiefs. 2. — To gather, revise, correct and record all published and unpublished Ancient Hawaiian History. 3. — To gather, revise, correct and record all published and unpublished Meles, and also to ascertain the object and spirit of the Meles, the age and the History of the period when composed and to note the same on the Record Book. 4. — To record all the tabu customs of the *Mois* and Chiefs."[22]

One of the main reasons for these goals was to identify the aliʻi nui and verify their genealogical claims, which constituted claims to leadership such as appointments to the House of Nobles. In this era, the acknowledged members of the royal lines (Kamehameha and Kalākaua) were lacking in progeny, so it was necessary to determine other genealogical lines that could be verified as aliʻi nui. Those considered for high positions had to have genealogies that went back to the origin of the world; their genealogies thus were indistinguishable from traditional cosmologies. According to John Charlot, aliʻi nui were considered "the link between the community, the gods, and the cosmos, and their mutual harmony depends on [them]."[23]

The projects of interest here performed by the Papa Kūʻauhau Aliʻi were done for specific political reasons and not simply as knowledge for knowledge's sake.[24] The reason for determining the aliʻi nui and reaffirming the sacred in tradition was to keep the rule of Hawai'i in Kanaka Maoli hands. The identification of ali'i nui and transcription of mele and mo'okū'auhau worked to define the nation as the lāhui Kanaka and began the development of national narratives. This functioned to interrupt the discourse that said that "progress" meant becoming more like the United States — that is, ruled by Euro-American immigrants. Viewed in this way, these activities can be seen to be direct resistance to colonization.

The report lists one hundred twenty-eight mele that were used in the genealogical studies, along with their approximate ages. In the list of mele we see that the board, representative perhaps of the educated ali'i and kahuna (spiritual adviser) classes, operates in this context within ancient Kanaka epistemologies. The first mele is the *Kumulipo*, said to be "ke Mele kahiko loa" (the most ancient mele).[25] Some of the mele are given actual dates; others are noted to be from a time the modern West would call historical, such as *Kamauli* [sic] *o Ku*, from the "time of Kaumualii"; others are what might now be called legends, such as the *Kau o Hiiaka*, from the "time of Pele," and the *Kau o Kawelo*, from the "time of Kawelo,"[26] but no distinction is made between the historical and the legendary. Likewise, all of the works are called "mele," ranging from the cosmogonic, genealogical prayer *Kumulipo* to the many hula songs listed.

The board derived these mele and other genealogical information from sources listed in the report, including the "na buke kuauhau" (genealogy books) of experts such as Davida Malo and Kamokuiki, who both trained under 'Auwae, "the great genealogist of Kamehameha's last days."[27] The report notes that the board would not attempt to "hooponopono i keia mau buke a me na moolelo i kakau ia e ka haole" (edit these books nor the histories written by foreigners), because they had so much work to do just to verify genealogies for certain persons listed in the Kanaka sources.[28] This indicates that the board did not feel a compelling need to rely on foreign historical sources to validate this part of their work; the genealogical information from the private books of the Kanaka experts was sufficient for verification. In fact, part of their work was to contest the historical accounts written by foreigners.

Another project of the board was to locate the bones of certain ali'i nui. It was the practice in ancient times to carefully prepare the bones of the dead in special wrappings such as fine tapa or specially woven baskets and then hide them inside caves so that they would not be disturbed by sorcerers or anyone else. For a bone to be chipped at or otherwise mutilated was the worst desecration an ali'i could suffer after death, so the bones were hidden and the secret of their location usually carefully guarded. The board claimed, however, to have located the bones of some of the most important ali'i and arranged to have them even more carefully hidden or moved for better preservation. They also recovered an artifact that Western science would relegate to the realm of mythology or legend: "Ka Ipu Makani a Laamaomao" (The wind gourd of La'amaomao). This gourd was said to contain winds that could be called on by a properly trained chanter to create favorable sailing conditions (or unfavorable, for one's enemies); the possessor would obviously have a great advantage in racing and in war. The board wrote: "O ka loaa ana o keia ipu kaulana kahiko, he mea nui no, oiai ua pili keia ipu kahiko me kekahi o na moolelo kahiko kaulana o ka wa kahiko" (Obtaining this ancient famous gourd is very important because this ancient gourd is associated with famous histories/legends of ancient times).[29] Again, we see that the board did not make distinctions between the mythological and the historical in the categorical way that we would expect if it were operating within a Western epistemology. Rather, it seems to be saying that the physical existence of the recovered gourd validates the ancient stories.

Recovering and properly caring for sacred items was of utmost importance to the consciousness of the nation. These actions were done with the view toward affirming that the lāhui had a long and proud history prior, and without reference, to the West. Showing that the sacred items of tradition were valuable and cared for were acts that resisted the discourse that called Hawai'i's precontact history the "brutal and degraded past."[30]

The remainder of the board's report concerns ocean measurements taken at the time by the government surveying office. The purpose of receiving such information was "e pau ai ka pohihihi o kekahi mau kumu hoopaapaa i hoopukaia e ka poe kakau i ka moolelo o na lahui kanaka o ka Moana Pacifica nei" (of great value to the board in solving many points and theories already advanced by writers of the history of the Polynesian races).[31] Here the board was trying to verify some of the genealogical information with the oceanographic information being gathered at the time. They state again that they did not use histories produced by foreigners but rather only relied on "na moolelo kahiko o Hawaii nei a me na mea i hoike ia ma na mele" (the ancient histories/legends of Hawai'i and what is said in the [various] mele).[32] Kanaka Maoli share with other Pacific Islanders theories about the migrations around the Pacific that are significantly different from those proposed by scholars such as Abraham Fornander. It was mainly the migration theory, preserved in genealogies, that the board was hoping would be verified by the ocean soundings. They were no doubt acutely aware that traditional epistemologies were dismissed by the Europeans and Euro-Americans, and they hoped to use the scientific tools available to contest that dismissal by showing that science proved what they had always known. Kalākaua and the Papa Kū'auhau o Nā Ali'i, especially Po'omaikelani, also used the *Kumulipo* to demonstrate that mo'okū'auhau and mo'olelo constituted valid knowledge.

THE KUMULIPO

By far the work with the most far-reaching consequences, and the most ambitious work accomplished by the board of genealogy was the collection and transcription of the *Kumulipo* (source of deep darkness). The *Kumulipo* is a cosmological chant/prayer that describes the genesis of living things on the earth, including humankind, and links them to the genealogy of Lonoikamakahiki, which then leads directly to Kalākaua. It is the only chant of its kind preserved in its entirety, and, in the words of Charlot, it exemplifies an important type of "genealogy that links the chief to his illustrious, perhaps now deified ancestors; to the first humans; sometimes to the gods; and backwards in time through the animals, plants, and elements to the beginning of the universe."[33] Valerio Valeri further observes that "native exegesis reads it at once as the description of the origins of the cosmos, of the life of an ali'i from infancy to maturity, and of the formation of a new dynasty. These interpretations are not mutually exclusive, for the conception, birth, and development of an ali'i or dynasty reproduce the cosmogonic process and thereby aid in reproducing natural and social distinctions."[34]

I will examine here at length aspects of this genealogical/cosmological mele/pule as a political text because of how it figures in the national consciousness of the lāhui and, thus, how it continues to function as resistance to colonization and the attendant project of assimilation. The collection and transcription of such a chant certainly served its narrow political function of the time — that is, it validated Kalākaua's claim to the throne. But the *Kumulipo* also functioned, and continues to function, as ideological resistance. Its recovery and transcription were part of Kalākaua's "rediscovery and repatriation of what had been suppressed in the natives' past by the processes of imperialism."[35] The age and artistry of the *Kumulipo* were and are sources of pride and identity for the Kanaka Maoli. Liliʻuokalani undertook her translation of it while imprisoned by the colonial oligarchy in 1896, and then published it in 1897 as a way of explaining to the people of the United States that the Kanaka Maoli were a people with a very long history. This act was, among others, an attempt to counter the discourse that disparaged the Kanaka Maoli in order to justify annexation and the military occupation of Hawaiʻi. The *Kumulipo* was the basis for much of the work of the Hale Nauā, as well as for a genealogy committee in 1904. It inspired published works by other Kanaka scholars, such as that of Joseph L. Kūkahi in 1902, Joseph M. Poepoe in 1906, and Rubellite Kawena Johnson in 1981 and 2000, and Martha Beckwith's 1951 translation along with Liliʻuokalani's of 1897 are both still in print. Finally Kameʻeleihiwa begins her 1992 book with a quote and discussion of the *Kumulipo*: "Hawaiian identity is, in fact, derived from the Kumulipo, the great cosmogonic genealogy. Its essential lesson is that every aspect of the Hawaiian conception of the world is related by birth, and as such, all parts of the Hawaiian world are one indivisible lineage. Conceived in this way, the genealogy of the Land, the Gods, Chiefs, and people intertwine with one another, and with all the myriad aspects of the universe. . . . Today we Hawaiians use geneaological relationships to establish our collective identity. . . . Our shared genealogy helps us define our *Lāhui* (nation) as an entity distinct from the waves of foreigners that have inundated our islands."[36]

The text of the *Kumulipo* as published by Kalākaua in 1889 is called *He Pule Hoolaa Alii* (A prayer to consecrate (an) Aliʻi). The title can be read two ways, as consecrating a particular aliʻi (Lonoikamakahiki) and as consecrating "aliʻi" as a system of government, which Kalākaua, Liliʻuokalani, and the lāhui were trying to preserve. The chant consists of 2,102 lines, divided into sixteen wā. The first seven wā (epochs) are the times of pō (darkness) and the last nine are times of ao (daylight).

The use of the words pō and ao in the *Kumulipo* text is important at several levels. Earlier, I demonstrated that the missionaries appropriated the words ao and pō to designate civilization and savagery, respectively, in the terms naʻauao and naʻaupō. The *Kumulipo* predates the missionaries, probably by hundreds of years, but in recorded history by at least thirty: Liliʻuokalani writes that the *Kumulipo* was sung to Captain Cook.[37] It thus reflects traditional conceptions of pō and ao, which Kalākaua and Liliʻuokalani recuperate. The first seven wā belong to the akua and are described as taking place in pō. The prologue to the first wā is an ode to darkness:

O ke au i kahuli wela ka honua
O ke au i kahuli lole ka lani
O ke au i kukaiaka ka la
E hoomalamalama i ka malama
O ke au o Makalii ka po
O ka Walewale hookumu honua ia
O ke kumu o ka lipo i lipo ai
O ke kumu o ka Po i po ai
O ka Lipolipo, o ka lipolipo
O ka lipo o ka La, o ka lipo
o ka Po
Po wale ho—i
Hanau ka po
Hanau Kumulipo i ka po
he kane
Hanau Poele i ka po he wahine
(The time of change, the earth was hot
The time of change, the heavens turned over
The time the sun stood in shadow
To illuminate the moon/To allow the moon to shine
The time when the Pleiades was dark
There was an earth-establishing slime
The source of the darkness that made it dark (or, The reason for the darkness was to be dark)
The source of the night that made it night (or, The reason for night was to be night)
The deep darkness, the deep darkness

The darkness of the Day, the darkness of the night
Only night
The night gives birth
Kumulipo give birth to [in the?] night,
a male
Pō'ele (dark night) gives birth to [in the?] night, a female.)[38]

The first through seventh wā end with the line "Po—no" (Indeed/ still night/darkness). Pō in the *Kumulipo* does not mean the time of ignorance and barbarism before enlightenment and (Western) civilization arrived, but rather the time of the gods before the first human and out of which humanity rose. Pō is positive rather than negative in this context: to be "Mai ka pō mai" (from the pō) is to be descended "from the gods; of divine origin."[39] "Po—no" can, moreover, be read as the word "pono," with the dash signifying a lengthening of the sound that the chanter would make. It is, in fact, more ambiguous because of the presence of the dash in the text. If "indeed night" were the only meaning, it would be more clear without the dash. The two words—pō (night) and nō (indeed)—would be distinctly separated. In the same way, if the word "pono" were the singular meaning, it would be more clearly one word without the dash. The technique of using the dash to signify length of sound was a common practice, and it is used later in the eighth wā, "A—o—," and the "lala no ka wa umikumamalua" (branch of the twelfth wā), "Pu—ka."[40] In each of these two examples, however, only one word can be meant, "ao" (day; daylight) and "puka" (came out; emerged). This strengthens the idea that "Po—no" can be read as one word as well as two. Many other examples can be found; for instance, in the text of *Ka Moolelo o Hiiakaikapoliopele* in *Ka Leo o ka Lahui*.[41] As noted earlier, the word "pono" has many meanings, almost all of them positive. According to Pukui and Elbert, some of the meanings of pono are "goodness, uprightness, morality, excellence, well-being, fitting, proper, in perfect order," and also "resources, assets."[42] "Po—no," then, means not only "it is indeed night," but also "it is right" or "it is good."

Ao, from the eighth wā on, designates the eras of human beings, but again its meaning is free of the connotation of Western civilization. Its use here, in fact, acts as resistance to that discourse. As seen in previous chapters, Kanaka Maoli had been countering the discourse of civilization and savagery since at least Kalākaua's work on *Ka Hoku o ka Pakipika* in 1861–1862. The use of these terms in the *Kumulipo* asserts the presence of ao thousands of years before the arrival of the missionaries. Thus publication of the *Kumulipo* may be related to the aforementioned attempt to validate Kanaka traditional knowledge through the science of the day. They are similar gestures that assert that the traditional philosophy, religion, and ways of life are as valuable as the "civilization" of the West.

It is worth noticing the dualism, characteristic of Hawaiian poetry and also Hawaiian cosmology, in the structure of the chant: besides pō and ao, the excerpt quoted above pairs earth and heavens, sun and moon, stars (Pleiades) and slime, male and female. The origin of the earth takes place in the context of these balanced pairs, as opposed to the Judeo-Christian singular, male creation. Creation and reproduction of life require both male and female.

The male role in reproduction is symbolized by Kamapuaʻa, the pig god, who makes his appearance in the fifth wā. This wā celebrates the establishment of taro (kalo) agriculture through the symbol of the rooting pig, which, according to Beckwith, is at the same time "an erotic symbol for the function of the male in the founding of a new family branch upon the old stock." Beckwith concludes that the fruitfulness of the cultivated earth symbolizes "the rise of a fertile new branch on the family line multiplying over the land," an interpretation consistent with Kalākaua's position as founder of a new Hawaiian dynasty.[43] Although the Kamehameha line had died out, the *Kumulipo* was important in reassuring the lāhui that the nation continued on in a state of pono (balance; well-being) through the new genealogical line. This is also linked metaphorically to Kalākaua's concern over depopulation and his efforts towards repopulation, which he called "Hoʻoulu Lāhui" ("Increase the lāhui" or, more literally, "cause the lāhui to grow").

Besides Kamapuaʻa, kalo is important symbolically to the identity of the lāhui in another way. Wākea and Papa, appearing in the twelfth wā, have a daughter named Hoʻohōkūkalani, who becomes pregnant by Wākea twice. The first child, named Hāloa, is stillborn. It is buried and from its burial place grows the first kalo. Because Hoʻohōkūkalani's second child was a Kanaka also named Hāloa, the kalo is a virtual kaikuaʻana to Kānaka that is owed filial love, loyalty, and care.[44] This story of Hāloa is often invoked to symbolize the Kanaka belief in a familial

relationship to the land and opposition to ownership over land. Beckwith quotes a document from the Hale Nauā thus: "Now you must
understand that the children born from Hāloa, these are yourselves."⁴⁵

Other plants besides kalo also appear in the genealogy. In the middle of the twelfth wā are the lines: "Hanau Kihalaaupoe he Wauke,
Hanau o Ulu he Ulu" (Born was Kihalaaupoe, a wauke plant, born was
ʻulu, a breadfruit).⁴⁶ The fifteenth wā tells of the mysterious akua/
wahine Haumea who disappears into a breadfruit tree. The chant explains poetically that the breadfruit is one of her many physical forms. In
other texts, Kanaka authors explain that the breadfruit kino lau of
Haumea is named Kāmehaʻikana, the goddess of childbirth but also of
war and government.⁴⁷

> O kino ulu o pahu ulu o lau ulu ia nei,
> He lau kino o ia wahine o Haumea,
> O Haumea nui aiwaiwa.
> (Breadfruit body, breadfruit trunk, breadfruit leaves,
> One of the body forms of this woman Haumea,
> Mysterious, great Haumea.)⁴⁸

Gods, plants, animals, even stars appear in the *Kumulipo*. The presence of all of these within the genealogy of human beings expresses
belief in the familial relationship of Kanaka Maoli to all the other life
forms in their environment. This genealogical world view gives rise to
the particular form that love of nation takes in Hawaiʻi, which is aloha
ʻāina (love of the land).

Haumea, Papa, and Laʻilaʻi are symbolic of the female role in creation and reproduction. Their stories recur many times in the second half
of the *Kumulipo*. According to Beckwith, Haumea "underwent strange
renewals of youth to become mother and wife of children and grandchildren."⁴⁹ Laʻilaʻi likewise gives birth countless numbers of times, by
both the god Kāne and the human man Kiʻi. Papa, as mentioned, is the
symbolic earth mother. All three are powerful and mysterious, and their
prominence in the *Kumulipo* means that women are not effaced in the
consciousness of the lāhui; both men and women take their parts in the
creation and reproduction of life, and in the moʻolelo that follow.

Another aim of the board of genealogy was the validation of Kanaka knowledge. The first human being in the *Kumulipo* is the Laʻilaʻi,
whose life story Beckwith calls "myth."⁵⁰ But the board and the Hale

Naua treat Laʻilaʻi's life as historical fact, both moʻokūʻauhau (genealogy) and moʻolelo (history/legend). They both use Laʻilaʻi as a starting
point for constructing other dates in history. They arrive at her date in
years by following the genealogy using a generational interval of thirty
years.[51] Hale Naua uses Laʻilaʻi's birth as a year zero, counting their own
date from the number of generations since Laʻilaʻi (as given in the epi-
graph to this chapter). In the same way, Wākea and Papa are not just
father sky and mother earth in mythology, they are real people in the
genealogy. Beckwith states: "At the time of foreign contact Hawaii . . .
counted its stock from Wakea and Papa as the official parent-pair. Their
names occur on the earliest genealogy of the race [written] . . . in
1838. . . . They are quoted by Malo and incorporated into the report
made in 1904 by a committee of native scholars."[52]

The story of the god Māui is also told in the *Kumulipo*. The six-
teenth, and last, wā is a genealogy that begins with Maui and ends with
Lonoikamakahiki, ancestor to Kalākaua and Liliʻuokalani. Fifty generations separate the god Māui from Lonoikamakahiki (also known as
KaʻīʻImamamao and KalaninuiʻĪamamao). Beckwith notes that "the name
song of Maui . . . tells the story of the struggle for power of a younger
son born into the family through an alien alliance, one entitling him to a
higher-ranking status than the natural heir."[53] This is much like the
theme of the younger or lesser branch of the family becoming the ruler,
which recurs in the Kawelo and the Kamehameha narratives. It rein-
forces Kalākaua's own position by likening it to that of Māui, Kawelo,
Kamehameha (and the similar story of ʻUmi, not yet mentioned).
When placed in the genealogy of stories Kalākaua's ascension to the
throne, in spite of being a lesser line, seems natural.

This *Kumulipo* thus links Kalākaua and Liliʻuokalani, and by extension the entire lāhui, genealogically to the god Māui, and further, to the
goddess(es) Haumea/Papa, the god/first man Wākea, the taro Hāloa,
and plants of the earth, and the stars in the heavens. If Kalākaua and the
Papa Kūʻauhau o Nā Aliʻi had not done this work of collecting and
recording the genealogies, such a consequential cosmological chant
might never have been transcribed. Even in the 1880s there were few
persons left with such knowledge. It is disheartening to realize that this
is "*He* Kumulipo no Ka-I-I-Mamao" (*a* kumulipo for KaʻīʻĪmamao),
meaning that this is one of a class of such cosmological chants but there
are no others like it preserved. This work of the Papa Kūʻauhau func-

tioned at the time and continues to function as effective resistance to cultural erosion and as support for anticolonial nationalism by bridging the present to the past and by providing a basis for self-definition of the lāhui as those who are connected to the ʿāina genealogically. This explains in part why so many Kanaka Maoli are researching family genealogies today. Although it is said that only the aliʿi classes have genealogies preserved, nearly all Kānaka Maoli now living have reconstructed family genealogies. This is because, as described earlier, aliʿi and makaʿāinana are related.

Genealogy continues to provide a way to clear confusion about claims to being "Hawaiian." In the context of Kanaka genealogy, a claim such as being "fifth-generation Hawaiian" is clearly understood as being made only by those of immigrant or colonizer descent and never by Kanaka Maoli, to whom such a phrase is meaningless. As Anne McClintock puts it, genealogy works to "distinguish between the beneficiaries of colonialism (the [descendants of the] colonizers) and the casualties of colonialism (the [descendants of the] colonized)."[54]

The important genealogical work of the Papa Kūʿauhau o Nā Aliʿi was expanded on by the Hale Nauā, a society of aliʿi nui whose genealogies were verified by the Papa Kūʿauhau. The Papa Kūʿauhau thus laid the foundation for development of the Hale Nauā. Both were necessary to Kalākaua's constituting the nation as the lāhui Kanaka Maoli.

THE HALE NAUĀ

The Hale Nauā was established in 1886 and, according to Mookini, "had genealogical studies as [its] basis."[55] Earlier, Kalākaua formed a committee of nine women and one man to plan a society "to further the humble and careful way of life as nurtured by our ancestors from the beginning of time, so that it will never be forgotten."[56] Shortly thereafter, officers for the organization were elected; four of them were women, including Mōʿīwahine Kapiʿolani, with one man, John Baker, serving as treasurer.[57] After the association was formed, Princess Poʿomaikelani, head of the Papa Kūʿauhau, served as president. Hale Nauā was called a "secret society," and it based some of its organizational structure on that of the Masonic societies.[58] There are, however, some major differences, most notably that the Masonic societies are based on the Western cosmology, in which male power is dependent on the exclusion of women from the centers of power. In Genesis, the Judeo-Christian god is able to create the whole universe with no female force evident. The Hale Nauā, on the other hand, was based in the Kanaka cosmology, in which excluding women would have been unthinkable because pono — balance and well-being — requires both male and female forces. Further, whereas the "outer domain," as Chatterjee terms it — that is, the political structure — is Western and thus excludes women, the Hale Nauā is an organization of the "inner domain," which recreates the traditional sacred space. Here Kanaka women are able to serve and be recognized for their genealogical place as well as for their work in genealogy and other traditions. Of the list of the first seventy-one members, at least twenty-four were women.[59]

The creation of the Hale Nauā provoked an onslaught of the discourse of civilization and savagery, as the missionary establishment expressed their outrage at the existence of an organization from which they were banned by virtue of their genealogies. As Mookini quotes from the *Pacific Commercial Advertiser*: "The membership appears to be presently limited to native Hawaiians. . . . [This] is a retrograde step. . . . From its constitution the country has a right to expect that any attempt to revive and vitalize the customs and usages of the barbarous and savage past would be promptly put a stop to. . . . No country can afford to abandon the light of contemporary civilization for the gross darkness and ignorance of a brutal and degraded past."[60] We can see very clearly here that traditional Kanaka practices were threatening to the project of colonization, which continued to be equated with "civilization." It is clear as well that the editor(s) of the *Advertiser* thought of Anglo-American culture as belonging to an enlightened present and future, while Kanaka culture, although actually concurrent in time, belongs to a "brutal and degraded past." This is also a discursive strategy that makes use of the developing theories of progress and evolution that propose that all peoples will eventually "progress" to resemble Anglo-Americans. McClintock calls this the trope of "anachronistic space" in which "the stubborn and threatening heterogeneity of the colonies was contained and disciplined not as socially or geographically different . . . and thus equally valid, but as *temporally* different and thus as irrevocably superannuated by history."[61] This trope is related to the categorization and hierarchical classification of colonized or colonizable peoples according to their state of primitivity or advancement, which in turn contributed to creating the idea of "race" in biology and anthropology.[62] Such categorization then conveniently justifies Euro-American rule over "primitive" peoples.

The *Hawaiian Star*, known for its hyperbole, contributed to the race discourse by calling attention to the Hale Nauā's possible political function: "The practices of sorcery are intimately connected with the worship of heathen deities . . . they are also allied to political tyranny. . . . Kalakaua undertook to propagate this unholy terror [Hale Nauā] in order to establish his own corrupt despotic power."[63] In its first annual report, Hale Nauā answered these charges: "There is nothing derogatory to reason or common sence [*sic*]. Nothing impure or indecent; but, [our] principal aim is to elevate the mind to high philosophical truths so that we may follow [our ancestors'] wise teaching and precepts, and learn more of nature and this world."[64] The annual report thus refuted the charges of barbarism and unholiness but sidestepped the question of political power. Kalākaua never accrued enough power to truthfully be called despot or tyrant, but there can be little doubt that Hale Nauā increased his prestige through its continuance of genealogical work: by expressing pride in Kanaka traditions, it allowed his people to think more highly of themselves and of him.

The Hale Nauā's constitution lists degrees of membership along with areas of study for each degree. These areas include astronomy and meteorology, agricultural science, the mechanical sciences, "the signs of Aliis," ancient priesthood, and the "Christian Order of Knighthood."[65] The constitution of the "secret society" was published twice: first at its inception and then in pamphlet form in 1890. Hale Nauā also sponsored lectures that were open to the public, generally on topics in science.

In addition to the association's work in science, Hale Nauā played an important role in the preservation of traditional knowledge. Mookini states that "Historically, the Hale Naua society was . . . the most reliable native source for ancient practice."[66] In their use of traditional methods of keeping historical time they were also to escape, if only a little, the cultural dominance of the United States that surrounded them in daily life. Every member, for example, had to memorize the Hawaiian moon calendar, where nights of the month are named, rather than days of the week. They honored the traditional way of counting time by generations rather than by years, in a continuous stream unbroken by the birth of a religious figure on a continent far away.

As members collected and recited incidents from the moʻolelo kahiko, they contested the discourse of savagery and civilization. The annual report contains a narrative of Hema and Kahaʻi, father and son who
voyaged on canoes to Tahiti and back. According to the report, "the
ability of the men who planned and carried out these expeditions shows
that they cannot be regarded as leaders of a barbarous Race." The Hale
Nauā also contested the representations made of Kanaka Maoli by the
missionaries, who described them as half-beast and later as the missing
link in evolution. The annual report says that this representation was
"applied in a spirit partial to their interests so that their work would
have the justification for taming, civilizing and christianizing [*sic*] these
wretched creatures."[67] This is clearly a direct resistance to the colonial
actions of the missionaries through the means of revealing the hegemonic functions of their discourse. Historiography was also contested
by the Hale Nauā: "The historian [as representative of the West] had
reached a point which he considered far in advance of the state of the
Islanders. Upon comparing these conditions it was natural for him to
express and emphasize his self-congratulation; but it would have been
far better if his utterances . . . carried more of a spirit of philanthropy,
than that of intolerance and bigotry. Such being the spirit in which the
character of our people was measured[,] we can dismiss the reverend
historian and look upon his comments as coming from a source irrever-
ently ignorant."[68]

The Hale Nauā was essentially an urban organization of the aliʻi
who attempted to preserve traditional knowledge, validate that knowledge with contemporary science, and counter the discourses of race,
civilization, and savagery deployed by the haole elite in efforts to subjugate them. The works of the Papa Kūʻauhau and the Hale Nauā, especially the genealogical work, were confined, however, to the small circle
of aliʻi. As the ʻōlelo noʻeau (wise saying) says, "i aliʻi nō ke aliʻi i ke
kanaka" (an aliʻi is an aliʻi only because of the people who follow her/
him).[69] It was thus necessary to make the moʻokūʻauhau and moʻolelo
real to the makaʻāinana publicly. Kalākaua did so through two festivals,
the first of which being the Poni Mōʻī (coronation) of 1883.

THE PONI MŌʻĪ

After touring the world and being received as the king of Hawaiʻi by the heads of other sovereign states, including Japan and many nations in Europe, Kalākaua decided that a coronation of himself and his mōʻī-wahine, Kapiʻolani, would arouse feelings of nationalism in the Kanaka Maoli and help to consolidate his power. Liliʻuokalani describes the event this way: "[T]he coronation celebration has been a great success. The people from the country and from the other islands went back to their homes with a renewed sense of the dignity and honor involved in their nationality. . . . It was necessary to confirm the new family '*Stirps*' [a branch of a family] — to use the words of our constitution — by a celebration of unusual impressiveness. There was a serious purpose of national importance; the direct line of the 'Kamehamehas' having become extinct, it was succeeded by the 'Keawe-a-Heulu' line. . . . It was wise and patriotic to spend money to awaken in the people a national pride."[70]

The coronation ceremony took place at the newly rebuilt ʻIolani Palace on February 12, 1883. The festivities then continued for two weeks thereafter, including feasts hosted by the king for the people and nightly performances of hula. Kalākaua had asked various kumu hula (hula masters) to bring their hālau (troupes) to Honolulu for public performances, which were carefully arranged in advance. It was on this occasion that musicians and hula choreographers created a new genre of hula, called hula kuʻi. In the hula kuʻi, practitioners sought to combine components of the indigenous Hawaiian music and dance traditions with elements of Western music and dance. Amy Kuʻuleialoha Stillman has observed that "the hula kuʻi embodied the social, cultural, and political polarization," and that "hula kuʻi was used as a vehicle for reinforcing pride in Hawaiʻi and being Hawaiian and also for validating Kalākaua's right to rule."[71]

A program titled *Papa Kuhikuhi o Na Hula Poni Moi* was printed for the occasion. It included the order of the performances (although the date of each is not given), the name of the kumu hula, the titles of the oli and mele, and what type they were. Although the lyrics to the mele and oli were not printed in this program, the missionary establishment denounced the program as obscene, as well as illegal under the statute against public nuisances. William R. Castle, son of missionaries Samuel and Mary Tenney Castle, demanded that the printers of the document be arrested and charged, in response to which William Auld and Robert Greive were then arrested. The *Pacific Commercial Advertiser*, at this time owned by Kalākaua's close associate, Walter Murray Gibson, reported that "the community has been stirred a good deal recently by the discussion of an alleged obscene publication, a programme of Hawaiian hulas or dances . . . mainly because William R. Castle, Esq., made a mistake in supposing that the *Advertiser* office had printed the programme and not the *Gazette* office. He has admitted that he made this mistake. If he had known that the friends of the opposition [the missionaries] had printed it, he would not have written the letter on the subject published in that paper."[72]

According to Gibson, then, Castle was attempting to hurt Gibson and Kalākaua politically through the charge of obscenity. However, regardless of the public admission of his error, the court case against Greive and Auld proceeded. Robert Greive claimed that he did not understand Hawaiian and so did not know what he was printing; that he merely received an order from the palace and filled it without question. In fact, even the prosecutor did not understand what was printed. He had to bring in several Kānaka Maoli willing to testify against Greive and Auld. The first was G. W. Pilipo, a Kanaka politician who would later be associated briefly with the Reform Party, which was composed of anti-Kalākaua haole. Pilipo testified, in part, "I have seen the word 'mai' [ma'i, or 'genitals'] used in hulas before, this is not proper for children to peruse[;] children [who are] advanced would understand these sentences."[73] Two other Kānaka gave similar testimony, followed by that of Kānepu'u, the founding member of the *Ka Hoku o ka Pakipika* 'ahahui and member of Hale Nauā. His testimony, apparently for the defense, appealed to the ambiguity of the words; he never agreed that the publication contained any obscenity. He stated that "the word 'mai' has many meanings, the common meaning is sickness[.] When I was young people called things by proper names but since we had a written language things are called by other names."[74] In the end Auld and Greive were found guilty and fined $15 each plus court costs. Greive appealed and won an acquittal, but Auld, a Kanaka Maoli conversant in Hawaiian, remained convicted. Auld remained in close association with Kalākaua, however, joining the same Masonic societies. Further, in the annexation battle of 1897–1898, Auld was selected as one of the four delegates to travel to Washington, D.C., to present the people's protest there.

It may not have been only other Kānaka who were willing to explain the "obscene" nature of the program to the prosecution. One of the surviving copies of the *Papa Kuhikuhi o na Hula Poni Moi* belonged to Nathaniel B. Emerson, author of two books on hula orature and literature, and is preserved with his handwritten notes on it. Some of his notes have to do with the meanings of the names of the songs, or information about the places mentioned in the names. But he also noted that he considered one song, "Ko mai kiliopu," to be "smut" and another version of the same song as "lewd." He made another note that a "hula puili" was performed by two girls and was "innocent, calisthenic."[75] Castle and Emerson surely knew each other because both were missionary sons in a small society of missionary families, and thus it is likely (but not proven) that Emerson communicated his knowledge to Castle for the purpose of prosecuting the printers of the program.

"Ko mai kiliopu" is no doubt a hula maʻi, defined by Pukui and Elbert as "a song in honor of genitals, as of a chief, as composed on his or her birth."[76] Elbert and Noelani Mahoe characterize these songs as "an eminently sane and healthy realization of the importance of the sexual aspects of life, and perhaps a wish for future vigor."[77] These hula were important to Kalākaua as part of the reenactment of the traditional cosmology/genealogy. The Kanaka Maoli had suffered depopulation caused by epidemics of foreign disease and also by childlessness. Prayers to the Christian god seemed to work only for the haole; the missionary families were large and healthy, while the Kanaka continued to die en masse. One of the basic values of a genealogical world view is that it places people in a great chain of being: it links them not only to the past but to the future through children and grandchildren. The hula maʻi invoke the old ways of spurring fertility against the seemingly merciless refusal of Iehova (Jehovah). In this world view hula maʻi are not obscene but rather are essential to the continuance of life. Another important concept is that hula maʻi are "always lively and fun" and thus contribute to the air of celebration of Kanaka tradition.[78] It was, of course, anathema to the missionaries to associate procreation with anything lively or fun.

Besides the hula maʻi, other types of hula included on the program were coronation hula, composed especially for the occasion; hula pahu, important ancient drum hula; mele inoa for Kalākaua, such as "Eia Davida o ka Heke o na Pua"; and many hula Pele, for the volcano goddess, her sister Hiʻiaka, and the lover, Lohiʻau.[79]

In spite of the controversy over the program, no one was arrested for the actual performances of these hula. And while the English press reported on the court case, of far more interest to the Hawaiian press was the genealogy battle that the poni mōʻī had reignited and that the Hawaiian-language newspapers waged among themselves. It may have been the performance of the mele and hula that started this more serious trouble. Many mele listed on the program were "mele koʻihonua" (genealogical chants). The word "koʻihonua" also refers to the style of chanting used to make sure the genealogical information in this kind of chant was clearly understood. Kamakau wrote of the koʻihonua that it "is one which relates to the forefathers of the Hawaiian people and to the history of the kings and their accomplishments. . . . In the *koʻihonua mele* of Kualiʻi, the Kumuliʻi and the Kumulipo were preserved, and in the mele of Peleiholani [*sic*] the genealogical tree of Ololo and Haloa was given."[80]

The recitation of such mele along with the hula in public performance bring the cosmology and genealogy to physical life; public performance enacts the traditional spiritual beliefs of the Kanaka Maoli. The meaning and significance of the mele and hula, especially in Kalākaua's time when there had been no public ceremonial performances for decades, were incomprehensible for the most part to the foreigner. In a more explicit way than the published moʻolelo or mele, the ceremonial performances of hula over that two-week period bound the Kanaka together in a way described by Chatterjee as "the inner domain of cultural identity, from which the colonial intruder [was] kept out."[81]

The original article that started the argument over Kalākaua's and Emma's genealogies has apparently not been preserved, so the origin of the controversy remains a mystery. At the time of the controversy, three newspapers were being published in Hawaiian: *Ka Nupepa Elele Poakolu*, owned by Walter Murray Gibson, a close associate of King Kalākaua; *Ko Hawaii Pae Aina*, owned by Henry Whitney and edited by Joseph U. Kawainui, who later would edit *Nupepa Kuokoa*; and *Kuokoa*, at this time edited by Thomas Thrum, a haole opponent of Kalākaua. The main argument was between *Ka Nupepa Elele Poakolu* on Kalākaua's

side and *Ko Hawaii Pae Aina* on Queen Emma's side; *Kuokoa* chimed in
occasionally against Kalākaua.

The first article I was able to recover is from June 1883; I do not
know how long before that the controversy was going on. It lasted until
at least December of that year, after which no copies of the newspapers
have been preserved. At the very least, it went on for six months in
nearly every issue of the two papers. In *Ko Hawaii Pae Aina*, it was
usually on the front page.[82] Interestingly enough, mele in fragments —
sometimes short, sometimes quite long — were printed as part of these
arguments, but no one was arrested for it. Most of what is preserved is
from *Nupepa Elele Poakolu*, which always refers to the ongoing debate
with *Ko Hawaii Pae Aina*. It is unfortunate that nearly half of the argument is lost; however, even though the arguments cannot be reviewed in
their entirety, the significance of the issue for Kanaka Maoli is clear. The
court case against William Auld was insignificant compared to the genealogical battle. Kanaka Maoli, at least those running newspapers, were
far more concerned with the composition of the nation and the identity
of the sovereign, an identity that depended on the ancient cosmology
and an individual's genealogical link to it. The nation's sovereignty and
the offices of monarch and nobles were at stake in these discussions,
whereas the obscenity trial, while symbolic of the struggle for hegemony, was more simply a case of an attempt to embarrass the Crown,
which itself went embarrassingly out of control. The genealogy discussion had far greater potential to significantly embarrass or elevate any of
the ali'i nui. For Emma it might mean winning the crown for herself,
and for Kalākaua it could mean the loss or gain of legitimacy.

THE JUBILEE

Three years after the poni mō'ī, hula and feasting celebrations were again
held at 'Iolani Palace in honor of King Kalākaua, this time to mark his
fiftieth birthday. For nearly two weeks various celebrations took place at
'Iolani Palace and other locations in Honolulu. On November 16, 1886,
there was a "grand reception at Iolani Palace" and a torchlight procession
by the fire department. Saturday, November 20, brought a parade. On
Tuesday, November 23, the "ahaaina luau" (lū'au feast) was held, at
which hula was performed. A birthday ball, haole style, was given on

Hula being performed at 'Iolani Palace during Kalākaua's jubilee.
(Courtesy of Hawai'i State Archives)

November 25. Finally, on November 27, in celebration of Lā Kū'oko'a
(Independence Day), "historical tableaux" were performed, including
hula.

The parade in Honolulu on November 20 contained the first of the
significant public performances of the jubilee: "O keia ka la i hooholoia
no na hana hoikeike o ke au kahiko" (This was the day decided on for
the exhibitions of the ancient times). Those displays included hula: "He
poe hula Hawaii olapa aku me na ipu hula iluna o ke kaa loihi i hoowe-
hiwehi ia me na lau nahele" (Hula dancers danced with hula gourd
drums atop a long car decorated with the greens of the forest). Most of
the parade consisted of floats in the shape of canoes depicting scenes
from various mo'olelo kahiko. One float showed "ke ano o ka hana ana o
ka upena luu a me ka laau ona ia e ka i-a, oia o Makalei" (the manner
of using deep-sea nets and the intoxicant ingested by fish, known as
Mākālei).[83] This was a representation of the story of Mākālei, a magical
tree whose roots attract fish. Others represented the soldiers of Ka-

mehameha, especially his war generals, Keaweaheulu (Kualaku) and Kameeiamoku (Namahoe), both ancestors of Kalākaua.[84]

"Waʻa peleleu," long canoes used in battle, were displayed in the parade. Another canoe represented Keawenuiaʻumi, with two kāhili (feather standard) bearers on the sides along with twelve paddlers. Yet another float represented Kaumualiʻi, undefeated aliʻi nui of Kauaʻi and ancestor of Queen Kapiʻolani. Some of the aliʻi nui represented on the various waʻa wore traditional feather cloaks. Another float represented the story of Kawelo and the supernatural fish, Uhumākaʻikaʻi, along with a mermaid. The story of Pākaʻa and Kūapākaʻa (represented by J. H. Kānepuʻu) was told in another. One float demonstrated a method of casting for bonito, "hi aku." Another told the story of the god Māui hooking an ulua fish named Pimoe. The Royal Hawaiian Band and school marching bands also participated in the parade. These descriptions all come from *Nupepa Kuokoa*, edited at this time, by Thomas Thrum. Although not a supporter of Kalākaua, he was interested in Hawaiian lore and would have been able to interpret the representations. Moreover, these descriptions may have been written by him or by an anonymous Kanaka staff writer, which it was the *Kuokoa*'s practice to employ.

By contrast, the English-language paper, the *Daily Bulletin*, also described the parade, but without any names of those on the floats, except "Maui." The writer knew neither the moʻolelo being represented nor the significance of the carefully selected representations. Of Kawelo and Uhumākaʻikaʻi, for example, he wrote: "Next came another canoe, with mermaids, and at the stern . . . was mounted a huge model of a black skinned fish labelled 'Makaikai' whether meant for a shark, whale or dolphin, no one seemed to know."[85] The writers in the Hawaiian press knew, but apparently no one close to the writer for the *Daily Bulletin*. This same report says "The natives in the procession were all curiously costumed in imitation of ancient times." Their costume seemed curious only to the English-language paper written by a foreigner who did not understand it.

At this time, Walter Murray Gibson was also running the *Pacific Commercial Advertiser*, whose account was more versed in Hawaiian lore than the *Daily Bulletin*, but nevertheless was the view of an outsider. The headline for the account of the parade reads, "History of the Hawaiian Islands Symbolized. The Barbaric Past Exhibited Side by Side with

Modern Civilization." Although Kalākaua had arranged the parade to be a celebration of the glories told in moʻolelo kahiko, Gibson interpreted it this way: "Rarely, if ever, has [a] nation contemplated with greater reason for rejoicing its rapid transition from the crude customs of . . . yesterday." In his rush to privilege European knowledge, he made this mistake as well: "Many were there whose educational attainments and whose general mental progress were such that they were as competent as Europeans to understand the symbols of the pageant."[86] It is clear that, for the most part, the Kanaka Maoli understood far more completely "the symbols of the pageant" than did the Europeans, especially as represented by the *Daily Bulletin*. The assumption that the Kanaka Maoli were but yesterday barbarians is a continuance of the discourse of civilization and savagery. It is deployed in this era not just by Walter Murray Gibson, a supposed friend of the Kanaka, but also by the *Daily Bulletin*, for the usual political reasons: "The Hawaiian, although awaking to the first light of liberty under the tutorship of the now much abused 'missionaries' of the American Board, and although living under an organized system of government in which he is supposed to have a voice, has yet much to learn before he is fit to graduate a free citizen of a free country."[87]

As we have seen, this discourse is used to keep the Europeans and Americans in power over the mass of Kanaka Maoli. We can also discern that the missionaries felt and resented the resistance to themselves and to their colonizing actions. It is important that this discourse was again deployed during the jubilee celebrations, just eight months before the haole oligarchy virtually deposed Kalākaua by threat of force. This discourse constructs justifications for the overthrow by insisting that Kalākaua and his people were unfit to rule themselves. The *Daily Bulletin* suggested as well that if the Kanaka Maoli were to govern themselves they had better leave their ancient customs and traditions behind: "Let the Hawaiian be once fully saturated with American ideas of liberty and personal independence. . . . While the Hawaiian is wedded by ignorance to superstitious ideas and practices, he can never stand side by side, on the same plane with Bulgarian or American, as a free citizen of a free country."[88]

This discourse attempts to trap the Kanaka Maoli in a cultural wasteland and historical vacuum by insisting that equality with Europeans and Euro-Americans can only be gained by a repudiation of every-

thing in their own traditions. This notion is effectively countered, however, by Kalākaua and others through the physical representations of
the moʻolelo kahiko of the parade, and later in the jubilee festivities
through the hula performances and historical tableaux. Kalākaua vehe-
mently insists through these activities that the Kanaka Maoli are proud
of their past (which is not forgotten) and so already consider themselves
the equals of the Europeans and Euro-Americans.

Hula at the Royal Lūʻau

The ʻahaʻaina lūʻau held at the palace on November 23 was attended by
1,500 to 2,000 people, who were entertained that night with food and
hula. *Ko Hawaii Pae Aina*, edited by Kawainui, an opponent of Kalākaua, reported that five types of hula were performed, including the
hula pahu (sharkskin drum hula). The *Pae Aina* also asserted that people complained when a certain hula was performed and it was stopped
before it was completely over, and also that some people struggled with
the dancers to force them to kiss their cheeks. Then the brief report says,
"Ua paia kuli makou i na kamailio kupono ole no kekahi mau mea i ikeia
ma ia anaina lealea, i ae ole makou e hoike aku i ka lahui" (We were
deafened by the improper talk of certain things seen at that gathering for
entertainment, which we did not consent to have shown in public).[89]
The newspaper writer apparently considered some of the performance
shameful or perhaps obscene.

Nupepa Kuokoa's account of the evening, probably written by
Thrum, was vague and lacked understanding of the content of the hula.
This lack is probably because Thrum was interested in collecting and
translating moʻolelo but had not studied hula, nor did he (or anyone else
outside the palace or hula schools) have many opportunities to witness
hula. Indeed, he could not identify the different types of hula being
performed. Here is part of his account: "I ka hula ana, haa like lakou
iluina [sic] a ilalo me ka niniu o na pa-u, e kuhi ana na lima io a ianei me
ka lelele o na wawae. . . . [U]wauwa . . . na kanaka i ka maikai paha, i ka
inoino paha? Aohe maopopo aku o ia wahi; aka hoike mai kahi poe no ka
maikai ke kumu nui o ka uwauwa." (When they danced, they danced in
unison up and down with skirts twirling[;] the hands were pointing this
way and that and the legs were jumping. . . . People/Hawaiians shouted
because it was good, or perhaps because it was bad? We have no under-

standing there[,] but certain people have said the main reason for the shouting was because it was good." Thrum also reported that the hula performance lasted from "ke ahiahi okoa a hiki wale i ke kani ana o ke oo o na moa ma na hora wanaao" (the early evening until the sound of the roosters' crowing in the dawn hours).[90] Gibson reported very little on the hula; his entire discussion of it is as follows: "In the evening a number of hula-dancers were called into requisition for their amusement. The proceedings throughout were characterized by the utmost decorum and good taste."[91] Unfortunately, it is not clear in any of these accounts how many of the people who attended the lūʻau stayed on to watch the hula performance. Although Kawainui suggested that something indecent or improper occurred, no calls for arrest were made, and neither he nor Thrum called for the hula performances to be banned in the future.

He Hoikeike Tabalo au Kahiko:
A Performance of Historical Tableaux

November 27 was designated for the Lā Kūʻokoʻa (Independence Day) celebration because the official date, November 28, fell on Sunday. The celebration included the performance of "historical tableaux," which included scenes from the life of Kamehameha I interspersed with hula performances. I was able to retrieve two accounts of the event: one by Gibson, in English, from the *Pacific Commercial Advertiser*, and the other by Thrum, from *Nupepa Kuokoa*. Gibson reported that an "ancient 'Punch and Judy' created much amusement" (most likely he refers to the hula kiʻi done with puppets). During this performance an ipu hula was played by a woman as accompaniment to the "antics" of the kiʻi. In the last scene, actors representing Kamehameha's soldiers performed a "spear dance," while "sixteen young girls gave an exhibition of Hawaiian dancing."[92]

The account from *Nupepa Kuokoa* is similar to that by Gibson, but with added details and commentary. It states that when the aliʻi entered (meaning, most likely, Kalākaua, Kapiʻolani, and other members of the royal family), "mele ia ke mele lahui me na panai pu ana a na mea kani" (the national anthem was sung with musical accompaniment). *Kuokoa* took a decidedly approving tone in its assessment of the evening, even though it included so much hula: "Maikai a nui ka mahalo ia o na hana. O ka pokole loa nae hoi ka hewa?" (The performances were good and appreciated/respectable [mahalo ia]. That it was so short was neverthe-less a fault?).[93]

Taken together, the parade and the tableaux can be seen as perfor-mances representing the masculine heroism of the Kanaka past, bal-anced a little each time by female dancers. It is emphatically masculine because that is what the Euro-American powers respect(ed) in a coun-try. Whenever possible, Hawai'i had to display proof of its eligibility in the exclusive club of sovereign nations. It was a small nation with a small to nonexistent military force: in the age of imperialism it kept its sov-ereignty, at the pleasure of the Mana Nui "Great Powers." At the same time, however, the activities of the jubilee served to bind together the Kanaka 'Ōiwi in national solidarity built on shared language, genealogy, and history, none of which could be fully shared by the foreigners look-ing to take over their country.

Na Mele Aimoku, na Mele Kupuna, a me na Mele Pono o Ka Moi Kalakaua I: The Sovereign's Songs, the Ancestral Songs, and the Pono Songs of King Kalākaua I

A book of songs was published in honor of Kalākaua for his fiftieth birthday jubilee. Several of the original copies are in the library of the Bishop Museum, and so we can see that it was published in book form, typeset and hardbound. The name of the collector or editor appears nowhere on it, nor does the name of the publisher, although a note is given that it was "pai ia no ka la hanau o ka Moi" (published for the birthday of the King).[94] It is 303 pages long and contains forty different mele, some of which are said to be traditional and some of which have composer's names appended. Songs, especially traditional mele, are not always discrete pieces. It is a characteristic of mele that parts of songs may reappear attached to new songs, and may be combined in a variety of ways. Songs are also often renamed for a living ali'i to keep the genealogical connection to a deceased one current, and also to preserve the song.[95] Thus the actual number of the mele may be more than forty, and parts of mele may be repeated in other mele within the same book. Some of the mele listed in the Papa Kuhikuhi o Na Hula Poni Moi coronation program are the same as those in Na Mele Aimoku. Judging by the titles alone (because we do not have the full text for the Papa Kuhikuhi) at least seventeen of the mele are the same.

The general tendency in Hawaiian language and thought is to put important things first, so let us look at the first mele in the book. It is entitled "He Mele Inoa no Aikanaka" (A name song for ʻAikanaka). ʻAikanaka was Kalākaua's maternal grandfather, who happened to share his name with the aliʻi nui of Kauaʻi who figures prominently in the Kawelo moʻolelo. The first part of the mele is clearly identifiable as the mele known as "ʻAuʻa ʻia" (Withhold/hold onto [your land]). This is one of three classical hula pahu. Hula pahu originally were heiau (temple) rituals that became performance hula after the collapse of the traditional religion,[96] and as such are important links to the ancient traditions. "ʻAuʻa ʻia" was performed on the occasion of the poni mōʻi as well as the jubilee. Kaeppler says, however, that "it was probably at the time of Kalākaua's jubilee celebration in 1886 that the text was presented and reinterpreted as an admonition to hold on to the Hawaiian heritage."[97] What follows is the beginning of the chant, with a translation by Mary Kawena Pukui:

> Aua ia e kama e kona moku
> E kona moku e kama e aua ia
> E kama kama kama kama i ka huli nuu
> Ke kama kama kama kama i ka huli au
> Huli hia papio a ilalo i ke alo
> Huli hia i ka imu o ku ka makii lohelohe
> (Kama (the chief) refused to part with his island
> This is the land held back by Kama
> The son Kama, Kama, Kama, the highest born
> The son Kama, Kama, Kama, who reigns
> He turns his foes face down (kills them)
> He turns them into the imus (earth ovens), then lays them
>   before his idols.)[98]

This section of the chant is clearly a statement by (and for) Kalākaua, that he is the proper ruler of his land, and that he intends to retain his rule over the land. The next section appears to be a kanikau, and invokes the gods Lono, Kanaloa, Hina, and Kū, in that order. The section following the kanikau links Kalākaua to Kawelo:

> O ka Kawelo welo kapu o Kaweloaikanaka,
> O Kawelo Alii makua Kūhaulua

(Kawelo's sacred heritage/progeny is Kaweloaikanaka,
Chiefly Kawelo, Kūhaulua is the parent)

Kalākaua's symbolic linkage to Kawelo is important. The story of Kawelo was the first to be published in *Ka Hoku o ka Pakipika*, and Kawelo was also represented in the jubilee parade. Like Kawelo, Kalākaua is of a lineage that is secondary to the ruling line. And like Kawelo, he becomes the sovereign through great efforts of his own, combined with his devotion to his gods. While his cousin/competitors learn mokomoko wrestling, Kawelo learns the prayers and care for the gods. He is a heroic as well as a supernatural figure who derives most of his mana from his spiritual/religious activities. Kalākaua likewise gained mana from his efforts to bring Kawelo and his gods back into the Kanaka collective consciousness.

" 'Au'a 'ia" is a song of sovereignty that also functions to invoke the gods and the traditional mo'olelo of Kawelo. The fact that it was set down on paper for Kalākaua, along with the thirty-nine other mele, is also important as an act of preservation for future generations.

CONCLUSION

In the words of Valerio Valeri, "the *Kumulipo* . . . makes explicit what seems implicit in all Hawaiian religious ideology: man's dependence on the gods in fact conceals the gods' dependence on men."[99] The gods who legitimated Kalākaua's rule do not exist if they are not evoked in prayer and ritual. Because all of the ali'i were at least nominally Christian, they sought out ways to accommodate their need for the traditional gods and the genealogy/cosmology that gave them the right to rule, while escaping censure from their Christian churches. Consecration of heiau, offerings to the gods, and other overtly religious rites were not safe to perform in this environment. Kame'eleihiwa explains: "When a *pono Mō'ī* was religiously devoted to the *Akua*, the whole society was *pono* and prospered. When disaster struck . . . these were signs that the *Mō'ī* had ceased to be religious, for the society was no longer *pono*."[100] Kamakau quotes an old saying, "O ke ali'i haipule i ke akua, 'o ia ke ali'i e kū i ke aupuni" (The ali'i who is devoted to the god[s] is the ali'i who shall rule the nation).[101] Through public performance of hula and the publication of the *Kumulipo* and *Na Mele Aimoku*, Kalākaua demonstrated that he too was devoted to the traditional religion, and was therefore a good and proper mōʻī. Such a mōʻī should be able to hold onto the nation's sovereignty.

In addition to fulfilling the need for the traditional gods and cosmology, the public celebrations of tradition served to alleviate some of the psychological harm done to the lāhui through the social and economic colonization. As I show in my examination of the missionary discourse, colonialism in Hawaiʻi, as elsewhere according to Ngugi Wa Thiongʻo, meant "the deliberate undervaluing of a people's culture, their art, dances, religions, history, geography, education, orature and literature."[102] These public performances demonstrated pride in Kanaka culture, art, dance, religion, and history, and in so doing they strengthen the collective identity of the lāhui as a nation. Albert Memmi says that "the most serious blow suffered by the colonized is being removed from history and from the community."[103] At that time, with English-language schools outnumbering Hawaiian (and receiving more funding), the process of writing Kanaka out of their own history had begun.[104] But the Papa Kūʻauhau, the Hale Nauā, as well as events such as the parade, historical tableaux, and hula performances, insisted on reinscribing and reenacting a history that is particularly Kanaka.

Murray Edelman wrote that "art should be recognized as a major and integral part of the transaction that engenders political behavior."[105] The historical tableaux, parade, and hula performances, I believe, worked to win over the hearts of many Kānaka Maoli, some of whom may not previously have supported Kalākaua. Edelman also says that "works of art generate the ideas about leadership, bravery, cowardice, altruism, dangers, authority, and fantasies about the future that people typically assume to be reflections of their own observations and reasoning."[106] The particular works of performance art that Kalākaua inspired in the events he sponsored contain the themes of leadership that supported his rule. I have spoken of the moʻolelo of Kawelo, the cousin of the younger line who prevails by devotion to his gods. The Kamehameha story contains this same theme (as does the moʻolelo of ʻUmi). When Kalaniʻōpuʻu, the mōʻī of Hawaiʻi Island died, he bequeathed the office of mōʻī to his son, Kiwalaʻō, but he left the war god, Kūkāʻilimoku (Island-snatching Kū), to Kamehameha. Kamehameha, through consecration of this god and temples, defeated Kiwalaʻō in battle and went on to become the conqueror of all the islands except Kauaʻi. A similar theme is given in the story of Maui, as we saw in the *Kumulipo*. Through

Kalākaua's efforts, these stories became part of the national narrative, which not only justified his rule but, as I demonstrate throughout this chapter, contributed to the identity of the lāhui as nation.

Although the mōʻī represented tradition through genealogy, they themselves were the most powerful members of the class that both facilitated and resisted colonization. Alexander Liholiho (Kamehameha IV), Lota Kapuāiwa (Kamehameha V), and Kalākaua all created policies and otherwise assisted the progress of colonial capitalism while retaining their cultural identity as Kanaka Maoli through both the secretive and overt practice of traditional ritual, ceremony, performance, and custom. They could never abandon genealogy because that is what empowered them in the minds and hearts of their own people. Further, it was linked to the very core of their identity; to abandon it would have meant severe psychological damage as well as damage to the collective identity of the lāhui.

When Emma died in 1885, she left the lāhui without a close link to Kamehameha. The loss of Emma, along with the previous losses of Kamehameha descendants Lunalilo, Pauahi, and Keʻelikōlani, no doubt brought more supporters to Kalākaua. This served to make the missionary sons, who began to be known at this time as the "missionary party," more worried about holding onto power. While the people were divided for and against Kalākaua, it had been easier for the missionary party to exert their will to rule. Now feeling their power slipping, they turned to more coercive measures.

Eight months after the jubilee the haole oligarchy coalesced and forced Kalākaua to sign the "Bayonet Constitution," so named because he signed it under threat of violence. (The kingdom's small militia was under the control of the oligarchy, who were, furthermore, associated with U.S. military forces.) This constitution stripped Kalākaua of his most important executive powers: every decision he made had to have the approval of the cabinet; he was no longer able to appoint the House of Nobles; and he was prevented from dismissing his cabinet himself, that power being given to the legislature.[107] It was in response to the Bayonet Constitution that Kānaka Maoli attempted to use the political system of the West to their own advantage. In 1889, Kānaka Maoli formed a political party to try to gain enough political power within the imposed system to take back control of their own country. In the next chapter, I examine their efforts.

4

The Antiannexation Struggle

I ʻāina nō ka ʻāina i ke aliʻi, a i waiwai nō ka ʻāina i ke kanaka.
(The land remains the land because of the aliʻi, and the land
prospers because of the people.)
— ʻŌlelo noʻeau (Hawaiian proverb)

Between 1893 and 1898 Kānaka Maoli mounted vigorous and organized
opposition to the annexation of their nation by the United States. I
begin here with a sketch of the events that led up to the U.S.-backed
coup dʼetat of Liliʻuokalaniʼs government in 1893, followed by a more
detailed account of the resistance to the annexation five years later. Because I concentrate on bringing forth the words and actions of the
Kanaka Maoli, I do not dwell on the discourse of the annexationists.
Much documentation and analysis has already been done of these events
and of the annexationist discourse.[1]

The resistance, in contrast, has not been well documented or analyzed, in part because historians do not generally read the archive in
Hawaiian. Much of what is in this chapter is taken from sources written
only in Hawaiian. Resistance to the 1887 Bayonet Constitution and the
oligarchy that produced itself through it has in recent years been documented by Kanaka Maoli and other scholars, in particular Davianna
McGregor-Alegado and Albertine Loomis, both of whom focus on the

Wilcox Rebellion of 1889.[2] In 1975, Nancy Morris documented some of the antiannexation activities of the Hui Kālai'āina in 1898. African American historian Merze Tate is the only one who even mentions the 1897 antiannexation petition (which contained over 21,000 names) and that was in a footnote.[3] The major historian of Hawaiian political history, Ralph Kuykendall, devotes only one paragraph and several footnotes to the Hui Kālai'āina, and he did not document the activities of Hui Aloha 'Āina except for a brief reference to "the ladies of the Hawaiian Patriotic League."[4] This is in striking contrast to his exhaustive and sometimes excruciatingly detailed accounts of the formation of the oligarchy's Annexation Club and Committee of Safety, and in spite of his obviously careful reading of the Blount report, in which many documents of these important organizations appear.[5] William Adam Russ, who undoubtedly wrote and researched more on the 1893 coup and the battle over annexation than any other historian, makes five references to the Hawaiian Patriotic League (Hui Aloha 'Āina), mainly documenting various protests.[6] Like Kuykendall, he displays a lack of curiosity about these large Kanaka Maoli political associations. Although Russ's research in the U.S. National Archives appears to have been thorough, he fails to mention the petition of 21,269 names. His work on the annexation is titled *The Hawaiian Republic (1894–1898) and Its Struggle to Win Annexation*, but for Russ the struggle over annexation took place in Washington, D.C., and it was a matter of whether or not the United States would agree to annexation. The consent or opposition of the citizenry of Hawai'i was insignificant in his particular historical narrative, which aimed to present the annexation as a triumph of American political values, and thus as a good thing for Hawai'i. In order to create such a narrative, however, it was necessary for him to overlook and to smooth over, as much as possible, the opposition of the Kanaka 'Ōiwi and their demands for a democratic decision-making process.

Lili'uokalani mentions both Hui Kālai'āina and Hui Aloha 'Āina in her 1897 book. And Kahikina Kelekona (J. G. M. Sheldon) describes the formation of the Hui Hawai'i Aloha 'Āina in his 1906 biography of Joseph Nāwahī. This important resource was translated into English by Marvin Puakea Nogelmeier in 1988 but received only limited publication and has long been out of print.[7] Albertine Loomis documents some of the activities of the hui in her book about the 1895 countertop, *For Whom Are the Stars?* However, outside of these volumes no one has chronicled the existence and works of the Hui Aloha ʻĀina except Tom Coffman, whose account is based on an earlier version of this chapter.[8]

The lack of historical reference to such a large and organized resistance is typical of colonial situations, in which the archive in the language of the colonizer is privileged to a high degree over that of the vernacular — that is, the language of the native people. As Gyan Prakash writes, "a profound sense of historical awareness guided the European colonial conquest of 'peoples without history.'"[9] Describing the colonized as "peoples without history" and then rigorously keeping them out of the history books is part of the process of what Ngugi wa Thiongʼo calls the colonizer's establishment of mental control. This effort for mental control requires "the destruction or deliberate undervaluing of a people's culture, their art, dances, religions, history, geography, education, orature and literature, and the conscious elevation of the language of the coloniser."[10] The existence of the resistance in this case has been nearly erased in historiography. In this chapter I demonstrate that attending to the archive produced by the colonized in their native tongue can restore the history of struggle suppressed by the forces of colonialism. I also show that language itself is important in the anticolonial struggle — another issue that historians (except Chapin) have failed to treat. Successfully obfuscating or erasing the resistance activities of the colonized in historiography depends on the public's inability to read the language as much as it does on a lack of access to education and facilities.

Using the archive in Hawaiian, let us begin our examination "against the grain," as Said puts it, of the historical events that led to the illegitimate annexation and the resistance to it.

EVENTS LEADING TO THE 1893 COUP

King Kalākaua reigned during a time when descendants of missionaries and other settlers from the United States and Europe were establishing sugar plantations in the islands. They pressured the king for a reciprocity treaty with the United States so that they could sell their sugar to the large U.S. market duty-free. King Kalākaua tried to win the support of the lāhui while facing continual conflict with the haole, who were convinced of their superiority and who were determined to rule over the

Kanaka Maoli. Jonathan Osorio states that "it was not merely the fate of reciprocity that drove the haole to ever escalating challenges to the King and the Ministry. It was their sense that the King . . . [and] the entire government was a foolish and comic apparatus without their leadership and control."[11] They were the sons of the missionaries who were determined to eradicate Kanaka culture because it was savage, dark, and inferior. The missionary sons and grandsons had been imbued from birth with a sense of their own superiority to the natives; their parents and grandparents had come to Hawai'i in order to bring enlightenment and civilization. The sons and grandsons had been sent to the United States to be educated in East Coast colleges, where racism, even in the abolitionist north, was the norm. Although the missionaries had originally concentrated on converting souls, increasingly throughout the nineteenth century they took over key positions in the government and instructed and advised the ali'i in all matters having to do with Western forms of politics and economy. Eventually, faced with obstinacy and what they saw as regression to a savage culture on the part of the mō'ī, they wrested control of the government away from Kalākaua by forcing the Bayonet Constitution upon him. A conspiracy of missionary sons and other businessmen, with support from the U.S. military, took over Kalākaua's government troops and, according to Clarence Ashford, "little was left to the imagination of the hesitant and unwilling Sovereign as to what he might expect in the event of his refusal to comply with the demands then made upon him."[12]

The Bayonet Constitution created an oligarchy of the haole planters and businessmen. This was accomplished by destroying the executive powers of the sovereign, and giving those powers to the cabinet; by making the cabinet voting members in the House of Nobles and allowing the legislature to dismiss any cabinet with a simple majority vote; by providing that white foreigners no longer had to become naturalized citizens in order to vote; and, finally, by creating a "special electorate" comprised of men of Hawaiian or European descent who could read Hawaiian, English, or any European language, and who also possessed property worth at least three thousand dollars or who had an annual income of at least six hundred dollars.[13]

Osorio notes that this "was the very first time that democratic rights were determined by race in any Hawaiian constitution."[14] Indeed, it meant that wealthy white foreigners could vote and working-class maka'āinana and Asian immigrants could not. Furthermore, the previous constitution had guaranteed that "The King's private lands and other property are inviolable," but the Bayonet had no such article. The 'Āina Lei Ali'i, or Crown lands, were thus vulnerable for the first time.

McGregor-Alegado notes that "the initial period of reaction to the 'Bayonet' Constitution and the new Reform Cabinet was marked by mass meetings, petitioning, delegations to the King, electoral campaigning, and conspiracy."[15] These protests of the Bayonet Constitution eventually culminated in the founding of the first Kanaka Maoli political organization, the Hui Kālai'āina. According to David Earle, D. H. Nāhinu of Ho'okena, Hawai'i Island, a former representative in the House, galvanized suggestions that "native Hawaiians . . . establish their own political association."[16] Haole newspaper editor Daniel Lyons used his newspaper office of the *Elele* for organizing the Hui Kālai'āina. He emphasized that "the executive committee would be made up only of Hawaiians and that his role was only to start up the association."[17] At the first meeting of Hui Kālai'āina, "estimates of attendance ranged from 500 to 1500."[18] John Ailuene (Edwin) Bush, a newspaper writer and editor, was elected president of the hui. Of both Kanaka and haole ancestry, Bush had been prominent in Kalākaua's cabinet. By June 1888, the hui had established a constitution as well as a platform for the upcoming elections. Among the issues on the platform were the preservation of the monarchy, amendment of the constitution, and the reduction of property qualifications for voters for the House of Nobles.

While Hui Kālai'āina was preparing for elections, Robert Kalanihiapo Wilcox of Maui grew weary of working quietly and waiting patiently for justice. Wilcox was of ali'i ancestry and had been sent by Kalākaua to study at a military academy in Italy; it was assumed by all that he would have a respectable position with the government when he completed his studies. However, the government, now a (colonial) oligarchy of missionary descendants and planters, abruptly recalled him and then refused to employ him in any position equal to his qualifications (he had completed military and engineering training). Eventually Wilcox went to San Francisco where he obtained a position. In April 1889, he returned to Hawai'i "to help his fellow countrymen in the coming elections." Wilcox's wife, in an autobiography that appears to be largely fictionalized, says that Wilcox was banished after a failed plot to kill Kalākaua. However, there seems to be no other evidence to support this charge, and, in fact, Wilcox seemed determined to reinstate Kalākaua to power.[19] On his return, Wilcox organized a rifle association that eventually grew to seventy or eighty men. He and his men set out to undo the Bayonet Constitution by the same means as it had been done, by threat of violence. According to Earle: "In the early hours of the morning of July 30, Wilcox and his men gained control of the palace grounds. . . . [The cabinet] quickly assembled armed forces to retake the palace. . . . [S]hooting broke out between the government troops and Wilcox's men. Several of Wilcox's men were killed or seriously wounded. . . . They were forced to surrender . . . and 100 armed soldiers of the U.S.S. *Adams* were landed to patrol the streets."[20]

For neither the first time nor the last, U.S. troops were the deciding force in an internal conflict in Hawai'i. This is not surprising, however, because the perpetrators of the Bayonet Constitution and the subsequent government overthrow always thought of themselves as U.S. citizens first. They clung to their white American identity even while serving as officials in the Hawaiian kingdom government, they sent their children to be educated at U.S. East Coast prep schools and colleges, and they carefully patrolled the boundaries that separated themselves and their children from the Kanaka Maoli.[21]

After the failed Wilcox Rebellion of 1889 the Hui Kālai'āina continued its political work in an atmosphere even more hostile than before. As Earle states, the hui organized "mass, peaceful protest[s]" of a new version of the U.S. reciprocity treaty, which were "successful in stalling the treaty negotiations" and "inspired the organization of a mass movement for the [coming Legislative] elections."[22] The hui, in fact, "became the main political organization of the Hawaiian community during the 1890 election campaign," according to McGregor-Alegado.[23] The hui joined forces with the Mechanics' and Workingmen's Political Protective Union to run candidates friendly to both labor and revision of the constitution. Together they formed the National Reform Party and in February 1890 they won by a landslide. Even with that victory, however, they did not accrue enough power to change the constitution.

Members of Hui Kālai'āina, along with a number of men who would later organize Hui Hawai'i Aloha 'Āina, including Joseph Nāwahī and James Kaulia, met together on July 24, 1890 "for the purpose of forming a new constitution."[24] They petitioned King Kalākaua, who in turn submitted their petition to the legislature. David Earle says that

"members of the Haole community were alarmed at the idea of a constitutional convention,"[25] so the U.S. and British commissioners intervened by visiting the king to "warn" him.[26] While the move for a convention ultimately failed in the legislature, the National Reform Party
did succeed in getting some laws passed that were beneficial to the
Kanaka Maoli.[27]

Kānaka Maoli persisted in agitating for a new constitution up until
Kalākaua's death in 1891. When Kalākaua's sister Liliʻuokalani took office in January 1891, she too was repeatedly pressed to rectify the Bayonet Constitution. For example, in July 1892 she received petitions from
men who were voters. Many concerned women crossed out the references to qualified voters, substituting their own wording so that the
petition read: "O makou, me ka haahaa, na poe o kou Lahui Ponoi,
nona na inoa malalo iho nei he mau wahine Hawaii Ponoi Maoli. Ke
nonoi aku nei me ka iini nui, e hookoia e Kou Kuleana he Moiwahine no
ke Aupuni Hawaii, ka hoohana ana aku e hiki ai e loaa koke mai he
Kumukanawai hou no ko kakou Aina a me ko kakou Lahui" (We, hum-
bly, the people of your own Lāhui to whom the names below belong . . .
are Hawaiʻi's own Native women. We ask with great desire that action
should be taken in your authority as Queen of the Hawaiian Government, that a new Constitution be immediately acquired for our Land
and our People).[28] But Liliʻuokalani's government, particularly the legislature and the Crown, was at a standstill because the Bayonet Constitution provided that the mōʻī could take no action unless approved by
the cabinet. At the same time, the constitution gave authority to the
legislature to dismiss the cabinet at any time. Liliʻuokalani commented
that "instead of giving attention to measures required for the good of
the country, [the legislature] devoted its energies to the making and
unmaking of cabinets."[29]

RESISTANCE TO THE 1893 COUP

In January 1893, Liliʻuokalani attempted to promulgate the new constitution that her people were demanding. As has been written about in
great detail elsewhere, a handful of U.S.-identified politicians and businessmen, mainly the same men who perpetrated the Bayonet Constitution, then overthrew her government.[30] They conspired with U.S. Min-

Hui Aloha ʻĀina, men's branch. (Courtesy of Hamilton Library, University of Hawaiʻi at Mānoa)

ister John L. Stevens, who ordered soldiers from the USS *Boston* to come on shore. They then occupied a government building, Aliʻiolani Hale, and declared themselves to be the provisional government of Hawaiʻi. As the minister of the United States, Stevens immediately recognized the usurpers as a legitimate government. On being asked to surrender, Liliʻuokalani made several protests, which I examine at length in the next chapter.

Her people also immediately organized in protest. They formed the Hui Hawaiʻi Aloha ʻĀina and a sister organization, the Hui Hawaiʻi Aloha ʻĀina o Nā Wāhine. Joseph Nāwahī was president of the men's branch and Mrs. Abigail Kuaihelani Maipinepine Campbell was president of the women's branch.[31] In English the Hui Hawaiʻi Aloha ʻĀina was called the Hawaiian Patriotic League, but "aloha ʻāina" means love of the land, which differs significantly in connotation and cultural coding from "patriotic." The Hawaiian term is not gendered male, as "patriotic" is, nor does it share the Western genealogy of the term "patriotic."[32] Instead, it has a genealogy of its own, based in traditional Kanaka cosmology. Throughout the struggle Kanaka Maoli who worked to retain the sovereignty of their own nation called themselves "ka poʻe aloha ʻāina" (the people who love the land).

When President Grover Cleveland took office in 1893, he rejected the provisional government's proposed treaty to annex Hawaiʻi. Instead he sent Commissioner James Blount to investigate. The Hui Aloha ʻĀina, both men's and women's branches, prepared testimony to present to Commissioner Blount, and the men's branch submitted a copy of their constitution. It reads, in part: "Article 1. The name of this association shall be the Hawaiian Patriotic League (Ka Hui Hawaii Aloha Aina). Article 2. The object of this association is to preserve and maintain, by all legal and peaceful means and measures, the *independent autonomy* of the islands of Hawaii nei; and, if the preservation of our independence be rendered impossible, our object shall then be to exert all peaceful and legal efforts to secure for the Hawaiian people and citizens the continuance of their civil rights."[33]

The Hui Aloha ʻĀina also presented two other documents to the commissioner. The first was a statement describing themselves as an association representing "over 7,500 native-born Hawaiian qualified voters throughout the islands (out of a total of 13,000 electors), and to which is annexed a woman's branch of 11,000 members." They asked for the assistance of the U.S. president in the restoration of the government, because "the fate of our little kingdom and its inhabitants is in your hands." They further stated that the people had not yet protested with violence because, "they are simply waiting, in their simple faith in the generosity and honor of the most liberal and honorable Government of the world; and they expect *justice*, id est, *restoration* of their legitimate sovereign."[34]

The second document presented to the commissioner is much longer, and it explains the events leading up to the overthrow. It also protests the representations made by those who overthrew the government that claimed the Kanaka Maoli were incapable of self-government. The poʻe aloha ʻāina contested that discourse by stating that "the natives when left alone have had a most satisfactory, peaceful, and progressive Government, while all the dissensions, riots, and troubles recorded in the annals of these islands have ever been *by* or *through* foreigners seeking to wrench the power and wealth from the poor natives, these being ever the peaceful and patient sufferers thereby, not 'misled,' but ter-

Hui Aloha ʻĀina, women's branch. The caption on the original reads "Executive Committee of the Hui Aloha ʻĀina for Women of Honolulu. They delivered the women's document protesting annexation to J. H. Blount." (Courtesy of Hamilton Library, University of Hawaiʻi at Mānoa)

rorized and oppressed."[35] There is much more in this statement, which takes up fifteen pages of the final report Blount submitted to Cleveland. The names of the men who signed the protest document include, among others, John A. Cummins, a prominent aliʻi and landowner; John E. (Ailuene) Bush, editor of the Hawaiian-language newspaper *Ka Leo o ka Lahui* (The voice of the nation); Joseph Nāwahī; J. W. Bipikāne; John Prendergast; James K. Kaulia; and J. Kekipi.

The women also petitioned Commissioner Blount. Their petition reads, in part: "We, the women of the Hawaiian Islands, for our families and the happiness of our homes, desire peace and political quiet, and we pray that man's greed for power and spoils shall not be allowed to disturb the otherwise happy life of these islands, and that the revolutionary

Joseph Kahoʻoluhi Nāwahīokalaniʻōpuʻu (Nāwahī).
(Courtesy of the Bishop Museum)

agitations and disturbances inaugurated here since 1887, by a few foreigners, may be forever suppressed."[36] The names of the women who
signed this statement include, among others, Mrs. Kuaihelani Campbell; Mrs. Emma Nāwahī, wife of Joseph Nāwahī; Mrs. Kahalewai
Cummins, vice president and wife of John A. Cummins; Mrs. Mary
(Parker) Stillman, secretary; and Mrs. Līlia Aholo.[37] Some of the
women of the Hui Aloha ʻĀina were married to haole men, but it appears that their love for their land was greater than their worry about
political disagreement with their husbands. The following statement
appeared in *Ka Leo o ka Lahui* in March 1893: "Nui ko makou mahalo ka
[*sic*] ike ana i ka papa inoa o na Lede i komo i ka Hui Hawaii Aloha Aina
a na Lede. O ka poe makahanohano no a pau i mare i na kane haole
kekahi i komo pu mai he hookahi wale no wahine i kanalua mai, a o kona
Kaikuana no hoi kekahi e lole lua nei" (We were grateful to see the list of

names of Ladies who joined the Hui Hawai'i Aloha 'Āina for Ladies. Some of them are distinguished women who are married to haole men; only one of them was uncertain, and her older sister is also ambivalent).[38]

The three hui succeeded in persuading Commissioner Blount that the overthrow was an illegal and unethical act. After reviewing Blount's report, President Cleveland announced his opinion that the provisional government had acted illegally. In fact, he stated that "the provisional government owes its existence to an armed invasion by the United States," and further, that "by an act of war, committed with the participation of a diplomatic representative of the United States and without authority of Congress, the Government of a feeble but friendly and confiding people has been overthrown."[39] He thus condemned the actions of John L. Stevens and asked for his resignation. However, even though President Cleveland supported the restoration of Lili'uokalani to the throne, he abdicated his responsibility to do so by leaving the decision to Congress. Cleveland was a Democrat and generally anti-imperialist and antiexpansionist, but many members of Congress favored the annexation of Hawai'i as part of an expansionist policy to develop markets in Asia.[40] Cleveland's initial gestures of support but failure to take action caused confusion and miscommunication between the queen and some of her people.

In addition to testifying to Blount, the Kanaka Maoli protested in many other ways. Some withheld ho'okupu (offerings) to their churches when the ministers supported the provisional government. The members of Kaumakapili Church in Honolulu said that they would no longer give money to the church when the minister was praying for the loss of their birth land.[41] Both men and women sewed quilts incorporating the Hawaiian flag, as a number of Kanaka Maoli continue to do this day: "Hawaiian Flag quilts of the nineteenth century were used to communicate loyalty and personal service to the Hawaiian nation . . . and protests to foreign domination."[42]

The Royal Hawaiian Band, originally founded during the reign of Kauikeaouli (Kamehameha III), had always been administered and funded by the government. But in 1893 the provisional government wanted band members to sign an oath of loyalty, swearing that they would not support the queen or her government. When the band refused they were told that they would be fired, and that they would soon be eating rocks (because they would have no paycheck to buy food). The band members remained loyal to the queen, however, and because they considered themselves poʻe aloha ʻāina they walked away from their jobs and their paychecks. When they told their story to Ellen Kekoʻaohi-waikalani Wright Prendergast, she composed a song for them called "Mele Aloha ʻĀina" (Song for the people who love the land) or "Mele ʻAi Pōhaku" (Rock-eating song) also known as "Kaulana Nā Pua" (Famous are the flowers).[43] Here are two verses from the song:

> ʻAʻole aʻe kau i ka pūlima
> Ma luna o ka pepa o ka ʻenemi
> Hoʻohui ʻāina kūʻai hewa
> I ka pono sivila aʻo ke kanaka.

> ʻAʻole mākou aʻe minamina
> I ka puʻukālā a ke aupuni.
> Ua lawa mākou i ka pōhaku,
> I ka ʻai kamahaʻo o ka ʻāina.

> (No one will fix a signature
> To the paper of the enemy
> With its sin of annexation
> And sale of native civil rights.

> We do not value
> The government's sums of money.
> We are satisfied with the stones,
> Astonishing food of the land.)[44]

This song is still sung by Kānaka Maoli today as a call to sovereignty. The band, now independent of the government, re-formed as Ka Bana Lāhui Hawaiʻi (The Hawaiian national band) and continued to represent the poʻe aloha ʻāina, who regarded the band members as heroes because of their sacrifice.[45] They traveled for some years around the United States, bringing their Hawaiian nationalist message to the common people through their music.[46]

The Kanaka Maoli continued to protest, and the provisional government continued to press the U.S. government for annexation. Both sides petitioned the United States for assistance.

RESISTANCE TO THE REPUBLIC

When President Cleveland withdrew the provisional government's annexation treaty, President Sanford Dole and his colleagues moved to establish a permanent government in order to legitimize their power and control over the resources of Hawai'i. In early 1894 they declared that there would be a constitutional convention held in May. They appointed nineteen delegates—themselves—to the convention, and called for eighteen more delegates to be chosen by popular election. But in order for people to vote in this election, they would first have to sign an oath of loyalty to the provisional government, promising to "oppose any attempt to reestablish monarchical government in any form in the Hawaiian Islands." The overwhelming majority of Kānaka Maoli refused to sign the oath, and boycotted the constitutional convention: only about 4,000 men, most of foreign birth, signed the oath and voted in the election.[47]

The po'e aloha 'āina protested this unfair election process in a resolution sent to the new U.S. minister, Albert Willis. The women of the Hui Aloha 'Āina wrote a statement of protest addressed to the foreign ministers of the United States, England, France, Germany, Portugal, and Japan. Their statement said that the entire Hawaiian nation had been protesting for seventeen months, and that during that time "the Hawaiian People, confident in the honesty and impartiality of America, [had] patiently and peacefully submitted to the insults and tyranny of the Provisional Government." At the same time, "the Provisional Government, without even the courtesy of waiting for America's final decision, [have] been straining every effort to transform themselves into a permanent government, based on the support of Alien bayonets, and are now preparing . . . to proclaim an assumed Republic, through a constitution which is acknowledged as the most illiberal and despotic ever published in civilized countries."[48]

The women called the constitution "illiberal and despotic" because it was designed to keep as many Kānaka Maoli from voting as possible and to prevent Asian immigrants from voting as well. To do so it made use of the "Mississippi laws" that had kept African American citizens from voting in that state. In short, these laws stipulated that any voter could be challenged to explain details of the Constitution before being

allowed to vote.[49] The proposed constitution also followed the laws of
the provisional government in restricting rights to freedom of speech
and freedom of the press. Any criticism of the government spoken or
published could be labeled "seditious" and therefore illegal. People
again were required to sign an oath of loyalty to the republic in order to
vote, sit on a jury, or hold any job with the government.

In spite of continual protest by the people the oligarchy proceeded
with the constitutional convention, at which they approved the constitution that they had drafted in advance. The provisional government
then selected July 4 to announce their new permanent government. The
po'e aloha 'āina found out about these plans just a few days ahead of
time, and they were outraged. They called a hālāwai maka'āinana nui
(mass meeting) for July 2. Between 5,000 and 7,000 people — almost
twice as many as had voted for the constitutional convention — showed
up at 5 P.M. at Palace Square to express their disagreement with the
republic's formation, and to approve a resolution drafted by the officers
of the Hui Aloha 'Āina to be submitted to the U.S. minister. Here is part
of that resolution: "Ke kue kupaa loa nei ka Hui Hawaii Aloha Aina a
me na Hui Aloha Aina e ae, a me na kupa aloha aina o ke Aupuni
Hawaii . . . i ke kuahaua ia ana o kekahi Kumukanawai Hou i hana ia me
ka ae ole ia me ka lawelawe pu ole hoi o ka Lehulehu" (The Hui Aloha
Aina, and other patriotic leagues together with the loyal subjects of the
Hawaiian Kingdom . . . do hereby most solemnly protest against the
promulgation of a new Constitution formed without the consent and
participation of the people).[50] Joseph Nāwahī gave a speech that evening, in which he said: "No kakou ka Hale e like me ka na Kamehameha
i kukulu ai. Ua kipaku ia ae kakou e ka poe i aea hele mai, a komo i loko o
ko kakou hale; a ke olelo mai nei ia kakou, e komo aku a e noho i loko o
ka hale kaulei a lakou i manao ai e kukulu iho a onou aku ia kakou a pau e
komo aku. O ka'u hoi e olelo aku nei ia oukou e o'u mau hoa makaainana, mai noho kakou a ae iki" (The house of government belongs to
us, as the Kamehamehas built it. We have been ousted by trespassers
who entered our house and who are telling us to go and live in a lei stand
that they think to build and force us all into. I am telling you, my fellow
citizens, we should not agree in the least).[51]

Nāwahī asserts here that the government properly belongs to the
Kanaka Maoli, that the Kamehameha line had established a foundation
of constitutional monarchy that gave voice and representation to the

people, and that the haole oligarchy sought to replace that constitutional government with a colonial government that lacked such a foundation in the consent of the people. The reference to the lei stand may also be indicative of Nāwahī's concern about the economic fate of the people: it can be seen as a symbol of the ways that the Kanaka Maoli would be reduced to selling exotic and ephemeral elements of their culture, instead of holding substantial places in the economy.

Although President Cleveland had declared the acts of the provisional government illegal, U.S. Minister Willis immediately recognized the Republic of Hawai'i as a legitimate government. The three hui continued to protest through peaceful and diplomatic means, but assistance from other nations never arrived. In the face of the failure of the Cleveland administration to act, which no doubt felt like a betrayal, and in despair of diplomatic solutions, some of the po'e aloha 'āina began to plan an armed takeover of the government. In October 1894, they bought arms in San Francisco, and had them shipped to O'ahu on the schooner *Wahlberg*. The steamer *Waimānalo* then received the arms offshore of O'ahu.[52]

Unfortunately, the republic learned of the plans, mainly through their paid spies,[53] and on December 8, 1894, they arrested John Bush and Joseph Nāwahī. Both were leaders of the Hui Aloha 'Āina and both were newspapermen. Bush was editor of both *Ka 'Oia'i'o* and *Ka Leo o ka Lahui*, and Nāwahī also worked at these papers. It is unclear what roles these two po'e aloha 'āina might have played in subsequent events were they not in jail, but the attempted countercoup was disorganized and unsuccessful. The republic government also shut down the rest of the opposition press, so the po'e aloha 'āina and their sympathizers were without reliable printed news for several months.[54] Bush and Nāwahī were held without bail for two months, then released on $10,000 bond. Joseph Nāwahī contracted tuberculosis while in jail.

On January 4, 1895, Samuel Nowlein and Robert Wilcox, who was drafted into the leadership at the last minute, directed the *Waimānalo* to unload the arms at Kāhala near Lē'ahi (Diamond Head). On January 5, they distributed the arms, and then made plans to march on Honolulu and seize both the palace and the police station. On January 6, republic officials learned that the arms were stored at Henry Bertelmann's Waikīkī home, and they sent armed police there. The aloha 'āina rebels, who had arrived at Bertelmann's home from Kāhala, exchanged gunfire with officials of the republic, killing one of the haole civilian guards and later wounding Kanaka Maoli police officer Lieutenant Holi. The police eventually gained the upper hand and entered the home and arrested Bertelmann.[55]

Wilcox and his remaining force retreated to Lēʻahi, where the republic's militia again fired on them. The rebels retreated through Pālolo Valley, over the mountain ridges into Mānoa, Pauoa, and Nuʻuanu. There they began to surrender individually to the republic's forces. On January 14, Wilcox and other leaders surrendered in Kalihi.[56] On January 16, the republic claimed that they found arms buried in Queen Liliʻuokalani's garden at Washington Place.[57] In response the queen was arrested and held prisoner in a room at ʻIolani Palace.[58]

The poʻe aloha ʻāina, about two hundred of them, were given sentences varying from one to thirty-five years in prison and fined $5,000 to $10,000. Many of their haole sympathizers who were not citizens were deported.[59] Wilcox was sentenced to hang, but the sentence was later commuted. Prince Jonah Kūhiō Kalanianaʻole was among those imprisoned, and he was not released until September 1895.[60] The poʻe aloha ʻāina called the prisoners "poʻe paʻahao kālaiʻāina" (political prisoners) because they went to jail for making a desperate move to express their political will under the colonial oligarchy that allowed them no participation. Some women made dresses of striped fabric resembling the prison uniforms to show their solidarity with the men in prison.[61] Women of the Hui Aloha ʻĀina also cared for the needy and homeless families of the men who were suddenly left without incomes. On July 4, 1895, a few of the political prisoners were released, mainly in Hilo,[62] and all of the remainder were paroled on January 1, 1896.

In May 1895, Joseph Nāwahī and his wife, Emma ʻAʻima Nāwahī, started a new weekly newspaper called *Ke Aloha Aina*. In this newspaper, Nāwahī wrote a series of articles expressing what aloha ʻāina meant for the Kanaka Maoli. Nāwahī was educated at Hilo Boarding School, Lahainaluna, and the Royal School, all of which were run by the American Board of Commissioners for Foreign Missions, and he served at one time as vice-principal at Hilo Boarding School. According to Osorio, "he was the living promise of the Calvinist mission and an exemplar of that mission's contradictions. He was a Christian Native who was, nevertheless, a firm and lifelong opponent of annexation."[63] That Nāwahī accepted Christian mission doctrine while opposing the political takeover of his country by the same missionary families is not necessarily contradictory. Like Davida Malo before him,[64] and like Ke Aliʻi ʻAi Moku Liliʻuokalani, Nāwahī retained his Kanaka identity while assimilating Christianity into his life and philosophy. In this essay, for example, he begins by quoting the Fifth Commandment: "E hoomaikai oe i kou makuakane a me kou makuahine, i loihi ai na la o kou noho ana maluna o ka aina a Iehova a kou Akua i haawi mai ai ia oe. Pukaana 20:12" (Honor your father and mother, that your days will be long of living upon the land that Jehovah, your God, has given to you. Genesis 20:12). He goes on:

> O ka makuakane a me ka makuahine mua loa o ka lahui kanaka, oia o Adamu a me Eva, he mau materia laua o ka lepo o ka honua i hoopiha ia me ka hanu ola. . . .
>
> O na lahui a pau loa e ola nei . . . he mau hunahuna lepo lakou, a he mau mahele hunahuna materia o ka aina a ke Akua i hana ai. Nolaila, ma kekahi olelo pololei ana ae; ke ola nei, a ke hele nei no ka aina maluna o ka honua: Ke ola nei a ke hele nei na keiki aina, na moopuna aina, na lahui aina, maluna o ko lakou makuahine nui, ka Honua.
>
> O wai kou makuahine? O ka aina no! O wai kou kupunawahine? O ka aina no! Pehea hoi o Eva, ko kakou kupunawahine mua loa? He lepo no ia no ka aina.
>
> (The first father and mother of human beings, Adam and Eve, they are material of the dirt of the earth who were filled with the breath of life. . . .
>
> All of the peoples living . . . are fragments of the dirt, and they are part of the material of the land that God made. Therefore, it may be correctly said, the land itself is living and walking upon the earth. Living and walking are the children of the land, the grandchildren of the land, the peoples of the land, upon their great mother, the Earth.
>
> Who is your mother? She is the land! Who is your grandmother? She is the land! What of Eve, our very first grandmother/female ancestor? She is the soil of the land.)

Nāwahī then departs from these biblically oriented musings and addresses his Kanaka traditions:

> Malia, ua nui loa ke kuhihewa o ko Hawaii nei poe kupuna, ma ko lakou moolelo kahiko, e olelo ana: Ua hanau maoli ia mai keia Paemoku

e Papa [wahine] nana me Wakea [kāne]. He mea hiki ole loa ia ma ka noonoo ana o ke kanaka; aka i na nae ma ka lawena olelo ana, a he wahi moowini malamalama iki ko lakou no na hana a ke Akua i ke au kahiko loa, alaila, o kela lawena olelo ana, ua ku no ia i ka oiaio . . .

Ua hoomoe ka moa wahine maluna o ka hua, a kiko ae la he manu moa opio! Ua noho aku o Wakea ia Papa alaila, hanau mai la keia mau Paemoku o Hawaii nei. . . . Oiai he hookahi wale no hana ia ana o Adamu mai ka lepo mai; aka, ke mau nei no nae ko kakou hoopuka mau ana i na huaolelo, *na ke Akua au i hana.* Pela ka lawena olelo no ka hanau ia ana o keia Paemoku e Papa.

(Perhaps the ancestors of Hawai'i's people were greatly mistaken in their ancient moʻolelo, saying: This Archipelago was truly born of Papa (woman) and Wākea (man). It is something impossible in people's thought; but, if in the stories, they might have had a glimmer [moowini malamalama iki] of the works of God in the old days, then, those stories are true.

A hen sits upon an egg, and a fully formed chick pecks out! Wākea lives with Papa and these Islands of Hawai'i are born. . . . While there was just one creation of Adam out of the dirt, yet we all continue to say the words, *God made me.* So it is with the story of the birth of the Islands by Papa.)

Nāwahī's weaving of the two belief systems together takes him to this conclusion:

Alaila, o ke aloha i kou makuahine, kou aina, kou wahi i hanauia ai, oia ka mea e loihi ai na la, na makahiki o ke ola ana. . . .

Nolaila, e ka Lahui Hawaii, e hoonui i ke aloha no ko kakou aina hanau, ka Paeaina o Hawaii, alaila, e ola loihi oukou me ka oukou mau mamo maluna o ka aina o Hawaii a ke Akua i haawi mai ai ia oukou.

(Thus, love for your mother, the land, the place where you were born, that is what will make the days and years of your life long.

Therefore, Hawaiian People, let us increase the love for our birth land, the Islands of Hawai'i; then, you and your descendants will live long upon the land of Hawai'i which God has given to you.)[65]

Aloha 'āina, then, meant more than an abstract or emotional love for the "one hānau" (birth sands). For Nāwahī and the other po'e aloha 'āina, it meant that people must strive continuously to control their own government in order to provide life to the people and to care for their land properly. Notice too, that "life" is neither an abstraction nor the Christian concept of everlasting life to be achieved after death: Nāwahī articulates his lāhui's desire to live in the flesh on their land. Mass death from epidemics and lack of children surviving into adulthood were immediate and cruel realities for the Kanaka Maoli throughout this period; Nāwahī and the other poʻe aloha ʻāina of his time believed that a colonial government would add to the harm already done to the Kanaka Maoli, as it indeed has.[66]

In late summer 1896, Joseph Nāwahī was suffering from the tuberculosis he had contracted in jail. A doctor prescribed a therapeutic trip to San Francisco, so he and his wife ʻAʻima sailed for California. But, as in King Kalākaua's case, the therapy proved useless. When Nāwahī died these two major proponents of aloha ʻāina were very far away from their ʻāina. On his deathbed, he apologized to his wife for taking her so far from the ʻāina and from her family and friends, to deal with his death alone in a foreign place. The English-language (but Hawaiian nationalist) newspaper, the *Independent*, reported: "The deceased had for some time past been a very sick man, suffering from consumption contracted during his prolonged imprisonment for alleged political offenses in the pest hole known as Oahu Prison. His offense was that he loved his Queen and his country, and through his untimely death another sufferer has been added to the cohorts of victims of the men of 1893."[67]

Mrs. Nāwahī brought her husband's body home. He was given a funeral in Honolulu befitting a head of state. Several hundred women of the Hui Aloha ʻĀina marched in his funeral procession, which also included a detachment of police; the government band led by Henry Berger; the Portuguese political societies; many regional branches of the Hui Aloha ʻĀina, both men's and women's; and the Hui Kālaiʻāina. He was honored with another funeral procession in Hilo on Hawaiʻi Island prior to his burial there; his body was taken into Hilo harbor by a procession of traditional waʻa. Letters of condolence and kanikau and other mele were printed in his honor continuously in *Ke Aloha Aina* through November 1896.[68]

Queen Liliʻuokalani wrote: "One morning, in the month of October, 1896, I heard of the death of Mr. Joseph Kahooluhi Nawahi o Kalaniopuu; and I shared the common sorrow, for this was a great blow to the people. He had always been a man who fearlessly advocated the

independence of Hawaii nei." She also wrote that the provisional government hoped that Nāwahī's death would cause the demise of both the
Hui Aloha 'Āina and the Hui Kālai'āina, because these, "with the organization of the Women's Patriotic League, are societies much dreaded
by the oligarchy . . . ruling Hawaii." The three hui did not disband,
however, because, as the queen said, "the cause of Hawaiian independence is larger and dearer than the life of any man connected with it."[69]
The hui appointed temporary presidents and continued their organizing. Both decided to hold conventions on Lā Kū'oko'a, November 28,
1896, Hawaii'i's Independence Day (no longer a holiday under the
republic). Delegates were elected from all of the islands to come to
Honolulu, vote for new permanent presidents and, for the Hui Aloha
'Āina, consider an amended constitution.

Before the convention, a letter appeared in *Ke Aloha Aina* urging
everyone to elect their delegates, except the women because they had
no kuleana in that activity. The letter writer was swiftly rebuked by a
"makuahine aloha aina" (aloha 'āina mother [probably Mrs. Nāwahī]),
who explained that the president of the central committee was to represent the entire lāhui, and that the lāhui includes women and children as
well as men. She further asserted that the women's central committee
would be sending delegates to the convention and that those delegates
each expected to have a vote.[70] In the end, the women's central committee members did attend but did not vote as a separate organization; one
woman voted as the delegate for the combined Hui Aloha 'Āina from
South Hilo.

Ke Aloha Aina's editorial page said the presence of women delegates
was a sign that the whole nation was working together toward progress
for their beloved 'āina. Before the convention, another writer to *Ke
Aloha Aina* proposed criteria for selection of the new president. Each
criterion began with the phrase, "I kanaka a wahine paha" (Should be a
man or a woman),[71] indicating that at least some men supported female
leadership of the hui. While not resolved, the question of women having
the right to vote and to lead in these public arenas, which in the Western structure were reserved for men, had been brought to the public
and would surface again the following year. While these organizations
were clearly modeled on Western political structures, the Kanaka Maoli
adapted them according to their world view, in which there is no inherent reason why women cannot participate in politics. Indeed, Mrs.

Kuaihelani Campbell was acknowledged all through the struggle as a leader of the nation along with the two male hui presidents.

At the conventions, the Hui Kālaiʻāina elected David Kalauokalani president,[72] and Hui Aloha ʻĀina elected James Keauiluna Kaulia. At this same time, Mrs. Nāwahī continued without Joseph as owner and business manager of the newspaper *Ke Aloha Aina*. She hired her young nephew, Edward Like, as editor, while actually doing much of the editorial work herself.

The year 1896 brought a final blow to the Hawaiian-language schools. The Republic of Hawaiʻi passed a law that decreed that "the English language shall be the medium and basis of instruction in all public and private schools."[73] Nāwahī had protested the law when it was a bill before the legislature in 1895.[74] Its passage into law marks the beginning of the generations of grandchildren immersed in the English language in school and thus no longer able to benefit from the moʻolelo, ʻōlelo noʻeau, and other traditional language forms of their grandparents.

In truth, the number of Hawaiian-language schools had already been declining for many years, taking the most precipitous falls after the Bayonet Constitution and 1893 coup. In 1886, there were seventy-seven Hawaiian-language schools; in 1894, the number was down to eighteen; and in 1896 there was only a single school.[75] The original two-tiered school system — where the select schools were taught in English and were college prep oriented and better funded and the common schools were taught in Hawaiian and were oriented to reproducing laborers — began to change when the oligarchy came into power, because it was more convenient for them to have the Kanaka Maoli and immigrant laborers understand English. Thus the Hawaiian-language schools began their sharp decline. At the same time, English was said to be the language of high economic status and opportunity, and anyone who wanted to retain an education in Hawaiian was likely to be characterized as backward and foolish. In 1896 the Board of Education reported to the legislature: "Schools taught in the Hawaiian language have virtually ceased to exist and will probably never appear again in a Government report. Hawaiian parents without exception prefer that their children should be educated in the English language. The gradual extinction of a Polynesian dialect may be regretted for sentimental reasons, but it is certainly for the interest of the Hawaiians themselves."[76]

Although the minister of public instruction asserted that there were no Hawaiians who preferred education in their mother tongue, the political circumstances must be taken into account before accepting that assertion at face value. The colonial government was in a constant struggle with the Kanaka Maoli, who did not approve of it. Neither the minister nor any of the members of the Board of Education were Kanaka Maoli. The assertion that the demise of the native language (which the minister himself equates with the loss of the Hawaiian schools) was actually good for the Kanaka Maoli reveals the colonial government's beliefs in the superiority of their language, but it does not reveal the beliefs of the Kanaka Maoli, which were probably diverse. The assertion was, moreover, an attempt to justify a policy that the government knew would result in the death of the language — which is unjustifiable. Predictably, and painful to realize, after all the schools became English-medium schools, greater economic opportunity did not come to the students of the common schools because they were still expected to become nothing more than laborers. The common schools continued to be poorly funded and the curriculum was not changed to that of the select schools.[77] The loss of the language proceeded, but it was also resisted effectively enough to allow, more than one hundred years later, for the current revival. This is attested to by the continued vitality of the Hawaiian-language press, which from time to time printed warnings and lamentations about the impending loss of the language. Daily and weekly newspapers in Hawaiian continued to be published and to be a political voice, all the way until 1948. Further, a few families were committed to raising their children in Hawaiian despite the immense outside pressure not to do so.[78]

In November 1896 William McKinley, a Republican, was elected president of the United States, replacing the Democrat Grover Cleveland. McKinley was far more inclined to consider annexing Hawai'i than was Cleveland, and in response the three hui mobilized again. This time they directed their protests toward the U.S. Congress.

THE 1897 PETITIONS PROTESTING ANNEXATION

President McKinley was open to persuasion by U.S. expansionists and by annexationists from Hawai'i. In spring 1897, he agreed to meet with a committee of annexationists, including Lorrin Thurston, Francis

Hatch, and William Kinney. By June 1897, McKinley had signed a treaty of annexation with these representatives of the Republic of Hawai'i. The president then submitted the treaty to the U.S. Senate for ratification.[79] The Hui Aloha 'Āina for Women, the Hui Aloha 'Āina for Men, and the Hui Kālai'āina, along with the queen, formed a coalition to oppose the treaty. Together, these three organizations represented a majority of Kanaka Maoli. The Kanaka Maoli strategy was to challenge the U.S. government to behave in accordance with its stated principles of justice and of government of the people, by the people, and for the people. They hoped that once the U.S. president and members of Congress saw that the great majority of Kanaka Maoli opposed the annexation, the principles of fairness would prevail and Lili'uokalani's government would be restored. To this end, the hui began to organize mass petition drives. The heading on Hui Aloha 'Āina's petition read: "Palapala Hoopii Kue Hoohui Aina" (Petition protesting annexation). Written in both Hawaiian and English, the text stated, in part, "We, the undersigned, native Hawaiian subjects and residents . . . who are members of the Hawaiian Patriotic League of the Hawaiian Islands, and other citizens who are in sympathy with the said League earnestly protest against the annexation of the said Hawaiian Islands to the said United States of America in any form or shape."[80]

On September 6, 1897, the Hui Aloha 'Āina held a hālāwai maka'āinana at Palace Square, which thousands of po'e aloha 'āina attended. President James Kaulia gave a rousing speech, saying, "Aole loa kakou ka lahui e ae e hoohuiia ko kakou aina me Amerika a hiki i ke Aloha Aina hope loa" (We, the nation [lāhui] will never consent to the annexation of our land to America, down to the very last Aloha 'Āina). He added that agreeing to annexation was like agreeing to be buried alive. He predicted that annexation would open the door for even more foreigners to come to Hawai'i and take jobs and resources away from the Kanaka Maoli. He asked, "A ihea kakou e noho ai?" (Then where will we live?). In response, the crowd yelled, "i ka mauna" (in the mountains), meaning that they would be marginalized because on Hawai'i's islands nearly all urban areas are at the shore and to be in the mountains is to be invisible. Kaulia tried to encourage the people by asserting that a mass refusal could prevent the annexation: "Ina e mau ke kupaa o ka lahui me ke kue aku i ka hoohuiia o Hawaii me Amerika ke olelo nei au, e noke wale no ka Aha Senate o keia wahi Aupuni a helelei na paia pohaku o

Iolani Hale, aole loa e hiki ke hoohuiia o Hawaii me Amerika" (If the nation remains steadfast in its protest of annexation of Hawai'i to America, I say, the Senate of this little Government can continue to strive until the rock walls of 'Iolani Palace tumble down, and Hawai'i can never be annexed to America!).[81]

The annexationist newspapers had published threats that the leaders of the mass meeting would be arrested for treason, but Kaulia assured the people that their assembly was within their rights. He said that it was because the brains of the government could not push over the brains of the Kanaka Maoli that the government had to resort to weapons of war. He stated: "E lawe kakou i ke Kahua Hanohano o ka paio ana he lolo me ka lolo" (Let us take up the honorable field of struggle, brain against brain), and he told the people, "mai maka'u, e kupaa ma ke Aloha i ka Aina, a e lokahi ma ka manao, e kue loa aku i ka hoohui ia o Hawaii me Amerika a hiki i ke aloha aina hope loa" (do not be afraid, be steadfast in aloha for your land and be united in thought. Protest forever the annexation of Hawai'i until the very last aloha 'Āina [lives]).[82] In response, the crowd cheered.

Following Kaulia, David Kalauokalani, president of the Hui Kālai'āina, explained the details of the annexation treaty to the crowd. He told them that the Republic of Hawai'i had agreed to give full government authority over to the United States, reserving nothing. It would also give the United States all the government's money, the government and Crown lands, government buildings, harbors, bays, military forts, military armaments and warships, and all resources claimed by the government of the Hawaiian islands. Furthermore, he explained, the laws of the United States would not extend to the Hawaiian islands, but the U.S. Congress would decide how Hawai'i was to be governed. It was uncertain whether the Kanaka Maoli would have the right to vote; he said that those who favored annexation would want to deny Kanaka Maoli voting rights because, from the very beginning, they knew that the Kanaka Maoli would overwhelmingly vote against annexation and anyone who supported it. This is the reason they were always afraid to put a vote to the people.[83] A resolution protesting the annexation was then read to the crowd, who approved it. It was announced that U.S. Senator Morgan, an advocate of annexation, would be arriving soon, and that there would be another mass meeting held during his stay.[84]

The petition drive started at about this time. On September 18 *Ke*

Aloha Aina reported that Mrs. Abigail Kuaihelani Campbell and Mrs. Emma ʻAʻima Nāwahī had boarded the interisland ship the *Kīnaʻu* and sailed from Honolulu to Hilo on a mission to gather signatures.

On September 14, Senator Morgan and four congressmen from the United States did indeed arrive, and the provisional government arranged for Morgan to give a speech at Kawaiahaʻo Church. Morgan had come prepared to persuade the Kanaka Maoli that annexation was in their best interests, but he met mass opposition composed not of the ignorant and illiterate he might have expected, but of thousands of well-informed people, who were organized, articulate, and literate in two languages. When Morgan assured them in his speech at Kawaiahaʻo that, under U.S. laws they would be able to vote just as blacks did in the American South, they were not so uninformed as to believe that Southern blacks were enjoying freedom and equality.[85] For fifty years or more Kanaka Maoli had been reading newspapers, and they had been surrounded by American racism even longer. They knew that race hatred was the root of what had been said about Kalākaua — that his father was not Kapaʻakea but an exslave named Blossom,[86] and they remembered Thurston's 1894 speech to the American League justifying the disfranchisement of American blacks.[87] On October 23, *Ke Aloha Aina* ran an editorial titled "E Like Ana Anei na Hawaii me na Negero?" (Are Hawaiians going to be like blacks?) in response to Morgan. It said that the haole hatred for and fear of the blacks and the Indians, "ka poe nona ka lepo a ua poe haole la e hehiku la" (to whom the land those haole trespass upon belongs), was well understood. It asked how they could possibly "pakele . . . mai keia mau omole laau make a lakou nei e ake nei e hanai mai" (escape from the bottles of poison [American race hatred] that they desire to feed us). At the end, the editorial said that yes, Hawaiians will be like American blacks if the islands are annexed because their freedom will be taken away.[88] The same week, Mr. Enoch Johnson and Mr. Simon Peter Kanoa boarded the *Claudine* for Maui, and Mrs. Kaikioewa Ulukou departed for Kauaʻi — all bound to gather signatures protesting annexation.

A branch of the Hui Aloha ʻĀina at Kalaupapa, on the island of Molokaʻi where people with leprosy were imprisoned, contributed to the effort as well.[89] The president of the Kalaupapa branch was Mr. Robert M. Kaaoao, who not only gathered signatures on the protest petitions, but earlier had organized a full day of activities to commemo-

rate the queen's birthday on September 2. The activities included a prayer service; boating, swimming, running, and horse and donkey races; as well as pole-climbing and apple-eating contests.[90]

When Mrs. Campbell and Mrs. Nāwahī arrived at Hilo Bay they were greeted with honors. A delegation of the Hilo chapter of the hui, consisting of Mr. Henry West, Mrs. Hattie Nailima, Mrs. Kekona Pilipo, and Mrs. J. A. Akamu, met the two women at the harbor. The Hilo delegation showered them with lei and proclaimed that a waʻa kaulua, a traditional double-hulled canoe, would carry them into the harbor. They had decorated five seats on the beautiful vessel with lei of maile, lehua, and other flowers, and a Hawaiian flag was waving at the back. The people of Laupāhoehoe had sent welcome gifts of ʻopihi (limpet), limu (seaweed), and fish. Mrs. Campbell and Mrs. Nāwahī attended meetings of the Hui Aloha ʻĀina all over the Hilo and Puna districts, and returned with thousands of signatures.[91] A reporter from the *San Francisco Call*, Miss Miriam Michelson, attended the meeting in Hilo at the Salvation Army hall on September 16. She traveled along with (but not as a part of) the U.S. congressional delegation headed by Morgan. Michelson wrote a series of articles in the *Call* supporting the poʻe aloha ʻāina, which included some details about the hui and their leaders.[92] She wondered how Mrs. Nāwahī and Mrs. Campbell would handle themselves in conducting a mass meeting; after all, they were breaking the Victorian code that discouraged women from participating in the public sphere: "I watched Mrs. Emma Nawahi curiously as she rose to address the people. I have never heard two women talk in public in quite the same way. Would this Hawaiian woman be embarrassed or timid, or self-conscious or assertive? Not any of these. . . . This Hawaiian woman's thoughts were of her subject, not of herself."[93]

Miss Michelson watched as the confident Mrs. Nāwahī took charge of the meeting, giving a speech about the petitions and then encouraging those present to express their sentiments against annexation so that Michelson could report it in the U.S. newspaper. Thrust into even more political activity after the death of her husband, Mrs. Nāwahī carried on his work, both organizing as she had already begun to do and taking over management of the newspaper. Accompanied by some of the other women of the Hui Aloha ʻĀina leadership, Mrs. Nāwahī seems to have quietly and competently entered the public sphere at a time when it was extremely difficult for women to do so.

Meanwhile Mrs. Laura Mahelona of the Honolulu committee was working hard in Kona and Ka'ū as the committee member delegated to gather signatures in those areas. She traveled from north Kona south to Ka'ū, leaving blank petitions with instructions to the chapter presidents to get the petitions signed and ready in a few days when her ship would stop again at the same harbors. When she returned, signed petitions were ready at every harbor and she was welcomed by the women of the Hui Aloha 'Āina branches and people from the villages who carried many lei over their arms. When she returned to the boat her clothes couldn't be seen because she was completely covered by lei. Mrs. Mahelona gathered 4,216 signatures.[94]

Mrs. Kaikioewa Ulukou gathered 2,375 signatures on the island of Kaua'i, and Simon P. Kanoa gathered 1,944 in the district of Hāna, Maui.[95] When all the work was done, there was a total of over 21,000 signatures — men's and women's in about equal numbers. The Hui Kālai'āina also had a substantial membership, and they conducted their own petition drive at the same time, collecting over 17,000 signatures.[96] Together, the two groups collected over 38,000 signatures. Even considering the likelihood that some people signed both petitions, the total number of signatures is impressive given that the population of Kanaka Maoli at the time was around 40,000.

To organize the protest of the annexation aimed at Senator Morgan and his delegation Kanaka Maoli in Honolulu formed an ad hoc Komite o ka Lehulehu (Citizens' Committee). Little information exists about this organization except notices in the newspapers calling for a mass meeting on October 8, 1897, to protest the annexation treaty, and a palapala hoopi'i (memorial) signed by the committee members, which was approved by the public at that meeting. Members of the committee were F. J. Testa, editor of the resistance papers *Ka Makaainana* and the *Independent*; J. Kalua Kaho'okano; C. B. Maile; Samuel K. Kamakaia, songwriter and member of Ka Bana Lāhui Hawai'i (the re-formed Royal Hawaiian Band) and frequent contributor to the newspaper *Ke Aloha Aina*; and Samuel K. Pua. James Kaulia, representing Hui Aloha 'Āina, and David Kalauokalani, representing Hui Kālai'āina, also appended their names to both the notice of the mass meeting and the memorial.[97]

The committee composed the text of the memorial in both English and Hawaiian, and it stands as a thirteen-paragraph distillation of the

Kanaka Maoli case against annexation, and thus for sovereignty. Part of the opening paragraph reads as follows: "O ko oukou poe hoopii, he poe lakou e noho ana ma ko Hawaii Paeaina; . . . he poe Hawaii oiwi kumu maoli ka hapanui o lakou" (Your memorialists are residents of the Hawaiian Islands; . . . the majority of them are aboriginal Hawaiians).[98] In the Hawaiian, the committee says that they are "poe Hawaii oiwi kumu maoli," a phrase that means, "Hawaiian, native, original, true/indigenous": the "aboriginal" identity is emphasized by stringing these evocative words together. In today's vernacular the phrase would translate something like, "we are the original and true Hawaiians, down to our bones." The word "'ōiwi" is translated as "native" but is related to the word "iwi" (bone) and therefore inescapably evokes that imagery, which is entirely lost in the English rendition.

The second paragraph states that the "supporters of the Hawaiian Constitution of 1887 have been . . . held in subjection by the armed forces of the Provisional Government . . . and . . . the Republic of Hawaii; and have never yielded, and do not acknowledge a . . . willing allegiance or support to said Provisional Government, or to said Republic of Hawaii." It is clear that many Kānaka Maoli, the Hui Kālai'āina particularly, were in no way "supporters of the Hawaiian Constitution of 1887." This statement must reflect either a conciliatory gesture toward the oligarchy, used as a negotiating tactic, or a compromise between the various factions making up the Citizens' Committee. If made as a conciliatory gesture, it might indicate that they would be willing to operate (temporarily perhaps, until changes could be made) under the 1887 constitution as long as the independence of the kingdom were preserved and the odious oligarchy dismantled.

In paragraphs 3 and 4, the committee declares that the Republic of Hawai'i was not "founded or conducted on a basis of popular government or republican principles," and that it thus "has no warrant for its existence in the support of the people of these Islands" and, further, that it "maintains itself solely by force of arms, against the rights and wishes of almost the entire aboriginal population (lahui kumu)." Paragraph 5 points out that the constitution of 1894 "has never been submitted to a vote of the people of these Islands," and paragraph 6 follows by saying that the illegitimate government just described, "ua lawe a ke hooia nei . . . i ke kuleana e kinai loa i ke kulana Lahui o na Hawaii . . . a e hoohui a hoolilo aku hoi i na kuleana a pau o ka noho mana kiekie ana maloko a maluna ae o ko Hawaii Paeaina . . . i kekahi mana okoa aku, oia hoi, ia Amerika Huipuia" (assumes and asserts the right to extinguish the Hawaiian Nationality . . . and to cede and convey all rights of sovereignty in and over the Hawaiian Islands . . . to a foriegn power, namely, to the United States of America).

Paragraph 7 states that the treaty "to extinguish our existence as a Nation" was received "with grief and dismay," and paragraph 8 asserts that the people of Hawai'i, for more than fifty years, "had been accustomed to participate in the Constitutional forms of Government." Paragraph 9 states that they "invoke in support of this memorial the spirit of that immortal Instrument, the Declaration of American Independence; and especially the truth therein expressed, that Governments derive their just powers from the consent of the governed," and paragraph 10 says that "the project of Annexation . . . would be subversive of the personal and political rights . . . of the Hawaiian people and Nation, and would be a negation of the rights and principles proclaimed in the Declaration of American Independence in the Constitution of the United States, and in the . . . government of all other civilized and representative Governments."

Paragraph 11 reminds U.S. leaders that "they, no less than the citizens of any American Commonwealth, are entitled to select, ordain and establish for themselves, such forms of Government . . . [as] shall seem most likely to effect their safety and happiness." Finally, the last two paragraphs ask that the U.S. president and Congress "take no further steps" toward annexation, and it proposes that the Hawaiian people "be accorded the privilege of voting upon said questions." It may seem ironic or absurd that the Kanaka were forced to appeal to the United States for the opportunity to vote on their own political status but they were prevented from doing so by the armed and racist oligarchy in their own land. The treaty had been ratified in Hawai'i by a government supported only by arms, as the women had said, and not by the consent of the people. The committee prayed that the superior power of the United States might be brought to bear on the oligarchy to force them to hold a vote on the question. This was a desperate tactic, as the U.S. military had historically and very recently sided with the American colonizers, but it was one of the few available choices.

In a tactic similar to that used by Nāwahī four years before, the text composed by the Citizens' Committee was an appeal to the U.S. president and Congress to live up to their own democratic principles and body of law. At the same time the committee expressed their desire to participate democratically in the government of their own choosing, which was that of Queen Liliʻuokalani. Even though the oligarchy represented the queen's government as a tyrannical monarchy and the very opposite of a democracy, this attempt at forming a contradiction was merely a discursive strategy to make the oligarchy appear to have more in common with U.S. history and its national narrative that opens with the story of liberation from the tyrannies of King George III. But our memorialists did not agree; in fact, they were pressing for restoration of the constitutional monarchy in order to regain their political rights.

In a way, the memorial served as a moral challenge to the United States, in the form of a tactic similar to that used by Gandhi. Ashis Nandy says that "Gandhi queered the pitch. . . . He admitted that colonialism was a moral issue and took the battle to [the British] home ground by judging colonialism by Christian values and declaring it to be an absolute evil."[99] The Citizens' Committee likewise judged the republic and annexation by the United States's democratic values and declared both to be illegitimate.[100] The United States had heretofore rationalized many immoralities, however: most of those in power had managed to rationalize slavery until 1861 and, further, had a long history of justifying genocide and colonization of the indigenous peoples of North America. Lorrin Thurston, a missionary descendant born in Hawaiʻi, also provided many convenient rationalizations. He wrote, for example, that "it is not un-American to annex territory without a vote of the inhabitants"; one simply needed to find a precedent, which he readily did.[101]

The Citizens' Committee used the word "civilized," as did the women of the Hui Aloha ʻĀina in 1894, to describe democratic governments. By doing so they appropriated the discourse and turned it around on the oligarchy and the U.S. government in another challenge to them to live up to their own principles. The Citizens' Committee sent its memorial to the U.S. president and Congress on the same ship that carried Morgan back home.

While during this period the resistance organizations seem to have accepted the outer structure of Western-style government and used the language of rights to make their case, they continued to insist on their identity as Kanaka. Their insistence on their own language forms was especially counterhegemonic. I wish to stress here that historians who do not read the Hawaiian language can have no idea of this type of resistance, and that readers of their work are consequently misled by the omissions.

In January 1893, for example, John Bush's newspaper, *Ka Leo o ka Lahui*, began to run a new version of *Ka Moolelo o Hiiakaikapoliopele*, the story of Hiʻiaka and her older sister, Pele. In it, Bush says that the moʻolelo will help to instill aloha ʻāina in the young people. He thus asserts that knowledge and appreciation of the traditional language and culture were integral components of aloha ʻāina.[102] In *Ke Aloha Aina*, headlines over the stories about the treaty and related developments were often done as colorful ʻōlelo noʻeau, whose meanings are not always readily apparent even to speakers of Hawaiian. One example is "Pau Peapea i ke ahi" (Peʻapeʻa is destroyed by fire). To understand the phrase one needs to know the story of Peʻapeʻa, one of Kamehameha's warriors, and the way he was accidentally killed by a keg of gunpowder, to fully appreciate the relationship of the headline to the story. In this case the story, unfortunately premature, was that the treaty was dead.[103] Liliʻuokalani is almost always referred to as "ko kakou Alii Aimoku" (our ruling aliʻi), which is an older term than "mōʻī."[104] *Ke Aloha Aina* refers to the main Protestant church, Kawaiahaʻo, as "ka heiau," although the word heiau is generally used for the ancient temples dedicated to the Kanaka Maoli gods.

Ke Aloha Aina also wrote that "ua kuauluhua maoli kekahi poe" (some people were truly offended) by Senator Morgan's speech style, "oiai, o ka hapanui o ka manawa he heluhelu buke wale no" (because most of the time he only read from a book). Even though Kanaka Maoli society was a fully literate one, the people retained their appreciation for oratory; to have to read any part of one's speech from a book was to show one's lack of skill or preparation. It seems that this was of such great importance that people were not just lacking in respect for Morgan but were insulted that he would not take the time to prepare to speak to them properly.

Particularly notable is an editorial written by either Edward Like or Emma Nāwahī (or both) in *Ke Aloha Aina* on October 23, 1897. We can see that when speaking to their Kanaka readers the editors use language different than that used by the leaders of the hui when dealing with the United States and the oligarchy. First, the language used for the Kanaka

is Hawaiian with no translation into English. The title of the editorial is
"Na ka Lahui na Alakai, a na na Alakai Ka Lahui" (The leaders belong to
the people/nation, and the people/nation belong(s) to the leaders).
The editorial calls for people to support the hui leadership, two members of which have been chosen as delegates to take their protests to
Washington, D.C. It further argues that when the people elected the
presidents of the hui they expressed their trust in them to undertake that
most important task. The trip to Washington thus became more their
kuleana than anyone else's. At the end of the argument, the author
writes that after they traveled personally to Washington, "hookumu hou
ke ola, hookumu hou ke Alii, hoolaupai hou ka lahui" (life will be re-
established, the Queen re-established, [and] the people will multiply
again), and that this is "ka makou e kahoahoa ae nei i ka pule hooku-
muhana" (what we are appealing for in the prayer to establish the
work). A prayer follows the editorial, but it has nothing to do with
Jehovah or Christianity. It invokes instead the traditional sacred trust
between the land, the ali'i, and the maka'āinana. Here is the ending
portion of the prayer:

> Ku ka lani iluna nei,
> Paa ka lani, paa ka honua,
> Paa ke Alii, paa ka lahui,
> I paa i na koo,
> na alakai o ka lahui Aloha Aina,
> Hanau ka aina, hanau na 'lii,
> a ola ka lahui.
> (The heaven [ali'i] stands above,
> [When] heaven is solid, the earth is stable,
> [When] the Ali'i [the queen] is secure, the lāhui is secure,
> To be secure in the supports,
> the leaders of the Aloha Aina people/nation,
> The land gives birth, the ali'i give birth,
> And the nation lives).[105]

This prayer has an ancient feel to it; it is reminiscent of the *Kumulipo*
in its language, and it was obviously modified and expanded for this
occasion in 1897. In any case it is clear that the editors of *Ke Aloha Aina*
were speaking to their readers in language that is culturally purely Kanaka; language that even a foreigner conversant in Hawaiian would find

difficult to understand. Similarly, in a previous issue of the paper, when the annexation treaty was first announced, the editors reproduced the first ten lines of the *Kumulipo,* appending these three lines:

Po-wale-ho-i-e.
Hanau ka po ia Hawaii
He Aupuni Moi.
(Only night.
Night gave birth to Hawaiʻi
A Kingdom.)[106]

This was termed "He Pule Ola Hawaii" (A prayer for the life of Hawaiʻi). The editors state that it is an appropriate prayer because the beginning of the *Kumulipo* describes a time when the heavens lacked an earthly foundation, just as the people now lack a stable government. These ancient traditions lived on and inspired the poʻe aloha ʻāina, who, simultaneously, were church-going Christians — among them were Mrs. Nāwahī, the wife of the Hilo Boarding School vice principal, and James Kaulia, who resided at Kaumakapili Church with his grandfather, who was employed there. They were Christians who did not allow their Christianity to obliterate their identity as Kanaka Maoli; rather, they drew on that Kanaka identity for strength in the times of crisis.

Another important difference between Western and Kanaka political practice is indicated by who participated in the antiannexation mass meetings and who signed the petitions. As Nālani Minton has pointed out, the organizers of the petition drive seem to have gone into nearly every ahupuaʻa (land district), including the quarantined area of Kalaupapa.[107] The signatures of women and children were obtained as well as those of men: this was clearly not a U.S.-style democratic process in which only the opinion of eligible voters (men) mattered. The three hui understood that the U.S. Congress might count only the men's signatures and, on the queen's direction, kept those on sheets separate from the women's. But to Kanaka, everyone's expression of opposition to annexation was important.

In November 1897, the coalition of hui moved to send delegates to Washington, D.C. to present the petitions to President McKinley and to the U.S. Congress. The executive committees of the three hui met and decided to send four delegates: James Kaulia of Hui Aloha ʻĀina; David Kalauokalani of Hui Kālaiʻāina; John Richardson, an attorney from

Maui; and William Auld as secretary. All four were Kanaka Maoli, which was an important sign to the nation. An editorial in *Ke Aloha Aina* suggested that previous delegates to Washington had failed because they were not Kanaka Maoli, or because they were too wealthy to truly have the nation's well-being in mind at all times. It is important to note that although a women's representative did not travel to Washington, Mrs. Campbell, president of the women's branch of Hui Aloha 'Āina, was part of the decision-making committee and was viewed as a leader of the nation along with the men.[108]

The four 'Elele Lāhui (national delegates) left Hawai'i on November 20, 1897. In San Francisco, on November 28, they commemorated Lā Kū'oko'a, Hawaiian Independence Day. They arrived in Washington on December 6, the day the Senate opened. They first met briefly with Queen Lili'uokalani, who was staying in Washington. They then met Senator Richard Pettigrew, who took them in to view the Senate's opening ceremonies. After the ceremonies, they returned to Ebbitt House where the queen was staying and where they would also stay. Although someone told them that their trip to Washington was useless because it was known that there were fifty-eight votes on the side of annexation, with only two more votes needed for the treaty to pass, they did not give up but continued on their mission.[109]

The next day, December 7, they met again with the queen to consider how to present the petitions. They chose her as chair of their Washington committee, then together they decided to present only the petitions of Hui Aloha 'Āina because the substance of the two sets of petitions was different. Hui Aloha 'Āina's petition protested annexation, but the Hui Kālai'āina's petitions called for the monarchy to be restored. They agreed that they did not want to appear divided or as if they had different goals.

The following day, the delegates met with Senator George Hoar. They reported that they braved snow, cold, and slippery streets to get to the senator's residence. The "elemakule" (old man) greeted them with a handshake.[110] He asked them what the people of Hawai'i thought about annexation. While John Richardson was explaining, they could see tears welling up in Hoar's eyes. Richardson told him that they brought petitions signed by the whole nation protesting the annexation. Senator Hoar told them to submit the petitions to him, and he would bring them before the Senate and then to the Foreign Relations Committee.

David Kalauokalani of Hui Kālaiʻāina also submitted an endorsement of those petitions that said that he represented over 17,000 more people. On December 9, with the delegates present, Senator Hoar read the text of the petitions to the Senate and had them formally accepted.

On December 10, the delegates met with Secretary of State John Sherman, and Kalauokalani submitted a statement protesting annexation (Ka Memoriala a ka Lahui) to him. In the following days, the delegates met with many different senators and congressmen. Senators Pettigrew and White encouraged them in the hope that the annexation treaty would be defeated.

On February 23, David Kalauokalani gave an affidavit concerning the petitions of the Hui Kālaiʻāina to Senator Pettigrew. The senator remarked that it was the first time he had ever received that kind of document, asking for the restoration of a monarchy, but he accepted it nonetheless.[111] During debates on the Senate floor, Senator Pettigrew and Senator Turpie insisted that the Kanaka Maoli be given a chance to vote on annexation. But Senator Morgan and the other proannexation senators knew that if a vote were taken it would be overwhelmingly in favor of Hawaiʻi's independence. In a report, these senators wrote that "if a requirement should be made by the United States of a plebiscite to determine the question of annexation, it would work a revolution in Hawaii which would abolish its constitution."[112] They knew, in other words, that if the people were allowed to vote not only would they reject annexation they would also reject the colonial government called the republic that had been forced upon them.

By the time the delegates left Washington on February 27, there were only forty-six votes in the Senate on the proannexation side, down from the fifty-eight when they had arrived. Forty-six votes was far too few for the treaty to pass — sixty votes were necessary.[113] Three of the delegates, James Kaulia, David Kalauokalani, and William Auld, returned to Honolulu victorious, sure that the treaty would fail, as indeed it did. They had carried the hard work and hopes of the whole nation to Washington in the form of the protest petitions, and they had succeeded in persuading many senators to vote against the treaty. John Richardson stayed behind to continue the work, along with Queen Liliʻuokalani, her secretary Joseph Heleluhe, and his wife, and the queen's devoted friend, J. O. Carter.

ANNEXATION WITHOUT A TREATY?

One annexation crisis was over, but another was soon to follow. That same year, the peoples of Cuba and the Philippines were fighting wars of independence against Spain. The United States also declared war on Spain after the U.S. warship, the *Maine,* blew up in a harbor in Cuba in February, 1898. The *Maine*'s presence in Cuba was questionable; the United States had no official involvement in the conflict until it involved itself by sending the ship there. Coffman reports that "nearly five weeks after the *Maine* disaster, a naval board of inquiry said the explosion probably was caused by an underwater mine, but could cite no evidence. The clock was ticking, and the mood of the public was becoming more belligerent. In 1976, Admiral Hyman Rickover [reviewed] the *Maine* tragedy and [said] the explosion likely resulted from internal combustion in the boiler room."[114]

Nevertheless, the explosion on the *Maine* provided the necessary pretext for the United States to declare war on Spain. Suddenly, the empire builders of the United States were claiming the need to send military troops on ships to the Philippines to fight Spain, and to do so they claimed that they needed Hawai'i as a coaling station. On July 6, in the midst of the fever of war, a Joint Resolution of Congress, called the Newlands Resolution, was passed by a simple majority of each house, thus supposedly making Hawai'i a territory of the United States. The three hui in coalition protested yet again. On August 6, 1898, they sent a document in Hawaiian, with an English translation, to the U.S. minister, now Harold Sewall. This document recounted the facts of the overthrow, reproducing Lili'uokalani's January 17, 1893, statement of protest as well as part of Grover Cleveland's statement condemning the overthrow. The document also recited the history of the failed annexation treaty, and pointed out that "by memorial the people of Hawaii have protested against the consummation of an invasion of their political rights, and have fervently appealed to the President, the Congress, and the People of the United States to refrain from further participating in the wrongful annexation of Hawaii." Finally, they made this statement: "Ma ke ano hoi he poe elele no kekahi mahele nui a ikaika o na kanaka Hawaii oiwi maoli ke kue aku nei makou me ka manao kulipolipo kukonukonu loa i ka hoohuiia mai ma ke ano i manaoia a me ka ui ole ia mai hoi a loaa aku paha hoi ka ae ana o ka lahuikanaka o ko Hawaii Paeaina nei" (As the representatives of a large and influential body of native Hawaiians, we solemnly protest against annexation in the manner proposed and without reference to or obtaining the consent of the people of the Hawaiian Islands).[115]

Once again, the translation (theirs) has stripped away the cultural codes and emotional language of the Hawaiian text. What is rendered in English as "native Hawaiians" is in Hawaiian "na kanaka Hawaii oiwi maoli," which contains four strong words in a row that connote Kanaka identity. What is given as "we solemnly protest" in Hawaiian is "ke kue aku nei makou me ka manao kulipolipo kukonukonu loa." "Kūlipolipo" is related to "Kumulipo": it means deep, dark, intense, and is used in conjunction with expressions of pain and grief. "Kūkonukonu" means excessive, profound, serious.[116] These are expressions evocative of deepseated grief, which then become flat and unemotional in the English translation of "solemn." The Hawaiian was written for the Kanaka Maoli to express their grief to each other, while the English was for the U.S. diplomats, in front of whom the Kanaka leaders remained coldly dignified.

The signers of this document were James Keauiluna Kaulia, president of Hui Aloha 'Āina; Mrs. Kuaihelani Campbell, president of Hui Aloha 'Āina o Nā Wāhine; David Kalauokalani, president of Hui Kālai'āina; Enoch Johnson, secretary of Hui Aloha 'Āina; and Līlia K. Aholo, secretary of Hui Aloha 'Āina o Nā Wāhine.

Despite the continuous mass protest, the flag of the United States was hoisted over Hawai'i on August 12 in a ceremony at 'Iolani Palace. The three hui organized a boycott of the ceremony.[117] Even so, nervous officials of the United States thought it necessary to surround 'Iolani Palace with flanks of troops.[118]

On August 13 *Ke Aloha Aina* reported "He oia mau no kakou" (We go on), and the Kanaka Maoli did indeed continue to protest. The Hui Kālai'āina concentrated on persevering to undo the annexation and restore the Kanaka Maoli government. Hui Aloha 'Āina published a series of essays by Edward Kekoa denouncing the legitimacy of the Newlands Resolution and urging readers to remember Nāwahī's dying words to "kupaa mau i ke aloha i ka aina" (persist in aloha 'āina).[119] In 1900, the two hui banded together as a political party called the Independent Home Rule Party. David Kalauokalani was elected president, and James Kaulia vice president.[120]

CONCLUSION

Hui Kālaiʻāina and the two branches of Hui Aloha ʻĀina were organizations recognizable in Euro-American tradition: they had presidents, secretaries, treasurers, branches, and central committees. They developed when U.S. hegemony had taken hold; the Kanaka Maoli, at least the politically active leadership, were persuaded of the workability (or the inescapability) of the Western political system to the extent that they organized themselves to strive for their goals within it, adopting its structural forms. One could even say that their primary goal — national sovereignty — was structured by the West, for the "nation-state" was not an indigenous governmental form but rather was created out of the necessity of surviving as a people against the threats of the armed nations of the West. The leadership of the three hui consisted primarily of the aliʻi class, as well, who would have benefited more than makaʻāinana from adapting to the Western system.

Documentation and analysis of the forms of resistance in the rural areas during this time is, unfortunately, beyond the scope of this chapter. I suspect that the country makaʻāinana were more resistant to assimilation into the Western system than were the urban aliʻi, but that is a question that remains to be answered through future research. Even so, we have seen that the Kānaka Maoli who were articulating the thought of the resistance through the newspapers and memorials, including Queen Liliʻuokalani, retained their own epistemology and patterned much of their behavior according to traditional cosmology. They held onto their Kanaka identity even while working politically in accordance with the forms of the colonizer. It was in part Kanaka tradition that encouraged the women to organize in opposition to annexation — at least nothing in Kanaka tradition would suggest that such activity was inappropriate for women. Many alive no doubt remembered when women were members of the House of Nobles. They were also no doubt aware of the movement in the United States for women's suffrage, although they did not focus much attention on that issue during the annexation struggle. The women were, nevertheless, quite assertive about their importance to the struggle, and demanding of recognition of their kuleana.

This chapter demonstrates that there is a history of resistance to

U.S. colonialism that has gone unrecorded in mainstream historiography. That erasure has had far-reaching consequences. It contributes to the perpetuation of the "lazy native" stereotype, which relies on the myth that indigenous peoples are passive and unwilling to exert any effort toward the preservation of their nations. It makes people such as the Kanaka Maoli nearly invisible in the historical narratives of their own places, while making the actions of the colonizers appear to be the only ones of any importance. The erasure of the history of struggle weighs heavily on the self-perception of the Kanaka Maoli of the present and past several generations, who carry the burden of resisting the ugly stereotype while also being handicapped by a lack of resources to effectively oppose it. The imposition of English in the public and private schools for the last hundred years guaranteed that the moʻopuna (descendants) of the antiannexation struggle would be unable to read their ancestors' side of the story. But as power persists so does resistance, finding its way like water slowly carving crevices into and through rock. The resurgence of the Hawaiian language through a popular movement consisting of both taro roots and academics is creating scholars like myself who are now able to read the archive and effectively challenge the misrepresentations and omissions of the Kanaka Maoli in historiography. The existence of the antiannexation petitions and the large organizations that protested annexation are now part of history for many Kānaka Maoli, mainly because of the knowledge brought forth during the centennial observations in summer 1998. Although historians like William Russ obviously saw the petitions in the course of their research in the U.S. National Archives, they appear to have considered them insignificant or, perhaps, dangerous as counterevidence to the narrative that claims that the 1893 coup and 1898 annexation constituted the establishment of good government in Hawaiʻi.[121] But the antiannexation petition has proved to be of great significance to Kanaka Maoli today. Activist and scholar Lynette Cruz states: "As our ancestors, by their signatures on the great petitions, stood by their country and by their queen in time of trouble, so must we continue to claim what, by law, by history, by culture and by spirit, is ours. We are the Living Nation because the Hawaiian people . . . continue to live — as a nation, as a country."[122]

5

The Queen of Hawaiʻi Raises Her

Solemn Note of Protest

No darker cloud can hang over a people than the prospect
of being blotted out from the list of nations. No grief can
equal that of a sovereign forcibly deprived of her throne.

— Liliʻuokalani

Queen Liliʻuokalani, known as Ke Aliʻi ʻAi Moku (the aliʻi who rules the
islands), was the central figure in the struggle against annexation, but
her role has not been analyzed much in histories.[1] Her strategies and
tactics included a series of formal written protests and other ways of
contesting how she and her people were represented in the news stories
of the time, which were directed at the American public and politicians.
Equally important were the ways she sought to keep her nation alive by
maintaining and strengthening close relationships with her lāhui. All of
these forms of resistance were nonviolent, primarily because Queen
Liliʻuokalani and her people were outnumbered, in the queen's words,
by the "superior force of the United States of America."[2] As Leilani
Basham put it, instead of engaging in a battle they could not possibly
win, "ʻimi naʻe lākou i mau ala hou aʻe e hele aku ai no ka hoʻihoʻi hou i

ke Ali'i kona wahi kūpono e noho, 'o ia nō ka noho kalaunu," (they searched for other paths to follow to return Ke Ali'i to her rightful place, that is, on the throne).[3] The desire to avoid bloodshed may also be understood as the response of a people still suffering from epidemics and a low number of births. Not yet sixty years old, Lili'uokalani herself was the only survivor of all her siblings, among whom there was only one surviving child, Ke Kamāli'iwahine Ka'iulani. Maka'āinana as well as ali'i were dying too young, and to lose even a few people to violence would have been foolish.

Although a single chapter is insufficient to tell the story of the queen's struggle, it is worthwhile nevertheless to present some highlights here. As elsewhere I draw on Hawaiian-language sources (including Hawaiian-language newspapers and letters from Emma 'A'ima Nāwahī to the queen), and I also draw on the formal diplomatic protests and on a "contrapuntal" reading, à la Edward Said, of mainstream historical accounts.[4]

The battles over representation took place on two related grounds: the first was in the newspapers of 1893 to 1898 and the second in the historiography based on those news stories. Historians have relied on English-language newspaper accounts of the coup and the struggle over annexation, as well as on the memoirs written by Sanford Dole and Lorrin Thurston, who actually perpetrated the coup. The nineteenth-century newspapers, as I have shown throughout this work, were overtly political or religious. The two communities, the English-language community and the Hawaiian-language community, were in a struggle or even at war with each other. The English-language papers minimized the resistance to annexation, actively campaigned against the queen, and, at their worst, ridiculed her. To say that the newspapers as well as Dole and Thurston's memoirs are biased would be an understatement. Historical accounts based on these works have resulted in gaps, erasures, and far less than a full understanding of the actions of the Kānaka Maoli, and particularly of Queen Lili'uokalani.

Two popular histories, *Hawaii Pono* by Lawrence Fuchs and *Shoal of Time* by Gavan Daws, as well as the less popular but major history of the annexation by William Adam Russ, all rely on these sources.[5] Fuchs characterizes the 1893 coup as a popular "revolution," which was "dignified through the support of one of the great names in Hawaiian history, Sanford Ballard Dole" who "represented the best of the haole missionary tradition in Hawaii." He unashamedly goes on to report that "Dole wanted a constitution that would protect haole rights and privileges." He mentions Queen Liliʻuokalani in a one-paragraph summary of the events of January 14 to 17, 1893, and thereafter he does not mention her at all until another single-paragraph description of the 1895 war, which included her imprisonment and (coerced) abdication. The paragraph ends with the statement: "Without the Queen's leadership, her supporters were broken,"[6] but later in this chapter, I show how the people were never really without the queen's leadership. Finally, Fuchs mentions nothing at all about the resistance of the queen or anyone else to annexation.

Daws treats Liliʻuokalani at somewhat greater length than Fuchs, but he draws a portrait of an autocratic, ineffective monarch. He writes, for example, that "she had a strong streak of unfeminine toughness, almost coarseness, that surprised those who ran up against it in conversation." He also repeats a comment made to Lorrin Thurston (taken from Thurston's *Memoirs*) by a newcomer to the islands that "Liliuokalani was a dangerous woman." On her desire for a constitution, Daws concludes, "Liliuokalani simply wanted her cabinet ministers to obey her; if they refused she might proclaim a new constitution that suited her better."[7] He notes some of the resistance activities, especially the 1895 war, and even reports that the queen traveled to Washington, D.C., but he does not say what she actually did there and he always characterizes her actions as ineffective. All in all, there is almost nothing in the account that informs the reader about the queen or about her relationship to her people.

Russ uses the same sources as Fuchs and Daws, supplemented with eyewitness accounts written by members of the American military and the diplomatic despatches written by John L. Stevens and Albert Willis, to create an even more detailed representation of the queen as childlike, incompetent, desirous of tyrannical power, and violently vengeful. This is in spite of his own statement that in 1936, "Julius W. Pratt gave convincing proof that her evil reputation arose from deliberate reviling by Annexationists, especially by Minister John L. Stevens and the Reverend Mr. Sereno E. Bishop," and his recognition that "it profited those republicans who later deposed the Queen to paint her in as unfriendly terms as possible." But because for Russ the oligarchy was legitimate (although clearly not based in the consent of the native people) and annexation was a worthy pursuit, he begins by asserting that "Liliuokalani was not a good Queen. That is certain,"[8] and elsewhere says that the queen and her people's protests constituted "the native 'menace.'"[9] He accepts without question Willis's report that the queen, if restored, would have had Dole and the others beheaded. (Queen Lili'uokalani strenuously objected on numerous occasions that she had said no such thing.) He also concludes that the coup of 1893 was justified because "there can be no doubt that Royal Government under Kalakaua and Liliuokalani was inefficient, corrupt, and undependable."[10] For Russ, the native people of Hawai'i, including the queen, serve as background for a story about American expansion and American politics. As for Daws and Fuchs, for Russ "the key to what happened in the Hawaiian Islands was not in Honolulu but at Washington."[11]

It is possible, and crucial, to contest these representations by reexamining the events from a standpoint in which the queen and her lāhui are central, rather than marginalized, in the history of their own nation. This is what I aim to do in what follows.

THE FORMAL PROTESTS

After receiving many petitions of support from her people, Ke Ali'i 'Ai Moku Lili'uokalani consulted with trusted advisers and with Hui Kālai'āina, and then attempted to promulgate a constitution that removed the race and language requirements for the franchise, restored her executive powers, restored the guarantee of inviolability of the sovereign's property, and either eliminated or lessened the property requirements for voters. The resulting draft constitution was nearly identical to the constitution of 1864.[12] After she attempted to promulgate the new constitution, the oligarchy conspired with U.S. Minister John Stevens to land U.S. troops on Hawaiian soil and proclaim themselves the provisional government of Hawai'i the following day.

Lili'uokalani immediately sent several letters of protest, the longest of which was addressed to Sanford B. Dole and others "composing the Provisional Government":

I, Liliuokalani, by the grace of God and under the constitution of the Hawaiian kingdom, Queen, do hereby solemnly protest against any and all acts done against myself and the constitutional government of the

Hawaiian kingdom by certain persons claiming to have established a Provisional Government of and for this kingdom.

That I yield to the superior force of the United States of America, whose Minister Plenipotentiary, His Excellency John L. Stevens, has caused United States troops to be landed at Honolulu, and declared that he would support the said Provisional Government.

Now to avoid any collision of armed forces, and perhaps the loss of life, I do, under this protest and impelled by the said forces yield my authority until such time as the Government of the United States shall, upon the facts being presented to it, undo the action of its representative, and reinstate me in the authority which I claim as the constitutional sovereign of the Hawaiian Islands.[13]

Ke Ali'i 'Ai Moku reaffirmed in this protest that she was the rightful head of state by virtue of the constution. She continued in future protests to assert that she was abiding by the constitution and laws of the kingdom, while the oligarchy was not. Ironically, it was the Bayonet Constitution that she references, a document that she and her supporters considered illegal and illegitimate and that they had intended to replace with a new constitution. However, rather than claim that the constitution was illegal, she claimed only that it needed to be amended and that she had the mana to do so, provided her cabinet supported her. If her cabinet did not support her, *which in itself was a requirement of the Bayonet Constitution,* she felt that she could not legitimately proceed. The day following the coup, her cabinet ministers issued a pronouncement giving "assurances that any changes in the fundamental law of the land would be sought by methods provided in the constitution itself and signed by [her]self and [her] ministers."[14]

There appear to be two reasons why Lili'uokalani and her people felt bound by the Bayonet Constitution. First, King Kalākaua had bowed to threats of violence and promised to work within it. Jonathan Osorio points puts that Kalākaua apparently felt that he and his people were helpless against the oligarchy, and that "he had no stomach for war."[15] The second reason is that within hours of learning of her brother's death, Lili'uokalani herself had been rushed into taking an oath to uphold the constitution. As a person of honor, she was bound by her word, despite her belief that the oligarchy had taken advantage of her state of shock and grief. It is also significant that she had sought her husband's advice and he had advised her to take the oath. She was thus triply bound: by the rule of law, the rules of civility, and the solemnity with which the spoken word is regarded in Kanaka culture. The spoken (and, by extension, written, word) has power: the people of old said, "I ka 'ōlelo ke ola, i ka 'ōlelo nō ka make" (life is in the word [or language], death is also in the word). Larry Kimura explains that in Kanaka thought, "language contains the power of life and death. . . . The basis of the Hawaiian concept is the belief that saying the word gives power to cause the action. For example, to say 'I wish you good health,' will actually help a person to recover, while an expressed wish for death could actually cause it. . . . The power of the word is increased by the seriousness and preciousness of the form in which it is offered, such as in a chant or formal speech."[16] Thus, within these confines Ke Ali'i 'Ai Moku continued to act, searching for ways to restore pono for her people.

One of the ways was to appeal for help from the president of the United States. The situation of the coup was similar in some ways to the Paulet incident of 1843. In that case, faced with a threat of attack from a British warship, Kamehameha III temporarily surrendered sovereignty to the captain of the ship, and then sent an emissary to appeal to the Crown. The sovereignty of the kingdom was then restored within a matter of months, without any violence.[17] Similarly, Ke Ali'i 'Ai Moku wrote a letter of protest to President Benjamin Harrison in which she said that some of her subjects had "renounced their loyalty" and "revolted against the constitutional government of my Kingdom." She reported that the provisional government was being proclaimed "in direct conflict with the organic law of this Kingdom" and that the U.S. minister had "aided and abetted their unlawful movements."[18] Once again, we can see that the queen's strategy was to position herself as working within the law and constitution of the kingdom, while observing that the provisional government was acting illegally. She also wrote a letter to president-elect Grover Cleveland, and she was able to send her representatives, the attorney Paul Neumann and her nephew Ke Kamāli'i Kawananakoa, to meet with him.

Persuaded by the queen's protests, Cleveland withdrew the treaty of annexation that the provisional government had proposed and sent James Blount to investigate. The queen submitted a long statement to Blount, recounting the events of the overthrow and what had led up to it. Her main points were that it had been "a project of many years on the part of the missionary element that their children might some day be rulers over these islands"; that the U.S. minister had interfered in the internal affairs of the kingdom; that her attempt to promulgate the constitution "was in answer to the prayers and petitions of my people" and would have been constitutional if her cabinet had signed on; and, finally, that U.S. troops had been landed to support the conspirators.[19] Here the queen began to appeal to principles of international law: there was a treaty of perpetual amity between Hawai'i and the United States, and Hawai'i had been an accepted member of the family of nations since 1843.[20] It was a violation of the principles of international law for the United States to invade a recognized sovereign nation with whom it held treaties, especially for the purpose of installing an oligarchical government.

With Blount as representative of President Cleveland, the queen was dealing with a friendly administration. She trusted that Cleveland would conduct a fair investigation and then withdraw U.S. support for the provisional government. In December 1893, after reviewing Blount's report, Cleveland made a long statement condemning the actions of Minister Stevens and calling on the provisional government to step down and restore the throne to the Queen.[21]

CLEVELAND'S ABSOLUTE DENIAL

After Cleveland called for the restoration of the queen, she entered into negotiations with the new U.S. Minister, Albert Willis, which she thought would lead to her restoration. Sanford Dole responded to Cleveland with the statement that "we do not recognize the right of the President of the United States to interfere in our domestic affairs," with no discernible acknowledgment of the ironies of such a statement.[22] Annexation to the United States had always been the goal of the provisional government and always would be, but because it was obvious that Cleveland would not allow it to happen, Dole perhaps disingenuously issued his statement. Immediately thereafter, Dole and his oligarchy instituted the deceptively named Republic of Hawai'i. The queen sent a letter of protest to the U.S. government through Minister Willis on June 20, 1894. As in her previous protests, she emphasized that she was the "constitutional sovereign of the Hawaiian Kingdom," and that she "most solemnly protest[ed] against . . . any and all . . . acts done against myself, my people, and the Constitutional government of the Hawaiian Kingdom." She also reiterated that she and her government "would never have yielded" but for "the United States forces" and that "the great wrong done to this feeble but independent state by an abuse of the authority of the United States should be undone by restoring the legitimate government." Her main and "earnest request" was that "the government represented by [Willis] [would] not extend its recognition to any pretended government of the Hawaiian Islands."[23] Unfortunately, despite Cleveland's condemnation of the coup as an act of war, and despite Secretary of State Gresham's distaste for Lorrin Thurston and others in the provisional government, and finally, despite the negotiations undertaken in good faith by Lili'uokalani, Albert Willis immediately recognized the oligarchic Republic of Hawai'i as the de facto government of the islands.

Ke Ali'i 'Ai Moku's responses to this betrayal included sending a commission to Washington to present a protest to the president. Cleveland did not meet with the commissioners but offered a written response in which he refused to accept responsibility to rectify what the U.S. minister (Stevens) had done, and what his present minister was doing. He wrote, "Fully appreciating the constititional [*sic*] limitations of my Executive power . . . I undertook the task [of attempting to rectify the situation]. . . . Having failed in my plans, I committed the entire subject to the Congress of the United States . . . The Executive branch of the government was thereby dischsrged [*sic*] from further duty and responsibility in the matter . . . The Congress has . . . signified that nothing need be done touching American interference with the overthrow of the Government of the Queen." The president went on to say that a government had been established which was "clearly entitled to our recognition without regard to any of the incidents which accompanied or preceded its inauguration." The final result was Cleveland's statement of his "absolute denial of the least present or future aid or encouragement on my part to an effort to restore any government heretofore existing in the Hawaiian Islands."[24]

Ke Ali'i was not given a copy of this letter and therefore did not understand the immovable nature of the opposition the commission had encountered in Washington. Cleveland's "absolute denial" of any further effort to help was not communicated clearly to her, as she wrote quite angrily in her book: "What was the result of this commission? That is impossible for me to say. They went and they returned. They brought me no papers giving an official account of their proceedings or actions while on the mission."[25] The queen considered Cleveland a trustworthy friend and believed in his good intentions; perhaps the commissioners decided not to give the letter to the queen because they wanted to protect her from disappointment in her friend and perhaps because they feared for her health. She reported in her book that in the autumn and winter of 1894, she had been given electricity treatments because she "was suffering very severely from nervous prostration."[26] It is also possible that they withheld the letter from her because they did not want her to lose hope. If she lost hope, where would the lāhui be? It could also be that they knew that an armed uprising was being planned that they could not tell her about, and they did not want her to attempt some new tactic with Cleveland at the same time.

PROTESTING THE TREATY OF ANNEXATION

Lili'uokalani also submitted formal protests of the treaty of annexation, which the republic negotiated with President McKinley in spring 1897. She wrote the document in English. It was a strongly worded protest calling once again on international law: "I declare such treaty to be an act of wrong towards the native and part-native people of Hawaii, an invasion of the rights of the ruling chiefs, in violation of international rights both towards my people and towards friendly nations with whom they have made treaties, the perpetuation of the fraud whereby the constitutional government was overthrown, and finally an act of gross injustice to me."[27]

She reminded McKinley that his predecessor, Cleveland, had determined that her government had been "unlawfully coerced" and that she had been "the constitutional ruler" of her people. She also reminded him that her "people, about forty-thousand in number, have in no way been consulted by those . . . who claim the right to destroy the independence of Hawaii." Finally, she reminded McKinley of the treaties made between the United States and the legitimate sovereigns of the kingdom, which the annexation treaty ignored, making it "thereby in violation of international law." Finally, she called on the Senate to reject the treaty for these reasons.[28]

We can see in Queen Lili'uokalani's writings that she always positioned herself as working within the law and continually protested the unlawful actions of both the oligarchy (the provisional government and the republic) and the United States. Her insistence on doing this is related to the charges continually made against her and her people that they were uncivilized, backward savages who behaved like children and therefore could not understand the law or government. The oligarchy, and later the historians, would claim that their coup meant the triumph of "good government" in Hawai'i nei. Thus the queen and her people continually had to demonstrate that they did indeed understand and live according to the rule of law.

REPRESENTATION

Following the U.S. military intervention and the oligarchy's coup, "a number of the American people [were] deceived by the most astounding and unblushing falsehoods disseminated through the States by the papers," according to the executive committee of the Hui Hawai'i Aloha 'Āina.[29] The discourse of the savage pagan was deployed against the queen and her people once again, as it had been throughout the nineteenth century. Michael Dougherty quotes Sereno Bishop, a missionary son who wrote for the United Press, defaming her as the "'debauched Queen of a heathenish monarchy where . . . the *kahuna* sorcerers and idolators, all of the white corruptionists, and those who wish to make Honolulu a center for the manufacture and distribution of opium lie together with the lewd and drunken majority of the native race."[30] Writing from Boston in 1897 the queen's secretary, Joseph Heleluhe, enclosed clippings from a newspaper there that quoted the republic's representative on "ko ke Alii ino, oia hoi, ka hupo, pegana, hookamakama, a me ka hoomanakii" (the Queen's evils, i.e., that she was stupid, pagan, a prostitute, and an idol worshipper).[31]

Lydia Kualapai also quotes Bishop claiming that "'disgusting orgies . . . polluted [the] palace'" and that Kalākaua and Lili'uokalani "had no 'real hereditary royalty' but were instead the illegitimate children of a mulatto shoemaker." Bishop claimed that because of that, "white Ha-

"We Draw the
Line at This." Cartoon
by Victor Gillam,
December 1893.
(Courtesy of the
Bishop Museum)
Caricature of
Cetshwayo, Zulu king,
from *Judy*, 1879.

"Lili to Grover." Cartoon by Victor Gillam, February 1894. (Courtesy of the Bishop Museum) Caricature of Emilio Aguinaldo of the Philippines, by Victor Gillam, *Harper's Weekly*, 1899.

Queen Liliʻuokalani; frontispiece to her autobiography,
Hawaii's Story by Hawaii's Queen, 1897. (Courtesy of
Hawaiʻi State Archives)

waii loathes them, and native Hawaii has no respect for them."[32] Such a
charge was a ridiculous one, rooted in American racism against Africans,
and used to justify the continued subjugation of the African Americans
in the post–Civil War period, then borrowed here to justify taking over
the government from Kalākaua and Liliʻuokalani.

American cartoonists borrowed stock images of Africans and African Americans that worked intertextually with Bishop's and others'

statements. As Stuart Hall has pointed out, the "stereotyping of blacks in popular representation was so common that cartoonists, illustrators and caricaturists could summon up a whole gallery of 'black types' with a few, simple, essentialized strokes of the pen. Black people were reduced to the signifiers of their physical difference — thick lips, fuzzy hair, broad face and nose, and so on."[33] These signifiers can be seen in caricatures of Lili'uokalani that appeared on covers of *Judge* magazine. One such cover ridicules the queen and President Cleveland's decision to support the Kanaka Maoli government through the use of images borrowed from earlier caricatures of the Zulu king Cetshwayo, who battled the British in 1879. According to Jan Pieterse, in the media at that time a discourse developed about saving Africa from the practice of human sacrifice, and that "abolishing human sacrifice was the pretext for the British invasion."[34] In the magazine images Lili'uokalani is meant to be seen as a similar type of savage. She is barefoot, a sign meant to show that she is not civilized. She sits in a chair, holding two documents labeled "Gross Immorality" and "Scandalous Government." These undoubtedly refer to the opium and lottery bills passed by the Legislature in 1892, which she signed before the coup. In her chair she is being held aloft by a circle of bayonets wielded by white sailors and soldiers. In the background on one side are palm trees and on the other what appears to be a depiction of Kanaka men in loincloths, who may be protesting or perhaps worshipping her (one of them has both arms raised). By borrowing the ready-made "black" stereotype the cartoonist was able to signify the queen's racial difference immediately, a shorthand way to convey that she was essentially, naturally, unfit to rule.

Another cartoon draws on the black stereotype of the "pickaninny," notably in the drawing of frizzy hair and the use of the exaggerated contrast in color between the dark skin and white eyes and teeth. The pickaninny is an infantilizing as well as racializing stereotype, and in this case it is also sexualized because the queen appears to be made up to look like a prostitute, an image that works intertextually with the written statements about orgies, etc. The cartoon bases some of its ridicule on the detail of the dress made of feathers: featherwork is an important signifier of ali'i nui status in Hawai'i, and not too many years previously Lili'uokalani and Queen Kapi'olani had gained some fame in London for the fine featherwork sewn as decoration on Kapi'olani's gown. The figure in the cartoon is wearing a feather skirt (but not a fine one), as well as a crown and prominent earrings and bracelets, which the queen usually wore. The background of the image is meant to represent a Hawaiian beach, which is gruesomely strewn with the evidence of the queen's (and by extension, the entire people's) savagery: a bloody axe and a chopping block inscribed "for Dole" on the left, and a cannibal pot on the right, accompanied by a skull and bloody crossbones. The cartoon implies that despite her finery — the feathers, high-heeled shoes, and jewelry — the queen cannot escape her nature, which is defined by her skin color and features. She is in essence a pickaninny, a foolish, childish woman from a savage and cannibal "race." An almost identical cartoon image during the Philippine-American war depicted the resistance leader Emilio Aguinaldo of the Philippines as a girl pickaninny, thereby reducing Aguinaldo to the same set of stereotyped characteristics.

The queen attempted to contest these representations in several different ways. First, in 1893, not long after the coup, she agreed to write an article for the San Francisco *Examiner*. The article was translated into Hawaiian and published in *Ka Leo o ka Lahui* shortly after it appeared in the *Examiner*. In it, Lili'uokalani again asserted that she was the legitimate sovereign and that the constitution she attempted to replace was fatally flawed. She also appealed to the readers' humanity, presenting herself as the champion of her people who were being oppressed by wealthy planters. She wrote, "I am a Hawaiian. I love and sympathize with my native poor." She used her considerable knowledge of politics and the haole principles of democratic government to make her case, turning the tables on the oligarchy by deploying the very discourse that they attempted to use against her. She wrote, for example, "the circumstances of the case do not call for a change of Government. Annexation is repugnant to the feelings of every native Hawaiian . . . Annexation is not necessary for the ends of peace or of civilization, or of commerce, or of security."[35]

While in Washington the queen published *Hawaii's Story by Hawaii's Queen*, which was meant to counter the racist representations, as well as the arguments that the Republic's delegates were making for annexation at the time. Lydia Kualapai, in her work "Cast in Print," makes a strong argument that the queen's discursive strategies in *Hawaii's Story* successfully countered both the negative representations and the arguments for annexation.[36] Included in the book as a frontispiece is a formal portrait of Lili'uokalani, another visual representation meant to counter the intertextual discourses of savagery. In the photo the queen wears a tiara, a white gown sewn with featherwork, and a sash with the royal order attached: she appears as a member of the upper class and royalty. Claiming this upper-class status is meant to strengthen her claim that she is the proper head of state of Hawai'i as well as counter the claims that she is incapable. The ostentatiously expensive gown and jewelry signify her real wealth. Simultaneously, her brown skin confounds the notion that upper-class, royal status belongs only to white people.[37] The portrait disrupts the meaning making of the aristocracy, which depends on the existence of a dark other who is the opposite — the savage for the civilized. The existence of real wealth also disrupts the racist stereotypes: this dark queen had been received by Queen Victoria and by many in the U.S. capital despite the color of her skin; she was able to present herself as an anomaly to the American racist imagination.

The queen also made appearances in society in Boston, New York, and Washington, D.C. to counter these misrepresentations. She used her body, her physical ability to carry herself as an aristocrat and thus ultracivilized, as a countertext. Her secretary, Heleluhe, wrote that although some people had initially been deceived by Gilman, the republic's representative who had been claiming the queen was a pagan and a prostitute, "i ka ike pono ana iho nei o ko onei poe a me na poe hoolaha nupepa, ke olelo nei lakou he kanaka hoopunipuni loa o Gilimana" (now that the people and the reporters here have actually seen her, they are saying Gilman is a liar). Heleluhe reports that several hundred people visited the queen in the first three days of her stay in Boston.[38] The queen then spent private time with family and friends, but after making a doll for a charity doll show she again received positive attention in a Boston newspaper. Her friend was quoted in the paper saying, "I have never found a more devout and perfect Christian under all circumstances than Liliuokalani."[39]

In Washington, wrote the Queen, "it was my custom to give a reception about every fortnight; to receive callers at eight to nine any evening . . . Both houses of Congress were well represented at my receptions, if not always by the gentlemen themselves, by their wives or daughters." These receptions were exceedingly well-attended; the queen notes that "there were seldom less than two hundred callers, and [the] largest reception numbered nearly five hundred persons." Ke Ali'i 'Ai Moku also received visits from, she adds, "many delegations of patriotic or literary societies" and from "all denominations of the Christian church."[40] She accepted invitations to the homes of dignitaries, and to the theatre and opera. Reports in the *New York Times* commented on her dignity and tasteful dress.[41] She thus attempted to demonstrate to hundreds of the most influential citizens of the United States that she was indeed a lady and a head of state, not the bloodthirsty and ignorant pagan she was represented to be.

In addition to these discursive and other actions directed at the American public the queen spent considerable thought and energy in maintaining the hopes and spirits of her own people. Let us turn now to an examination of some of the ways that she attempted to keep the lāhui together in the face of sustained efforts by the oligarchy and United States to dismantle it.

KONA LĀHUI ALOHA

In January 1895, after the frustrated po'e aloha 'āina unsuccessfully attempted to overthrow the provisional government in an armed countercoup, Queen Lili'uokalani was arrested and imprisoned in 'Iolani Hale, the palace that the oligarchy had taken over and renamed the Executive Building. The provisional government convened a military tribunal, and, according to the queen's account, forced her to abdicate with the threat that she and her most loyal supporters would be executed if she did not. Shortly after signing the abdication, she was subjected to trial by the military tribunal. Osorio has written that "this trial was not simply about establishing the Queen's guilt. It was also a demonstration of the power and the right of the new government to arrest and convict the previous head-of-state."[42] Ke Ali'i 'Ai Moku strongly denied that the republic or the tribunal had any such power or right. She prepared a long statement in her own defense that was read in court; and although the tribunal was conducted in English she submitted her written statement in Hawaiian, which had to be translated for the officers. In translation, her statement reads in part: "I must deny your right to try me in the manner and by the Court which you have called together for this purpose. In your actions you violate your own Constitution and laws . . . All who uphold you in this unlawful proceeding may scorn and despise my words, but the offense of breaking and setting aside for a specific purpose the laws of your own nation and disregarding all justice and fairness may be to them and to you the source of an unhappy and much to be regretted legacy."[43] The queen was sentenced to five years of hard labor, but her actual punishment was eight months imprisonment in one room of 'Iolani Palace; five months house arrest at her home, Washington Place; and eight months confinement to O'ahu.[44]

During the months Lili'uokalani was held at 'Iolani Palace she was not allowed to communicate with her people. At the start of the conflict, the republic had declared martial law and then arrested all those it believed to have worked for its downfall, including all newspaper editors who supported the queen. The prorepublic paper *Pacific Commercial Advertiser* sarcastically reported that "the native and English papers troubled with a leaning towards the resumption of royalty are enjoying a long-needed term of rest. The editors are passing their vacations in the Oahu prison."[45] The *Advertiser* also opined that "the right to a free and untrammeled expression of opinion on the conduct of national affairs is causing any quantity of trouble in more than one nation in the world."[46] What this meant for the po'e aloha 'āina was that the only news they were getting about the queen and the situation of the people who were imprisoned was from the progovernment newspapers, that is, from their enemies. The prorepublic *Nupepa Kuokoa* was the only source of news in Hawaiian.

Up until this time, Ke Ali'i 'Ai Moku had been working closely together with Hui Aloha 'Āina, Hui Kālai'āina, and others. News about her activities was reported on a weekly basis, and her opinions were made known to the people through the papers. But now the newspapers were reporting that she willingly gave up everything, even her claims to her own land. *Nupepa Kuokoa* claimed that the queen had independently signed a statement drafted by her own advisers. They reported: "Ua kakau inoa iho o Liliuokalani Dominis moiwahine hope o ko Hawaii Paeaina malalo o kekahi palapala ano nui loa iloko o ka moolelo o ko Hawaii nei noho ana, e hookuu ana, haalele loa a hoopau loa i kana mau koi a pau, kona mau hooilina a mau hope i ka nohoalii o Hawaii no ka manawa mau loa" (Liliuokalani Dominis, formerly queen of the Hawaiian islands, signed on a document very important to the history of the life of Hawai'i, releasing, abandoning completely, and completely quitting all her claims, and [those of] her heirs and other claimants to the throne of Hawai'i forever).[47]

The stories in the *Kuokoa* and the *Advertiser* were intended to lead the people to think that Ke Ali'i 'Ai Moku had abandoned them and their struggle. Then, in March, F. J. Testa, editor of *Ka Makaainana,* and the other newspapermen were released from jail, and allowed to resume publication of the opposition papers. The second week of publication *Ka Makaainana* ran an anonymous mele in the top left corner of the front page. It was titled "Mai Wakinekona a Iolani Hale" (From Washington Place to 'Iolani Palace). This title, along with the first line, "Ia'u e nanea ana ma Wakinekona" (While I was relaxing at Washington Place), identified the composer as Ke Ali'i 'Ai Moku. This was the first in a four-week series of mele written by her that appeared in the same position on the front page. Thus it was only through lyric composition that Ke Ali'i was able to communicate with her people and to bear witness to what she suffered at the hands of the provisional government, expressing her thoughts and feelings in the language of her ancestors, family, and community. Amy Ku'uleialoha Stillman has laid the groundwork for understanding nineteenth-century Hawaiian politics through analysis of mele, noting that study of song and poetic forms are particularly important "in situations of colonization, where histories from generations past [have been] produced largely or even solely from records of the colonizers." Stillman has found that "the political turmoil of the late 1880s and 1890s contributed to a dramatic increase in the use of poetic texts for political and explicitly nationalist commentary," and that these texts created "nationalist poetic discourse [that] took place in arguably the most public of forums—Hawaiian language newspapers."[48] Lili'uokalani, like her siblings, was a haku mele (composer), and we can better understand her songwriting if we view it in its political context as well as in the context of the traditional culture.

Haku mele had and have important roles to play in the life of the community. In the ancient world, says Kamakau: "'O ka haku mele kekahi hana akamai a na'auao o ka po'e kahiko, a ua kaulana loa ia po'e ma ia hana" (Mele composition was an activity of the people of old requiring education and skill, and composers became very famous for their work).[49] This was in part because haku mele were responsible for remembering and composing mele ko'ihonua, the cosmogonical chants that linked ali'i to the birth of the land itself and to the gods, and so legitimated their rule. Haku mele had the mana to select among different lineages to create and maintain the illustrious names of their ali'i nui. Mele ko'ihonua such as the *Kumulipo* were thus the most political of all mele forms. Kamakau explains that the composition of mele ko'ihonua was kapu, meaning both sacred and restricted; only those who were most knowledgeable in all of the three fields of genealogy, oratory, and land distribution — that is, politics (kālai'āina) — composed mele ko'ihonua. The kapu were the same as those that governed genealogies.[50] In addition, mele contained the memory of the people, so the haku mele had to be trustworthy as well as talented. Kamakau, Poepoe, members of Hale Nauā, and other Kanaka authors relied on mele for evidence for their accounts and analyses of the wā kahiko (ancient times). Kamakau celebrates "ka waiwai i loa'a ma loko o nā mele a ka po'e kahiko i haku ai" (the riches found inside the mele that the people of old composed). And he states that "he nui nā loina a me nā kaona i loko" (much lore and kaona are contained within [mele]), because "ua hana 'ia ko ka lani, ko ka lewa, ko ka moana, ko ka honua, ko ka lā, ka mahina, nā hōkū a me nā mea a pau" (that of the heavens, the sky, the sea, the earth, the sun, the moon, the stars, and everything were made [into mele]).[51]

Haku mele composed many other kinds of mele, including name songs, or mele inoa; mele ma'i that celebrated sexuality and fertility; songs that honored deities; songs that extolled certain places, and so on. Name songs often served political functions, as they were usually composed for mō'ī and other ali'i, and often for parents and children, as well. Kamakau says that they were sung with happiness, but the kaona in them could contain riddles and metaphors about an ali'i's weakness or character failures, such as stinginess or withholding. The public would enjoy the mele in its celebratory aspect, which was the main idea, but they would not understand the kaona of the mele; only certain other ali'i might appreciate the criticisms hidden in the kaona.[52]

When Lili'uokalani lived and composed, mele had changed in both form and function. Haku mele remained central to the life of both ali'i and maka'āinana, but in ways different from the ones Kamakau describes for the old world. Genealogies were still of the greatest importance and cosmologies were recited and recorded, but only at the risk of direct opposition by the increasingly wealthy missionary camp. Many cosmogonical chants were lost, and the composition of new ones ceased to be part of the nineteenth-century haku mele's profession. The interwoven nature of politics, religion, and mele continued in name songs for ali'i, and also in mele lāhui that were used as national anthems in the

European style. Liliʻuokalani was an important composer both of mele lāhui and of mele inoa.

Since the advent of the print media starting in 1834, mele also became a genre of resistance to cultural imperialism. Even in the first missionary newspaper, the student page (written by the Kanaka students of the missionaries) contained a traditional kanikau. Recall that it was a mele (ironically a parochial school hīmeni [hymn] of particularly Kanaka style) that began the struggle over whether or not Kanaka could continue to publish their own paper. It was mele that Kānepuʻu felt should be written and published in their entirety for posterity because the knowledge of the kūpuna was being eroded by the demands of the missionaries. Mele were crucial to Kalākaua's formulation of himself and the legitimation of his reign — he had the *Kumulipo* written down and published (which Queen Liliʻuokalani later translated while imprisoned), and he also had *Na Mele Aimoku* published as a book. Further, in the era of print, mele composition became a popular literary form. Ordinary people as well as the highly trained aliʻi were literate in great numbers, and many composed various kinds of mele (although not the types previously guarded by kapu).[53] Mele was a primary genre through which women were able to express their political views in the nineteenth century. Many ordinary people, including women, published kanikau to honor deceased family members or aliʻi.[54]

Mele communicate in ways prose cannot. Mele functioned then (and now) both as carriers of messages of opposition and as signs of Kanaka identity, in that they indicate mastery of cultural knowledge and poetic language, which few foreigners, even orientalists like Nathaniel Emerson or Thomas Thrum, possessed.[55] As Kameʻeleihiwa has explained about prose in Hawaiian, which is intensified in mele, "there is the tale at face value ... An additional level is introduced by innumerable allusions to ancient events, myths, gods, and chiefs that have become metaphors in their own right. This includes the use of place names and the symbolism attached to the names of winds, rains, plants, and rocks, evoking a certain emotional quality on all levels. ... This device not only creates a certain mood but adds to the beauty of the work, as what is seen on the surface can be interpreted simultaneously on other levels."[56] I would suggest that the understanding by both poets and audiences that mele should contain these several levels of meaning made the genre particularly well suited to communicating thoughts and feelings undetected but yet in plain sight of hostile forces. The shared understanding also bound the lāhui together.

In 1861 mele had been used to oppose the increase in cultural oppression. Later, during her brother's reign, when Kalākua battled the missionary sons, Liliʻuokalani composed at least one song, "He ʻAi na ka Lani," that talks back to his detractors and defends her family's right to the throne. The first verse is:

Ke ʻai nei ʻo ka lani,
Hāmau ʻoukou lākou nei aʻe
Mai noho a pane aʻe,
Ua kapu ʻē ka ʻaha i ke aliʻi.
(The royal one is dining now,
You should all be silent,
Make not a sound,
The assembly is *kapu* in the presence of the chiefly one.)[57]

The word ʻai has been translated here as "dine" in keeping with the surface meaning of the rest of the song, which refers to eating various types of foods.[58] However, because ʻai also means "rule" (as in aliʻi ʻai moku), the first two lines can also be understood as "The king is ruling now / You should all be silent." The single-meaning translation of ʻai as dine effectively depoliticizes the song. The remainder of the song refers to food being brought to the king from the uplands, the kula (plains), the freshwater streams, and the sea, indicating in the usual language of Hawaiian poetry that he rules over the entire country.

Liliʻuokalani also composed a mele inoa for her niece and heir apparent that similarly defends the family's genealogy:

Lamalama i luna ka ʻōnohi lā,
Kāhiko uakoko ʻula lā,
Ka hōʻailona kapu o ke kama lā,
He ēwe mai nā kūpuna.
(The display of a rainbow illuminates above,
An adornment with the blood red rain,
This is the sacred sign of the princess,
The lineage passed down from the ancestors).[59]

The two kinds of rainbows, ʻōnohi and uakoko (the "blood red rain"), are hōʻailona (cosmic signs) that validate aliʻi nui status, which are common in moʻolelo kahiko as well as in moʻolelo contemporary to that time. Kalākaua's funeral was attended by many such hōʻailona that were recorded in the newspapers. In that case, John Bush asserted that the presence of the hōʻailona proved Kalākaua's genealogy against his racist detractors.[60]

Ke Aliʻi ʻAi Moku shared this language and understanding with her lāhui and, as I have stressed, many foreigners, although functionally fluent in Hawaiian, could not understand such poetic references and did not share these beliefs. Her mele worked differently from the other genres of resistance. The formal protests; articles in newspapers; publication of books; and presence in Washington were directed at U.S. politicians and the American public, but her mele were primarily for her people. Kanaka were the only ones who could understand the language and the form, and a handful or more of them understood the kaona. Communicating through mele was a way of keeping the lāhui together when they were the most isolated from each other.

Moreover, the idea that the spoken (and written) word has mana continues to this day among Kanaka, and the well-composed mele was and is a particularly potent mode of communication. Elizabeth Tatar quotes one nineteenth-century Kanaka expert as saying "he pule ke mele" (mele are prayers).[61] Mary Kawena Pukui explains that "the kaona of a chant was believed to be potent . . . but it was ineffective unless chanted before a gathering of people."[62] When mele were published in the newspapers, they reached a large number of people, and as such were meant and perceived to have such mana.

During the period 1893 to 1898 there was an outpouring of song in the nation. According to J. J. Leilani Basham, there were approximately 250 mele lāhui published in the Hawaiian papers in this five-year period.[63] Love for the land and loyalty to the queen were the major subjects of these songs.

Basham explains that "he mana ko nā mele [lāhui], no ka mea, hōʻike mōakāka aku nā haku mele i ko lākou manaʻo kūpaʻa no ka pono o ka ʻāina" (mele [lāhui] have mana because composers clearly show their commitment to what is pono for the land). She adds further that "he waiwai a koʻikoʻi ia mea he mele lāhui i ka hoʻomaopopo pono ʻana i ka moʻolelo Hawaiʻi" (mele lāhui are valuable and extremely important for understanding Hawaiian history).[64] The category mele lāhui originally referred to national anthems composed in the mid-nineteenth century, when Hawai'i was constructing itself as a nation-state in the Euro-American tradition. Lili'uokalani composed "He Mele Lāhui Hawai'i," which was used as the national anthem from 1866 to 1874; it was followed by "Hawai'i Pono'ī," which was composed by her brother Kalākaua.

But in 1895 the meaning of mele lāhui had changed because although the nation or lāhui was alive in the people there was no government attached to it, so mele lāhui could no longer be "national anthems." In some ways the meaning of the term intensified because instead of simply celebrating an existing nation, the songs were a powerful expression of the people's commitment and desire for the nation to be restored. The term mele lāhui now came to signify all the songs in honor of the mō'īwahine and the po'e aloha 'āina who were trying to restore her government.[65] This included songs that protested the oligarchy, U.S. intervention, and the proposed annexation of Hawai'i and supported the restoration of the native government. Or, as Basham says, mele lāhui became "nā mele a pau i haku 'ia no ka ho'ohanohano 'ana a me ke kāko'o 'ana i ka Mō'ī, ka 'āina, ke aupuni, a me ka lāhui o Hawai'i" (all mele composed to honor or support the Mō'ī, the 'āina, the government, or the people of Hawai'i).[66]

Four mele were apparently smuggled out of the queen's prison room to the newspaper *Ka Makaainana*, where they were published in weekly installments. Her main message in these mele was that her heart was still with her people and her nation, and that contrary to the representation being made by the prorepublic papers she had not abandoned the po'e aloha 'āina or the struggle for their nation. In the first mele are the lines:

Eia ko hewa la e Kalani
No kou aloha i ka lahui
(This is your offense, Kalani
It is because of your love for your people.)

And in the second part are these lines:

Anoano ke aloha ka hiki'na mai
No kuu lahui i ke ehuehu
(Sacred is the aloha that comes
For my people in the spray [of bullets])[67]

The first of these verses recounts the "hauna o ke Aupuni" (blows of the Government); Lili'uokalani's experience of being carried to the palace in "ke kaa pio Hope Ilamuku" (the deputy sheriff's carriage); and of her view from the window of her prison room of Lae'ahi (Diamond Head), where the po'e aloha 'āina "i imi ai i ka pono o ka lanakila" (had sought the pono of victory). She also prays to the heavenly powers to release her distressed people.

In the next installation, in the second week, the song is titled "Lokahi ka Manao me ka Lahui" ([My] mind is one with the people), which again stresses the queen's desire to tell the lāhui that her heart and mind are with them. In this song, the queen angrily criticizes her former appointee, William A. Whiting, along with William Kinney, who told prisoners they would hang if they did not tell all to the republic's police. Whiting was the head of the military tribunal that convicted her, a matter than Jon Van Dyke says "must have been particularly painful, because Queen Lili'uokalani had picked Whiting to serve as her Attorney General in her first cabinet in February 1891."[68] Kinney had been the law partner of Lorrin Thurston and was one of the original organizers of the bayonet coup.[69] In January 1893 he had been one of the provisional government representatives that traveled to Washington to propose the treaty of annexation.[70] He now served as prosecutor at the tribunal. Here is most of the song:

Ka aku ke aho ia Waitina
Ka peresidena nui o ka Aha-Koa,
Nana e kaana mai i ka pono,
No kuu lahui i alohaia,
Hana e launa ole o Wi[l]i Kini,
Haole lelepi o Waialae,
Kana hana o ka pelo i ke kanaka,
E hai pau mai i ola oe,
Mai puni aku oe i kana mali,
E i aku e ke ola ia Kalani,
I molia kona ola no ka lahui,
I ola nou e ke aloha aina.
(The line was thrown to Whiting,
President of the Military Tribunal,
It is he who will mete out "justice,"

To my beloved people,
Inexplicably strange are the actions of Willy Kinney,
The hot-tempered haole of Wai'alae,
His act was to lie to the people,
"Tell all so that you will live,"
Do not be deceived by his cajolery,
Say that there is life through Her Majesty,
Who sacrifices her life for the lāhui,
So that you patriot(s) may live.)[71]

These lines refer to the queen's attempt to prepare herself for the death sentence to which she had been alerted.[72]

The third week's installation — a mele inoa for the queen's nephew, Kalaniana'ole (Prince Kūhiō), imprisoned in a republic jail — was published under the title "Umia ke Aloha i Paa Iloko" (The love held inside).

Hiki mai e ka lono i o'u nei,
Aia o'u pokii la i Kawa,
. . . .
Umia ke aloha i paa iloko,
No ke one oiwi ou e Hawaii,
Eha ai ka ili ou kupuna,
O Keawe, O Kalani-I-a-Mamao,
(The news has come to me,
My younger brother [nephew] is at Kawa jail,
. . . .
The love held inside is choked back,
For your native sands, Hawai'i
For which the skins of your ancestors were injured,
Keawe and Kalaniiamamao).[73]

Here the queen reminds her nephew and her people of the genealogy that gave her and Kalaniana'ole membership in the royal family and that links his struggle and sacrifice to the struggles of their warrior ancestors, Keawe and Kalani'īamamao. Later in the song, she says he is decorated with "aloha 'āina," a lei of honor to be cherished, and that together they all know the same hardship of imprisonment. These songs, smuggled out to be printed in the newspaper, let Kūhiō and the public know that Ke Ali'i approved of his joining the maka'āinana aloha 'āina attempt to regain the government. She must have hoped that the newspaper would be smuggled in to him, or at least that he would hear of the song and know her feelings.

The following week, Lili'uokalani published another mele inoa for Kūhiō, continuing the series. This mele concentrated on the people who were caring for her and expressed gratitude that none of her people had received a sentence of death. Here is an excerpt:

> Ke aloha hoohakukoi waimaka,
> Mai na puka alohi ka ikena iho,
> Ka maalo ana 'e ku'u maka,
> I ka poe i aloha i ka aina,
> I ukali ia ma na aoao,
> E ka poe menehune aiwaiwa,
> Ua ko ae nei ku'u makemake
> Ua hookuu ia ku'u lahui.
> (A troubled aloha that brings tears,
> From the bright windows the sight,
> Passing before my eyes,
> Is of the people who love the land,
> Attended at their sides,
> By the supernatural menehune,
> My desire has been fulfilled,
> My people have been released.)[74]

But not only did the queen express solidarity with her people by smuggling mele out to *Ka Makaainana*, the people responded by expressing their solidarity with her. They also sent mele out from their jail cells to be printed in *Ka Makaainana*. The mele acted like conversations between people who were physically unable to talk to each other because they were imprisoned in different locations and separated on different islands. This situation is apparent in the endings of the songs; the queen echoes the ending of "Mele Aloha Aina" or "Kaulana Na Pua," when she states "Haina ia mai ana ka puana / Na pua i aloha i ka aina" (The story is told / Of the flowers who love the land) or "Haina ia mai ana ka puana / No ka poe i aloha i ka aina" (The story is told / For the people who love the land).[75] The pieces in the queen's series all end with "Hookahi puana ko'u puuwai / No ka poe i aloha i ka aina" (My heart has one refrain / For the people who love the land) or some variation thereof, which is very similar. Other haku mele responded, as in the next song composed by two po'e aloha 'āina, Kapu and Kaulia, in prison; their refrain is "Hainaia mai ana ka puana / Makou o na poe aloha aina" (The story is told / We are the po'e aloha 'āina).[76]

Another example is the queen's description of her location imprisoned within "Na paia hanohano o Iolani Hale," (The grand walls of 'Iolani Palace).[77] Kapu and Kaulia echo her words, locating themselves inside "Na paia laumania o Kawa," (The smooth walls of Kawa [jail]";[78] and then Heleluhe (her secretary) and Koa in turn locate themselves imprisoned in "Na paia pohaku o ka Halekoa" (The rock walls of the Barracks).[79]

Po'e aloha 'āina communicated in mele their continuing love and loyalty to the queen. On May 6, a mele titled "Liliu Lei a ka Lahui" (Lili'u, "lei" of the people) by W. Olepau appeared in the same space the queen's had in previous weeks. Here lei is a metaphor for a cherished one, someone who might put their arms around one's neck. The mele compares the queen to a precious feather lei, urges her to put on the royal feather cloak, and prays that the Crown flag will fly again. On May 20, an anonymous mele titled "Kupaa ka Manao me Liliu" ([My] mind is steadfastly with Lili'u) appeared in response to her "Lokahi ka Manao me ka Lahui." This mele calls her the queen who is draped in aloha.

These mele served as a way for Ke Ali'i 'Ai Moku to communicate to her people that she shared their anger, sorrows, and desire to regain their nationhood, and for them to communicate to her that they were still loyal, no matter what the haole newspaper said. For her and her lāhui, the mele also functioned as pule, praying for the life of the nation, published as if chanted before the large gathering of newspaper readers. The queen's message in the various mele was consistent: she was with them, she had not abandoned them, and she was fighting the provisional government in every way she could, including through spiritual appeals. The people were po'e aloha 'āina, and so was she.[80] At the end of the year the four songs, (under the pseudonym Ha'imoeipo), were included in F. J. Testa's collection *Buke Mele Lahui*, and two years later the queen included them in her own (unpublished) songbook "He Buke Mele Hawaii."

"I KISS YOUR SOFT HANDS":
LETTERS TO KE ALIʻI ʻAI MOKU

The bonds between the lāhui and Liliʻuokalani are also reflected in a series of letters to the queen written by Mrs. Emma ʻAʻima Nāwahī between December 1896 and August 1898. Liliʻuokalani wrote back to Mrs. Nāwahī regularly — sometimes once a week, sometimes more or less. All of the letters are in Hawaiian. Although I have not been able to locate the queen's letters to Mrs. Nāwahī, Mrs. Nāwahī, in her newspaper, *Ke Aloha Aina*, excerpted the letters she received from the queen, so we do have some fragments.[81] We also have letters and excerpts from Ke Aliʻi's secretary, Joseph Heleluhe, published in *Ka Makaainana*. These letters are further demonstration that without reading the archive in Hawaiian it is not possible to gain a full understanding or analysis of the politics of the era. Although some of the letters have been translated, many have not, and the context for them is missing unless one also reads the newspapers.[82] And as we have seen many times now, translations by themselves of works in Hawaiian tend to leave out the multiple meanings and Hawaiian cultural connotations present in the originals.

In this case, the letters help to answer some questions about the role of the women of Hui Aloha ʻĀina. Through the letters a picture emerges of mature and politically engaged women trusted by the queen to guide the younger men who were the presidents of the hui. The letters also reveal that Ke Aliʻi ʻAi Moku directed the 1897 antiannexation petition drive through the exchange of letters with Mrs. Nāwahī, David Kalauokalani, and James Kaulia. It was she who suggested the petition drive, directed that the three hui work together, and suggested the content of the heading of the petition.

THE QUEEN SAILS TO AMERICA

As soon as the queen's full civil rights had been restored, and with no warning except to her retainers and to the republic government from whom she needed passports, she boarded a ship for the United States. ʻAʻima Nāwahī and David Kalauokalani learned of Ke Aliʻi ʻAi Moku's departure and were able to go to her home to say goodbye; F. J. Testa of

Ka Makaainana happened to be at the harbor for another reason and was startled to see the queen and her retainers, Joe Heleluhe and Mrs. Nahaolelua, boarding the ship. Mrs. Nāwahī described in a letter how the lāhui felt when she left: "Ua hoopuiwa loa ia ko ke kaona nei poe a nui ka pioo ame ka nune ia la a po" (The people of this town were very surprised and there was a lot of upset and questions all that day). She goes on to describe hō'ailona traditionally associated with ali'i that had appeared as Ke Ali'i 'Ai Moku was leaving: "Auwe! Aloha nohoi na hiohiona eehia oia la au e Kalani i haalele iho ai i ka aina nei, e nee ana nohoi ka ua liilii, e pipio ana hoi ke anuenue, ku ka onohi, ka punohu ua koko i ka moana. Ae, e hoike mai ana na Lani a me ka po, he hoailona kapu ia no Kalani Aimoku o Hawaii no Liliu no Loloku no Walania i ke kiionohi" (Auē! So awe-inspiring were the phenomena on the day that you left, Your Majesty, a fine rain moved in, a rainbow arched in the sky, and the blood-red rainbow appeared on the sea. Yes, the Heavens and the pō [the spirits of ancient past, and those who have passed on] were showing sacred signs for Kalani Aimoku of Hawai'i, for Lili'u, for Loloku, for Walania i ke ki'i'ōnohi). The signs continued through the night: Mrs. Nāwahī lamented that "oiai ka ua me ka makani e nu mai ana iluna ae nei o ka laalaau o Muolaulani . . . Auwe! aohe hiki pono ia'u ke moe, e hiolo mau ana ko'u mau waimaka, e pule ana, a e nonoi mau ana i ke aloha o ka makua mana loa e malama a e kiai hoi i kana kauwa wahine, ka makuahine o keia lahui kanaka nawaliwali" (Since the rain and wind were roaring above the plants of Mu'olaulani [Lili'u's home in Kapālama] . . . Auē! I could not sleep well, my tears were falling, I was praying, asking continuously for the mercy of the almighty father to care for and watch over his servant, the mother of this powerless people).[83]

Mrs. Nāwahī was understandably anguished and worried over the queen's departure. In January 1891, Kalākaua had sailed to San Francisco and later passed away there. And just three months before the queen left, Joseph Nāwahī had made the same journey and also died in San Francisco. The po'e aloha 'āina had just suffered the failed countercoup and the mass arrests and imprisonment in places like "the pest hole known as Oahu prison,"[84] which caused death and illness like the tuberculosis that killed Nāwahī. These experiences had also apparently tamed the spirits of some of the strongest advocates for Hawaiian autonomy. John Bush and Kahikina Kelekona, for example, were never again as outspoken as they had been prior to being imprisoned. Just the week before, the Hui Aloha 'Āina and Hui Kālai'āina had convened to elect their new presidents, Kaulia and Kalauokalani, who had not yet had a chance to exercise their leadership. It was a shock, then, to lose the guiding presence of the queen at this time. But, as the queen herself explained, "I felt greatly inclined to go abroad, it made no difference where"; and as the ship pulled out of the harbor, "for the first time in years I drew a long breath of freedom. For what was there worthy of that sacred name under the circumstances in which I had lived on shore?"[85] She had suffered not only the isolation of imprisonment but the indignity of imprisonment in her own palace. She had been terrorized with the threat of execution and by displays of American military power, as when the soldiers of the USS *Philadelphia* were "marched in front of my windows with their guns pointing at the building."[86] She also suffered from the betrayal of some whom she had thought were friends, such as the marshal Charles B. Wilson and the policeman Robert Waipā Parker, now both in the employ of her jailers. Being under constant surveillance had caused a great strain and strengthened her desire to sail away. Besides the relief from surveillance, Kualapai has argued that the queen had carefully planned the journey in conjunction with a handful of advisers as a tactic to fight annexation.[87] The planning had to have been kept secret, or the republic would have withheld their passports.

The day the queen left, Kuaihelani Campbell, president of the women's Hui Aloha 'Āina, telephoned 'A'ima Nāwahī and asked to meet with her the following morning. They shared stories of their sorrow at the queen's departure and of their restless night, and then got down to work. 'A'ima suggested to Kuaihelani that they draft a document protesting annexation to be presented to President McKinley along with a similar document from the men's hui, and she assured Kuaihelani that as president of the hui she had the kuleana to sign the document on behalf of the entire group.[88] Again, this was all done secretly so that the republic would not sabotage their plan. In 'A'ima's letters to the queen, it is clear that she and the queen had discussed the idea prior to her departure, and that the queen had trusted 'A'ima to present it to Kuaihelani. 'A'ima and Kuaihelani became close friends from that day on, and, although Kuaihelani was the hui president, 'A'ima was the one who corresponded most often with Ke Ali'i and she shared her letters with Kuaihelani.[89]

Emma 'A'ima Nāwahī in her *Ke Aloha Aina* newspaper office. (originally published in John
G. M. Sheldon, *Ka Buke Moolelo o Hon. Joseph K. Nawahi*, Honolulu: Bulletin Pub. Co., 1908;
Courtesy of Tom Coffman)

    In her letters, 'A'ima describes how she watched over Kaulia and
Kalauokalani, even temporarily taking away from them the project of
drafting their protest document because some "traitorous friends" of
Kaulia's had gotten him drunk in an attempt to find out what the queen
was planning.[90] In other letters, 'A'ima said she mediated between Kaulia and Kalauokalani and even assisted in straightening out internal
problems within Hui Kālai'āina.[91] In December, 1896, 'A'ima told the
queen that she had to restrain the young men from conducting a petition drive before the proper time.[92]

    'A'ima also stressed to the queen the importance of letters from her
or her staff to the newspaper. In her letter of December 25, 1896, which
began, "E honi aku au i na lima palupalu i aloha nui ia" (I kiss your soft
hands which are dearly loved), she wrote, "E oluolu Kelii, e mea iho ia
Joe, a i ole ia Mrs. Nahaolelua paha, i kahi o laua e kakau mai no kahi
Nupepa Ke Aloha Aina. O ka ka Lahui ia e noke mai nei i ke kakau ia'u.
He makemake loa lakou e lohe mau no ka huakai a Kelii ame ka ike mau i
ko Kelii ola kino oiai oia i ka aina mamao" (Please, Ke Ali'i, mention to

Joe or Mrs. Nahaolelua for one of them to write for *Ke Aloha Aina* newspaper. The Lāhui persist in writing to me. They want to hear regularly about Her Majesty's trip and her health while she is in that distant country).[93]

In February, ʻAʻima reiterated the people's desire to hear from and about the queen: "Ua kohu pula kau maka kahi Nupepa i nei wa, kohu ipo aloha na ka lahui, oiai, o ko lakou aniani kilohi a hoonui ike ihola ia e ike ai i ke aka o Kalani e maaloalo ala i ke Kapitela hanohano o Wasinetona" (The newspaper is now the obsession of the people, it is like a darling sweetheart, since it is their mirror and magnifying glass through which they may see the reflection of Your Majesty moving around in the glorious Capital of Washington).[94] For ʻAʻima the newspapers, especially her own, were crucial in keeping up the spirits of the people. She wrote: "Ke hooikaika like nei maua me J. K. K. e hoolana mau i ka manao o ka lahui mamuli o ko maua wae ana ae i na mea ano nui i kupono no ka lehulehu mailoko ae o na Nupepa a me na leta nohoi a maua, a ma ia ano, ua like me he ume makeneki ala e hoopipili paa ia ana ka manao o ka lahui, a lilo na hana hapai kumuhana o na ano a pau e manao ia nei i mea ole" (I am working with J. K. K. [Kaulia] giving hope to the people by our selecting the important matters pertaining to the people from [other] newspapers and our letters. And this is like a magnet's pull firmly bonding the feelings of the people. And this makes all the different projects being planned seem easy).[95]

Both Testa's *Ka Makaainana* and *Ke Aloha Aina* ran news and commentary about the queen in every issue, assuring the public that her health was good and that she was in the United States to carry on the fight. Both papers selected and translated stories from newspapers in San Francisco, as ʻAʻima said. Joe Heleluhe seemingly preferred to send his letters to Testa, which appeared regularly in *Ka Makaainana* and infrequently in *Ke Aloha Aina*, and ʻAʻima apparently continued to excerpt her own personal letters for her paper.[96]

ʻAʻima wrote to the queen in March reporting that the republic also depended on the papers for news about her, but she added that her own newspaper was in danger of being shut down by them. The queen had offered to contribute toward a new printing press (apparently in order to free them from renting from the establishment press), but ʻAʻima refused by saying that the queen's living expenses were great in the foreign land and that instead she would "quietly bear it."[97] Then, the very next day, ʻAʻima wrote another letter reporting that a member of the oligarchy was trying to buy out her paper in order to stop it because of its advice to the people to continue their resistance as was done in the time of Joseph Nāwahī. 'A'ima laughed that they thought they could outwit her because she was a woman: "Keu nohoi ka hilahila ole la o ka manao ana o ka hana ihola keia e loaa ai ka lakou. No ka ike mai paha he wahine au a e puni wale hoi i ka lakou. Auwe! hilahila o — le —. Akaaka loa au i ko'u lohe ana ihola" (They are so shameless to plan to do this to get theirs. Because they know I am a woman they think I will be easily deceived by them. Auē! Shameless! I laughed long when I heard that).[98] The threats were serious, however, and later when the petition drive was going strong the republic shut down *Ke Aloha Aina* temporarily on the grounds that the paper was in debt $168 to Thrum's printing house. Fortunately, 'A'ima was able to raise the funds to pay Thrum and the paper resumed publication immediately.[99]

NĀ PALAPALA HO'OPI'I KŪ'Ē HO'OHUI 'ĀINA (PETITIONS PROTESTING ANNEXATION)

It was through these and other letters that the queen, 'A'ima Nāwahī, Kuaihelani Campbell, James Kaulia, and David Kalauokalani jointly planned the petition drive and other actions to protest the annexation treaty in 1897. When the queen heard about the treaty in June, she immediately wrote to the leaders of the hui: it became more urgent that McKinley receive the protests of the lāhui. The "fans," as Mrs. Nāwahī called them in code, actually letters of protest to McKinley, "woven" months earlier, had not been delivered to the president, because neither Joe Heleluhe nor Lili'uokalani had been granted an appointment. Now the queen wrote a cover letter sending the documents to McKinley. The "fans" informed McKinley that the people of Hawai'i trusted the U.S. government, and that their trust was partially based on the recognition of the independence of the kingdom supported by the United States in 1843. Their main message was "aole loa he kumu e keakea ia ai ka manaopaa luli ole o ka lahui Hawaii, no ka manao kuio, e hoihoi hou ia mai ke Aupuni Moi o Hawaii, a me ka Noho Moi o ka Moiwahine" (that no cause whatever can arise that will alter or change the mind of the Hawaiian people, and their desire to see the Monarchy restored, and the Throne occupied by [the] Queen).[100]

The queen understood that, however strongly worded, these letters were not sufficient to stop the treaty because Thurston, Kinney, and others were in Washington telling the press that the majority of Hawaiians desired annexation to the United States.[101] American politicians apparently cultivated a willful amnesia about the recent events in Hawaiʻi, which Cleveland had termed illegal and an act of war on the part of the United States. Thus a much bigger protest had to be mounted. The queen notified the hui presidents that it was time to carefully plan the petition protesting annexation. The project that the young men had been anticipating since December now saw its proper time.

Ke Aliʻi and the three hui were successful in planning over long distance, but it was not without difficulty. Their letters often used code because the republic officials were opening all mail to and from Ke Aliʻi. Sometimes one person would receive instructions in a letter from Ke Aliʻi before the others, which caused confusion and jealousy. In addition, they could not agree on the heading for the petitions. In early August 1897, Kalauokalani apparently received a letter from Heleluhe on behalf of the queen advising him to have everyone sign one petition protesting annexation, including the members of Hui Aloha ʻĀina. Shortly thereafter, rumors began that Hui Kālaiʻāina members, and perhaps Kalauokalani himself, were telling people that they should leave Hui Aloha ʻĀina and join Hui Kālaiʻāina. This naturally made ʻAʻima and the other members of Hui Aloha ʻĀina angry. However, the leaders met together soon thereafter to form a joint committee to coordinate their efforts.[102]

Ke Aliʻi ʻAi Moku saw the necessity of mounting a massive coordinated action, so she was not pleased to hear of the strife among the three hui. ʻAʻima published a letter dated "Ebbitt House, September 1, 1897," addressed to Kaulia. Although no signature was printed, it is clear that the letter is from Heleluhe on behalf of Ke Aliʻi. It reads in part:

> Kai no paha e hana ana la hoi oukou elike me ka maua i hai aku ai ia olua, oia hoi, e kuka like la olua, a e kahea ia la hoi ka Papa hooko a me ka Aha Kuwaena o na Hui a elua a iwaena oia halawai ana e noonoo ai oukou i ke poo o ka ka lahui kue no ka hoohui aina, a malalo la hoi oia poo e kakau inoa mai ai na makaaina [sic] aloha aina a pau loa, eia ka e lilo ana keia hana i mea e kuee ai
>
> (We thought that you folks were doing as we told you two [Kaulia and Kalauokalani], that is, for you two to confer together, and then call the

executive board and coalition committee of the two hui together and in that meeting to consider the heading for the lāhui's protest of annexation, and below that heading, all of the aloha 'āina maka'āinana are to sign their names, however, this is now becoming something to fight over.) [103]

This letter directed Kaulia to "hoopau i na manao kuee mawaena o oukou" (stop the conflicts among all of you) and ended with an order to them to separate the signatures of the women on pages marked "Hui Aloha Aina o na Wahine," which they did.

Around the same time 'A'ima wrote to the queen saying how important the queen's voice was to the people, and about her worry that Kalauokalani might be rushing his own petition. She wrote about the process this way: "O ko Kelii leo he mea nui ia. Ua hoao maua e kaomi a hiki i ka wa kupono o ka hana . . . a i loaa ai ka hoonaauao e i ka lahui, a i loaa like hoi he lokahi, alaila hapai no ka hana a hele like i mua" (Ke Ali'i's voice is the most important thing. We two ['A'ima and Kuaihelani] tried to hold back until the right time for the action . . . in order that the people get educated beforehand, and in order to get unity, and then take up the work and go forward together). [104] In addition to Ke Ali'i's direction and approval, we see here again the importance of the mature women's leadership and their care in handling the petition drive slowly and properly so that it would succeed. 'A'ima represents the young men, especially Kalauokalani, as impetuously rushing ahead. But eventually he responded to the women's direction and all three hui finally managed to coordinate their efforts. The three hui seem to have done little without the queen's knowledge and approval during this time. These coordinated actions between the three hui in Hawai'i and the queen and Heleluhe in Washington resulted, as we know, in the defeat of the treaty of annexation.

BONES OF MY BONES: CONCLUSION

In spite of the written protests, the defeated treaty, and the queen's contestation of the racist representations of herself and her lāhui, in May 1898 Lili'uokalani heard that the U.S. Congress had decided to take Hawai'i. In her diary that day she wrote "Auwe! Kuu aloha i kuu Aina hanau ame kuu lahui aloha. Ka iwi o kuu iwi ke koko o kuu koko. Aloha! Aloha! Aloha!" (Auē! My love for my birthland and my beloved people. Bones of my bones, blood of my blood. Aloha! Aloha! Aloha!).[105] At home in Hawai'i, the po'e aloha 'āina had already been experiencing the ill effects of the United States's war to take the Philippines. *Ke Aloha Aina* reported that the streets were full of U.S. soldiers, and the paper protested that the government of Hawai'i had spent $10,000 to host the soldiers who were not fighting on behalf of Hawai'i's people.[106] In the midst of the U.S. drive for empire, there was little left for Ke Ali'i 'Ai Moku to do except to go home to her people. She arrived home on August 2 just past midnight, greeted by a crowd, including her niece Ke Kamāli'iwahine Ka'iulani, her nephew Ke Kamāli'ikāne Kawananakoa, and the presidents of the hui. She spoke, in tears, to the crowd, saying that the news about annexation was very painful to all of them but that she felt the circle around her there at the wharf in the middle of the night meant they were saying "eia no makou a pau mahope Ou e ke alii, no ke kupaa i ke aloha i ka aina" (we are all still behind You, Ke Ali'i, steadfast in love for the land).[107]

The crowd then followed her to Washington Place, where the columns, doors, and chairs of the house had been draped in forest greenery by a reception committee. James Kaulia read an official welcome from the lāhui, and Rev. E. S. Timoteo said a prayer. In the morning, the Bana Lāhui serenaded Ke Ali'i 'Ai Moku while she ate breakfast. For the readers who couldn't be there, 'A'ima's newspaper reported:

> Ua kipa aku makou e ike i ke Alii ka Moiwahine Liliuokalani a ua ike kumaka aku hoi Iaia, me he mea la, aia no Oia iluna o Kona nohoalii kahi i noho ai, a o Kana mau kamailio ana, me he mea la, e rula ana no Oia i ka pono o Kona lahuikanaka Ana i aloha ai. He oia mau no Kona kulana kapukapu alii, a aole loa e hiki ke hoololi ia ae ia mea mai Iaia ae, a hiki i na la hope o Kona ola ana.
>
> (We went to see the Ali'i, Mō'īwahine Lili'uokalani, and we did see her in person, and it was as if She were still on her throne, and her conversation was as if She were [still] ruling for the pono of Her people whom She loves. Her stature as a sacred ali'i continues, and this can never be changed or taken from Her, until the last days of her life.)[108]

Indeed, the po'e aloha 'āina continued to regard her as their ali'i for the rest of her life. She lived to the age of seventy-nine, passing away on

November 11, 1917. Her funeral was the last grand, solemn ceremony of the ali'i nui culture. Since then, descendants of the po'e aloha 'āina have remembered her with deep respect and admiration. Although she suffered the loss of her nation, she did not have to suffer the shame she feared because, in her words, she was the ruler "from whose hands national independence was forcibly wrested."[109] Instead, her own generation and the generations after have respected her for her decisions to work within the law, because her doing so now means that her lāhui are able to press their claims under international law.[110] Although, as Siba Grovogui so concisely states, "the aim of international law has been to justify or facilitate Western hegemony,"[111] Hawai'i's unique position as the first non-European member of the family of nations may allow it to regain its status as an independent nation, and, further, to join the movement to reform international law so that other indigenous peoples are treated fairly. The queen's careful actions have, at the very least, kept these possibilities open at the international level.

In addition, Lili'uokalani is still highly regarded as a composer; over thirty of her songs have been recorded by many different contemporary artists. Through these recordings and the *Queen's Songbook* people are able to hear and read her mele. Ke Ali'i 'Ai Moku also left a substantial legacy in writing, including her book *Hawaii's Story by Hawaii's Queen* and her translation of the *Kumulipo*, both still in print.

It is important to emphasize that all Lili'uokalani's official protests were translated into Hawaiian, as was *Hawaii's Story* and many of the magazine and newspaper articles written about her, which included excerpts of her letters in the newspapers. The newspapers played an important role in sustaining the lāhui as one across the archipelago, while people were separated when imprisoned and while the queen was far away. More important, perhaps, is that the newspapers provided a site for the practice of freedom in a time of repressive policy by a colonial government. These newspapers now perform a similar function: when they are used to restore Kanaka Maoli in history and deepen an understanding of these events, the connection to the ancestors and the queen is restored. Today, the knowledge that is reemerging similarly helps to keep the lāhui together.

Lili'uokalani's dedication and commitment to the welfare of her nation were extraordinary, and her commitment to peaceful resistance was celebrated both in its time and, perhaps even more so, now. A mele composed for her in 1893 by Mrs. Kawohikapulani contains the line, "Kaulana o Liliu i ka maluhia / Ma na welelau o ka honua" (Liliu is famous for peace / To the ends of the earth).[112] The queen's insistence on peace but also on active resistance forms part of her important political legacy; her country's government was taken not because she was weak but because she acted boldly.

Queen Lili'uokalani served as the ali'i nui within a constitutional monarchy that was a blend of Hawaiian, English, and American political traditions. She was the only woman of color at the time who was a head of state recognized and respected around the world. At the same time, she was an ali'i hānau o ka 'āina, born with the mana and kuleana to lead the nation. An equally important part of her legacy is that she was committed to democratic ideals and processes, even though she is portrayed by haole historians as a tyrannical monarch. In fact, in 1897, when a reporter told her that perhaps her niece Ka'iulani would take the throne, Ke Ali'i responded, "na ka lahui ke Alii, a no ka lahui na Alii" (it is up to the lāhui who the Ali'i is, and the Ali'i are of or belong to the lāhui).[113] This means that the people decide who their leader is to be. The queen's commitment to open and inclusive processes, and to working with her people and encouraging them to work in coalition despite their differences, serve as inspiration to her lāhui today, who are carrying on the struggle for their land.

The act of deposing Queen Lili'uokalani was the culmination of seventy years of U.S. missionary presence in Hawai'i. Step by step, the religion, the land, the language, and finally the government were overtaken by the drive for imperial domination. We Kanaka Maoli have now suffered more than one hundred years of nearly total U.S. hegemony: of being made into a minority without voting power in our own land; of being excluded and marginalized in important institutions, such as higher education; of being drafted to fight the U.S. wars in foreign lands; of fighting for scraps of entitlements to housing, education, and health care funding; of watching our language nearly become extinct; of watching the poorest be evicted from their tents on the sand; and of experiencing the psychic confusion of being raised ignorant of the mo'olelo, 'ōlelo, and culture of our own grandparents. But as the po'e aloha 'āina said on August 13, 1898 — he oia mau nō kākou: we endure.

We are inspired today by Ke Ali'i 'Ai Moku's strength, intelligence, dignity, and commitment to what was pono for her land and her people.

She skillfully moved in both haole and Kanaka worlds. So it is now up to us to weigh how much and which aspects of haole culture have been (and are) harmful to us and which are useful, and which aspects of the culture of our ancestors we wish to revive and perpetuate. We too are cloaked in haole culture and language but remain 'Ōiwi as the descendants of the people who have lived in the islands from time immemorial. Now *we* must decide how to govern ourselves and how we want to live together as a lāhui.

Appendix A

TEXT OF THE OBJECTIVES OF *NUPEPA KUOKOA*,

AS PUBLISHED THEREIN, OCTOBER 1861

Akahi. He olelo hoike i na mea nui a maikai a pau, i hanaia ma na aina e, e ku ana i ka pono o na kanaka Hawaii ke ike.

Alua. E hoolaha ia ana na manao haole o kela aina o keia aina; ke ano o ko lakou noho ana, hana ana, ao ana, ikaika ana, kuonoono ana, ia mea ae, ia mea ae, i hiki ai i kanaka ke ike ia mau mea, a e lilo ai i poe like me na mea naauao.

Akolu. E hoolahaia hoi na oihana mahiai pono, a e hoike i na mea paahana maikai e hiki ai ke mahi e like me na haole naauao. E paipai hoi keia pepa i na hana me ka molowa ole.

Aha. A loaa mai na mea pai kii, e hoonaniia ka pepa i na kii e hoike ana i ke ano o kanaka, a me na mea o na aina e.

Alima. E kupaa ana na mea o keia pepa ma ka oiaio o na olelo a pau, aka, aole e paiia na olelo hoopaapaa o na aoao hoomana.

Aono. E ku no keia pepa ma ka malama aloha i ka Moi kane, ame ka Moiwahine, i ka Haku o Hawaii, a me na alii iho, e ao aku ana i ka hoolohe i na kanawai, a me ka malama i ka moi, oia ka pono mua o na kanaka a pau.

Ahiku. E paiia ana hoi ma keia pepa, na nuhou o keia pae aina, i na lohe pono a pau e ku i ka makemake o kanaka ke heluhelu. O ka manao nui ma keia pepa, ka hoolaha aku i na mea hoonaauao a pau i ku i ko kanaka pono ke ike maopopo, i hoolikeia i ko lakou noho ana me ko na haole.

Appendix B

SONGS COMPOSED BY QUEEN LILIʻUOKALANI

DURING HER IMPRISONMENT

TITLE	DATE	SOURCE	NOTES
Kilioulani	Mar. 22, 1895	"He Buke Mele Hawaii"	
Mai Wakinekona A Iolani Hale/	Apr. 1, 1895	*Ka Makaainana*	First and
Hoonanea A Hookuene O Liliu		*Buke Mele Lahui,* 4	second verses
		"He Buke Mele Hawaii," 126	of Hoonanea
Lokahi Ka Manao me ka Lahui/	Apr. 8, 1895	*Ka Makaainana*	
Aha-Koa Keikei o ke Kulana		*Buke Mele Lahui,* 11	
Umia ke Aloha i Paa Iloko/	Apr. 15, 1895	*Ka Makaainana*	
Inoa Wehi No ka Oiwi Pokii/		*Buke Mele Lahui,* 10	
He Inoa Wehi no Kalanianaole (1)		"He Buke Mele Hawaii," 127	
Ike Hou Ana i ka Nani/	Apr. 22, 1895	*Ka Makaainana*	Third verse of
			Hoonanea

TITLE	DATE	SOURCE	NOTES
Hoonanea A Hookuene O Liliu/		*Buke Mele Lahui*, 5	
He Inoa Wehi no Kalanianaole (2)		"He Buke Mele Hawaii," 128	
He Inoa Wehi no Kalanianaole (3)		"He Buke Mele Hawaii," 129	
He Inoa Wehi no Kalanianaole (4)		"He Buke Mele Hawaii," 130	
Ke Aloha a ka Haku	Mar. 22, 1895	*Queen's Songbook*, 60	
Kuu Pua i Paoakalani	Mar. 20, 1895	*Queen's Songbook*, 65	
Ka Wai Apo Lani	Oct. 1, 1896	*Queen's Songbook*, 185	
Ke Aloha Aina/		*Queen's Songbook*, 195	
Kānaenae no Iosepa K. Nāwahīokalaniʻōpuʻu	Oct. 5, 1896 Sept. 30, 1896	*Ka Makaainana*, 1 Sheldon, *Ka Buke Moolelo o Hon. Joseph K. Nawahi*	

Notes

Introduction

1 Caroline Ralston, "Hawaii 1778–1854: Some Aspects of *Maka'āinana* Response to Rapid Cultural Change," *Journal of Pacific History* 19, no. 1 (1984): 21.

2 Haunani-Kay Trask, *From a Native Daughter: Colonialism and Sovereignty in Hawai'i* (Monroe, Maine: Common Courage Press, 1993), 154–55.

3 Gavan Daws, *Shoal of Time: A History of the Hawaiian Islands* (Honolulu: University of Hawai'i Press, 1968), 291.

4 Ralph S. Kuykendall, *The Hawaiian Kingdom. Vol. 3: 1874–1893, The Ka-lakaua Dynasty* (Honolulu: University of Hawai'i Press, 1967), 187.

5 Amy Ku'uleialoha Stillman, "Of the People Who Love the Land: Vernacular History in the Poetry of Modern Hawaiian Hula," *Amerasia Journal* 28, no. 3 (2002): 85.

6 Trask, *Native Daughter*, 153.

7 Nancy Jane Morris, "Ka Loea Kalaiaina, 1898: A Study of a Hawaiian Language Newspaper as a Historical Reference Source," (master's thesis, University of Hawai'i, 1975).

8 Ngugi wa Thiong'o, *Decolonising the Mind: The Politics of Language in African Literature* (Portsmouth, N.H.: Heinemann, 1986), 3.

9 Trask, *Native Daughter*, 147–49.

10 The committee consisted of physician and activist Kekuni Blaisdell, indigenous rights activist Nālani Minton, activist Leandra Wai, entrepreneur

Maile Meyer, and me. We met with Guy Kaulukukui and Tom Cummings of the Bishop Museum Education Department.

11 See documents filed at The Hague at www.AlohaQuest.com/arbitration/memorial_government.htm (annex 22).

12 James Baldwin, "A Talk to Teachers," in *The Graywolf Annual Five: Multi-Cultural Literacy*, ed. Rick Simonson and Scott Walker (Saint Paul: Graywolf Press, 1988 [1963]), 8.

13 Ibid.

14 An exception is Tom Coffman, *Nation Within* (Kāneʻohe, Hawaiʻi: Epi-Center Press, 1998), whose account is based on earlier versions of this work.

15 Michel Foucault, *Power/Knowledge: Selected Interviews and Other Writings, 1972–1977* (New York: Pantheon Books, 1980), 81.

16 Vilsoni Hereniko, "Indigenous Knowledge and Academic Imperialism," in *Remembrance of Pacific Pasts: An Invitation to Remake History*, ed. Robert Borofsky (Honolulu: University of Hawaiʻi Press, 2000), 82.

17 Edward Said, *Culture and Imperialism* (New York: Vintage Books, 1993); Michel de Certeau, *The Practice of Everyday Life*, trans. Steven Rendall (Berkeley: University of California Press, 1984), 23.

18 Lawrence W. Levine, *Black Culture and Black Consciousness* (New York: Oxford University Press, 1977), 12.

19 Ashis Nandy, *The Intimate Enemy: Loss and Recovery of Self under Colonialism* (New York: Oxford University Press, 1988), xv.

20 Michel Foucault, "The Subject and Power," in *Michel Foucault: Beyond Structuralism and Hermeneutics*, 2nd ed., ed. Hubert L. Dreyfus and Paul Rabinow (Chicago: University of Chicago Press, 1983), 83.

21 Ibid., 81–83.

22 Nandy, *Intimate Enemy*, xiv.

23 Michel Foucault, *Discipline and Punish: The Birth of the Prison*, trans. Alan Sheridan (New York: Vintage, 1995).

24 Foucault, "Subject and Power," 210.

25 Ibid., 211.

26 Certeau, *Practice*, xiii.

27 Levine, *Black Culture*, 11.

28 Partha Chatterjee, *The Nation and Its Fragments: Colonial and Postcolonial Histories* (Princeton: Princeton University Press, 1993), 6.

29 Ibid., 7.

30 See Chandra Talpade Mohanty, "Under Western Eyes: Feminist Scholarship and Colonial Discourses," in *Third World Women and the Politics of Feminism*, ed. Chandra Talpade Mohanty, Ann Russo, and Lourdes Torres (Bloomington: Indiana University Press, 1991), 51–80; Anne Mc-

Clintock, *Imperial Leather: Race, Gender, and Sexuality in the Colonial Contest* (New York: Routledge, 1995); Gayatri Chakravorty Spivak, ed., *In Other Worlds: Essays in Cultural Politics* (New York: Routledge, 1988); Ruth Elynia Mabanglo, "Metaphors of Protest: Anti-Colonial Themes in Tagalog Poetry," paper presented at the conference "Multi-Ethnic Literatures of the United States," University of Hawai'i, Honolulu, 1997.

31 Gayatri Chakravorty Spivak, "Can the Subaltern Speak?" in *Colonial Discourse and Post-Colonial Theory*, ed. Patrick Williams and Laura Chrisman (New York: Columbia University Press, 1994), 104.

32 Ibid.

33 Mary Kawena Pukui and Samuel H. Elbert, *Hawaiian Dictionary*, rev. ed. (Honolulu: University of Hawai'i Press, 1986), 130.

34 Levine, *Black Culture*, 8.

35 Ibid., 11.

36 Certeau, *Practice*, xix.

37 Ibid., 32.

38 Larry Kimura, "Native Hawaiian Culture," in *Report on the Culture, Needs, and Concerns of Native Hawaiians*, vol. 1 (Washington, D.C.: Native Hawaiians Study Commission, 1983), 182.

39 Pukui and Elbert, *Hawaiian Dictionary*, 240.

40 See Joyce N. Chinen, Kathleen O. Kane, and Ida M. Yoshinaga, eds., *Women in Hawai'i: Sites, Identities, and Voices, Social Process in Hawai'i* 38 (1997); Sally Engle Merry, *Colonizing Hawai'i: The Cultural Power of Law* (Princeton: Princeton University Press, 2000).

41 Hereniko, "Indigenous Knowledge," 84.

1   Early Struggles with the Foreigners

1 See Merry, *Colonizing Hawai'i*, for a good discussion of the adoption of Western law in Hawai'i.

2 Gananath Obeyesekere, *The Apotheosis of Captain Cook: European Mythmaking in the Pacific* (Princeton: Princeton University Press, 1997), 163.

3 Thos. G. Thrum, "Brief Sketch of the Life and Labors of S. M. Kamakau, Hawaiian Historian," in *Twenty-Sixth Annual Report of the Hawaiian Historical Society* (Honolulu: Paradise of the Pacific Press, 1918), 47.

4 S. M. Kamakau, *Ruling Chiefs of Hawaii*, rev. ed. (Honolulu: Kamehameha Schools Press, 1992), vii.

5 Samuel Mānaiakalani Kamakau, *Ke Kumu Aupuni* (Honolulu: Ke Kumu Lama, 'Ahahui 'Ōlelo Hawai'i, 1996), 27–45.

6 Ibid., 27.

7   Ibid., 28.

8   Ibid., 33.

9   Ibid., 29.

10   Ibid., 36–40.

11   Ibid., 34–35.

12   Ibid., 41.

13   Herb Kawainui Kāne, in *Current Anthropology*'s forum on Robert Borofsky, "Cook, Lono, Obeyesekere, and Sahlins," *Current Anthropology* 38, no. 2 (April 1997): 265.

14   Kanaka nicknamed others with Hawaiian names, and also Hawaiianized their English names. Cook was also called "Kuke," which is now the standard way to refer to his name in Hawaiian (Albert J. Schütz, personal communication, 2003).

15   Dipesh Chakrabarty, *Provincializing Europe: Postcolonial Thought and Historical Difference* (Princeton: Princeton University Press, 2000), 72.

16   Kamakau, *Ke Kumu Aupuni*, 41–42.

17   Ibid., 42.

18   Ibid., 43.

19   Ibid., 44.

20   For an excellent analysis of the first conflicts over "property" and "stealing," see R. D. K. Herman, "The Dread Taboo, Human Sacrifice, and Pearl Harbor," *Contemporary Pacific* 8, no. 1 (spring 1996): 86–89.

21   See Obeyesekere, *Apotheosis*; Marshall Sahlins, *Islands of History* (Chicago: University of Chicago Press, 1987), 104–135; Kamakau, *Ke Kumu Aupuni*, 55–56; Kamakau, *Ruling Chiefs*, 101–3.

22   Ralph S. Kuykendall, *The Hawaiian Kingdom. Vol. 1: 1778–1854, Foundation and Transformation* (Honolulu: University of Hawai'i Press, 1938), 19.

23   Kamakau, *Ke Kumu Aupuni*, 57 (my translation).

24   Kamakau, *Ruling Chiefs*, 104.

25   Kuykendall, *Hawaiian Kingdom*, vol. 1, 24–25.

26   Ibid., 39–44.

27   Greg Dening, *The Death of William Gooch: A History's Anthropology*, rev. ed. (Honolulu: University of Hawai'i Press, 1995), 41.

28   Kuykendall, *Hawaiian Kingdom*, vol. 1, 40–41.

29   Kuykendall, *Hawaiian Kingdom*, vol. 1, 57.

30   A. W. Crosby, "Hawaiian Depopulation as a Model for the Amerindian Experience," in *Epidemics and Ideas: Essays on the Historical Perception of Pestilence*, ed. Terence Ranger and Paul Slack (New York: Cambridge University Press, 1992), 177.

31   Ibid., 190, 192–93.

32   Joseph M. Poepoe, "He moolelo no Kamehameha I Ka Na'i Aupuni o Hawaii," *Ka Na'i Aupuni*, 5 Sept. 1906.

33 David Malo, "On the Decrease of Population on the Hawaiian Islands," trans. Lorrin Andrews, *Hawaiian Spectator* 2, no. 2 (April 1839): 122–24.

34 Ibid., 125.

35 Ibid., 128.

36 Ibid., 130.

37 Denise Noelani Manuela Arista, "Davida Malo: Ke Kanaka O Ka Huliau/David Malo: A Hawaiian of the Time of Change" (master's thesis, University of Hawai'i, 1998), 109.

38 Lilikalā Kame'eleihiwa, *Native Land and Foreign Desires: Pehea Lā E Pono Ai?* (Honolulu: Bishop Museum, 1992), 69.

39 Kamakau, *Ke Kumu Aupuni*, 229.

40 Ibid., 230. Compare the English version in *Ruling Chiefs*, 237. I am indebted to Puhi Adams and Kalani Makekau-Whittaker for bringing to my attention this particular example.

41 Marshall Sahlins, *Historical Ethnography. Vol. 1, Anahulu: The Anthropology of History in the Kingdom of Hawai'i*, by Patrick Kirch and Marshall Sahlins (Chicago: University of Chicago Press, 1992), 57–82, cited in Merry, *Colonizing Hawai'i*, 40.

42 Carol A. McClennan, "Hawai'i Turns to Sugar: The Rise of Plantation Centers, 1860–1880," *Hawaiian Journal of History* 31 (1997): 111.

43 Harold Napoleon, *Yuuyaraq: The Way of the Human Being* (Fairbanks: Center for Cross-Cultural Studies, College of Rural Alaska, 1991), 10, 11.

44 "No Ka Pono Kahiko A Me Ka Pono Hou," *Ka Lama Hawaii*, 1 Aug. 1834.

45 Napoleon, *Yuuyaraq*, 12–13.

46 Ibid., 15.

47 Crosby, "Hawaiian Depopulation," 183–84.

48 Napoleon, *Yuuyaraq*, 16.

49 Ibid., 17.

50 Kamakau, *Ruling Chiefs*, 9.

51 Kamakau, *Ke Kumu Aupuni*, 209.

52 Ibid.

53 Kuykendall, *Hawaiian Kingdom*, vol. 1, 64.

54 Kame'eleihiwa, *Native Land*, 76.

55 Ibid., 78.

56 Ibid.; Kamakau, *Ke Kumu Aupuni*, 216.

57 Kame'eleihiwa, *Native Land*, 79.

58 Kuykendall, *Hawaiian Kingdom*, vol. 1, 64.

59 Kame'eleihiwa, *Native Land*, 81, 82.

60 Hiram Bingham, *A Residence of Twenty-One Years in the Sandwich Islands* (Rutland, Vt.: Tuttle, [1849] 1981), 17.

61 For the pro-missionary view, see Bingham, *Residence*; William Ellis *Poly-*

nesian Researches: Hawaii (Rutland, Vt.: Tuttle, 1969); Mary C. Alexander, *William Patterson Alexander in Kentucky, the Marquesas, Hawaii* (Honolulu: privately printed, 1934); LaRue W. Piercy, *Hawaii's Missionary Saga: Sacrifice and Godliness in Paradise* (Honolulu: Mutual Publishing, 1992); and others. For the view of missionaries in a less-favorable light, see Kameʻeleihiwa, *Native Land*, and Kamakau, *Ruling Chiefs*.

62 Lawrence E. Fuchs, *Hawaii Pono 'Hawaii the Excellent': An Ethnic and Political History* (Honolulu: Bess Press, 1961), 8–12; William Adam Russ Jr., *The Hawaiian Revolution (1893–1894)* (Selinsgrove, Pa.: Susquehanna University Press, 1992 [1959]), 3–6; Daws, *Shoal of Time*, 61–105. The most balanced account in Hawaiian historiography is probably Kuykendall, *Hawaiian Kingdom*, vol. 1, 100–52; for the history of U.S. missions, it is William R. Hutchison, *Errand to the World: American Protestant Thought and Foreign Missions* (Chicago: University of Chicago Press, 1993).

63 Albert J. Schütz, *The Voices of Eden: A History of Hawaiian Language Studies* (Honolulu: University of Hawaiʻi Press, 1994), 85–87.

64 Hutchison, *Errand to the World*, 5, 7.

65 Ibid., 65.

66 Ibid., 67.

67 Bingham, *Residence*, 58–59.

68 Hutchison, *Errand to the World*, 67.

69 Hawaiian Mission Children's Society, *Missionary Album: Portraits and Biographical Sketches of the American Protestant Missionaries to the Hawaiian Islands*, enlarged, sesquicentennial ed. (Honolulu: Hawaiian Mission Children's Society, 1969), 7.

70 Patricia Grimshaw, *Paths of Duty: American Missionary Wives in Nineteenth-Century Hawaii* (Honolulu: University of Hawaiʻi Press, 1989), 27.

71 Kamakau, *Ke Kumu Aupuni*, 246.

72 Ibid., 242.

73 Schütz, *Voices of Eden*, 71.

74 See Walter D. Mignolo, *The Darker Side of the Renaissance: Literacy, Territoriality, and Colonization* (Ann Arbor: University of Michigan Press, 1995), 82–83, 122.

75 Andrews, quoted in Schütz, *Voices of Eden*, 157.

76 Schütz, *Voices of Eden*, 157.

77 Hiram Bingham, *O Ke Kumumua na na Kamalii; He Palapala E Ao aku i na Kamalii Ike Ole i ka Heluhelu Palapala.* (Oahu: Mea Pai Palapala Na Na Misionari, 1835), 16.

78 Ibid., 123.

79 Kamakau, *Ke Kumu Aupuni*, 259.

80 Bingham, *Residence*, 178.

81 Marjorie Sinclair, *Nāhiʻenaʻena: Sacred Daughter of Hawaiʻi* (Honolulu: University of Hawaiʻi Press, 1976).

82 Marion Kelly, *Loko Iʻa o Heʻeia: Heʻeia Fishpond* (Honolulu: Department of Anthropology, Bishop Museum, 1975), 7.

83 In Bingham, *Residence*, 457; quoted from a resolution of "the mission, at their convention in June [1834]."

84 See Benedict Anderson, *Imagined Communities: Reflections on the Origin and Spread of Nationalism*, rev. ed. (New York: Verso, 1991).

85 Kamakau, *Ruling Chiefs*, 330–32.

86 Ibid., 366.

87 Ibid., 362.

88 David Keanu Sai, personal communication, 2001; Kuykendall, *The Hawaiian Kingdom*, 221–26.

89 See Kameʻeleihiwa, *Native Land*, for "pono" as the legitimating concept for government.

90 Merry, *Colonizing Hawaiʻi*, 89.

91 Kamakau, *Ruling Chiefs*, 370.

92 For a short time after Kamāmalu's death, and the ascension of Lot Kapuāiwa to the throne (Kamehameha V), the mōʻī's father Kekuanaoa served as kuhina nui, but that was a temporary measure until the mōʻī could abolish the office as he planned.

93 *Kumu Kanawai a me Na Kanawai o ko Hawaii Pae Aina* (reprint; Green Valley, Nev.: Ted Adameck, [1842] 1994), 5. The five aliʻiwahine were Kekauonohi, Kekauluohi, Konia, Keohokalole, and Hoapiliwahine (Kaheiheimalie).

94 For Kekauonohi, see Kamakau, *Ruling Chiefs*, 397; for Keʻelikōlani, see Merry, *Colonizing Hawaiʻi*, 163.

95 Kamakau, *Ruling Chiefs*, 370.

96 *Ka Elele* (Honolulu), 15 July 1845, 57–59; *Friend* (Honolulu), August 1845, 118–19.

97 Ibid.

98 Ibid.

99 W. D. Alexander, "A Brief History of Land Titles in the Hawaiian Kingdom," in *Hawaiian Almanac and Annual for 1891* (Honolulu: Press Publishing Co., 1890), 105.

100 Keanu Sai has pointed out, however, that neither was the Hawaiian system "communal," as Kameʻeleihiwa and others sometimes describe it (David Keanu Sai, personal communication, 2001).

101 Kameʻeleihiwa, *Native Land*, 26.

102 See Moses N. Nakuina, *Moolelo Hawaii o Pakaa a Me Ku-a-Pakaa* (Ho-

nolulu: Kalamakū Press, 1991 [1902]), or the translation by Esther T. Mookini and Sarah Nākoa, *The Wind Gourd of Laʻamaomao* (Honolulu: Kalamakū Press, 1990).

103 "No ka Pono Kahiko a me ka Pono Hou," *Ka Lama Hawaii*, 1 Aug. 1834.

104 Kameʻeleihiwa, *Native Land*, 22.

105 Joseph M. Poepoe, "Ka Moolelo Hawaii Kahiko," *Ka Naʻi Aupuni*, 1 Feb.–4 Aug. 1906.

106 Kamakau, *Ke Kumu Aupuni*, 33.

107 Jonathan K. Kamakawiwoʻole Osorio, *Dismembering Lāhui: A History of the Hawaiian Nation to 1887* (Honolulu: University of Hawaiʻi Press, 2002), 49.

108 Alexander, "Brief History," 109.

109 Ibid., 112.

110 Osorio, *Dismembering Lāhui*, 44.

111 Ibid., 50.

112 Kameʻeleihiwa, *Native Land*, 155.

113 Ibid., 52.

114 Ibid., 54.

115 "No ka Pono Kahiko."

116 Osorio, *Dismembering Lāhui*.

117 Ibid., 49.

118 "No ka Pono Kahiko."

119 Kameʻeleihiwa, *Native Land*, 302–6.

120 *Kumu Kanawai*, 5; Osorio, *Dismembering Lāhui*, 45, 69, 109, 118, 138, 149, 163, 228, 247.

2 *Ka Hoku o ka Pakipika*: Emergence of
the Native Voice in Print

1 Ralph S. Kuykendall, *The Hawaiian Kingdom. Vol. 2: 1854–1874, Twenty Critical Years* (Honolulu: University of Hawaiʻi Press, 1953), 110.

2 Sinclair, *Nāhiʻenaʻena*.

3 Kuykendall, *Hawaiian Kingdom*, vol. 2, 106–7.

4 Edward D. Beechert, *Working in Hawaiʻi: A Labor History* (Honolulu: University of Hawaiʻi Press, 1985), 61.

5 Ibid.

6 See Kuykendall, *Hawaiian Kingdom*, vol. 2, 65–66.

7 Ibid., 86.

8 Ibid., 95.

9   Noel J. Kent, *Hawaii: Islands under the Influence* (Honolulu: University of Hawaiʻi Press, 1993), 36.

10   *Polynesian*, 17 Apr. 1858.

11   Ibid.

12   Anderson, *Imagined Communities*, 14.

13   Michel Foucault, *The History of Sexuality. Vol. 1: An Introduction*, trans. Robert Hurley (New York: Vintage, 1990), 140–41.

14   Hawaiian Mission Children's Society, *Missionary Album*, 34–35.

15   Quoted in Alexander, *William Patterson Alexander*, 456.

16   Ibid., 454.

17   Arthur C. Alexander, *Koloa Plantation, 1835–1935: A History of the Oldest Hawaiian Sugar Plantation* (Līhuʻe, Hawaiʻi: Kauaʻi Historical Society, 1937), 4–5.

18   Max Weber, *The Protestant Ethic and the Spirit of Capitalism*, trans. Talcott Parsons (New York: Scribner, 1958), 157, 158, 159.

19   See Beechert, *Working in Hawaiʻi*, 59–60.

20   *Pacific Commercial Advertiser*, 2 July 1857. For more on the attempted legal ban of hula, see Noenoe K. Silva, "He Kanawai e Hoopau i Na Hula Kuolo: The Political Economy of Banning the Hula," *Hawaiian Journal of History* 34 (2000): 29–48.

21   *Polynesian*, 1 May 1858.

22   Weber, *Protestant Ethic*, 157.

23   Ibid., 172.

24   Ibid., 166.

25   Castle, quoted in Kent, *Hawaii*, 28.

26   Benjamin R. Tillman, "The Race Question," *Van Norden's Magazine* (April 1907): 19–28, quoted in Lee D. Baker, *From Savage to Negro: Anthropology and the Construction of Race, 1896–1954* (Berkeley: University of California Press, 1998), 75.

27   Winthrop D. Jordan, *The White Man's Burden: Historical Origins of Racism in the United States* (New York: Oxford University Press, 1974), 129.

28   Baker, *Savage*, 13–14.

29   Hutchison, *Errand to the World*, 70.

30   Baker, *Savage*, 12.

31   Ibid., 12.

32   Thomas F. Gossett, *Race: The History of an Idea in America* (Dallas: Southern Methodist University Press, 1963), 31.

33   Helen Geracimos Chapin, "Newspapers of Hawaiʻi, 1834 to 1903: From 'He liona' to the 'Pacific Cable,'" *Hawaiian Journal History* 18 (1984): 67.

34   Helen Geracimos Chapin, *Shaping History: The Role of Newspapers in Hawaiʻi* (Honolulu: University of Hawaiʻi Press, 1996), 60.

35 John E. Reinecke, *Language and Dialect in Hawaii: A Sociolinguistic History to 1935* (Honolulu: University of Hawai'i Press, 1969), 70.

36 Esther K. Mookini, *The Hawaiian Newspapers* (Honolulu: Topgallant Publishing 1974), 15; Chapin, *Shaping History*, 56.

37 J. H. Kānepu'u, "Mooolelo o ka Hookumu ana o ka Hoku o ka Pakipika," *Ka Hoku o ka Pakipika*, 14 November 1861.

38 Kuykendall, *Hawaiian Kingdom*, vol. 2, 99.

39 *Ka Hoku Loa*, 2 July 1859.

40 Ibid., Sept. 1861.

41 *Ka Hoku Loa*, Dec. 1861.

42 *Ka Hoku Loa*, Jan. 1862.

43 The first editor of *Ka Hoku o ka Pakipika*, J. W. H. Kauwahi, also resisted this cultural imperialism by insisting on the legitimacy of native medicinal practices; in 1867, he helped to form the 'Ahahui Lā'au Lapa'au to challenge the laws forbidding use of native medicine. See Malcolm Nāea Chun, *Must We Wait in Despair: The 1867 Report of the 'Ahahui Lā'au Lapa'au of Wailuku, Maui on Native Hawaiian Health* (Honolulu: First People's Productions, 1994).

44 John Emerson, writing in *Ka Hoku Loa*, Nov. 1861. Emerson uses the word "lapuwale" in the first two quotations, which I have translated as "worthless" (following Pukui and Elbert, *Hawaiian Dictionary*); the word "lapu," however, Pukui and Elbert gloss as "ghost, apparition, phantom, specter." Emerson may (also) have intended the latter.

45 Pukui and Elbert, *Hawaiian Dictionary*, 257.

46 Chapin, "Newspapers," 52.

47 *Ka Hae Hawaii*, 5 Mar. 1856.

48 Ibid.

49 Kamehameha IV, writing in *Ka Hae Hawaii*, 5 Mar. 1856.

50 *Ka Hae Hawaii*, 18 Sept. 1861.

51 Ibid., 25 Sept. 1861.

52 Ibid., 19 Mar. 1956.

53 Ibid., 11 Sept. 1861.

54 Kamakau, *Ruling Chiefs of Hawaii*, 335.

55 Ibid., 337.

56 *Ka Hae Hawaii*, 11 Sept. 1861.

57 Ibid., 28 Aug. 1861.

58 Ibid., 18 Sept. 1861.

59 Ibid.; G. W. Kahiolo, *He Moolelo no Kamapuaa*, tran. Esther T. Mookini and Erin C. Neizman, with David Tom (Honolulu: Hawaiian Studies Program, University of Hawai'i, Mānoa, 1978 [1861]).

60 Mookini et al., in Kahiolo, *He Moolelo*, xii.

61 Joseph S. Emerson, "The Lesser Hawaiian Gods," *Hawaiian Historical Society Papers* 2 (1892): 14.

62 Kānepuʻu, writing in *Ka Hoku o ka Pakipika*, 28 Nov. 1861.

63 I've borrowed the term "orature" from Ngugi, *Decolonising the Mind*.

64 This is most likely the same mele reproduced by Sahlins in *Islands of History* (13), but as the reader will see, its context within *Hoku o ka Pakipika* and the explanation by Puni Nūpepa below give it a completely different meaning than that claimed by Sahlins. To be fair, the file in the Hawaiʻi State Archives in which Sahlins found the mele does not mention *Ka Hoku a ka Pakipika*. A note says that most of the mele in the file were published in *Ka Hae Hawaii*. This one was not.

65 Reprinted in *Ka Hoku o ka Pakipika*, 26 Sept. 1861.

66 "Maʻemaʻe" means "cleanliness, purity, or chastity," and is associated with the puritan missionaries.

67 *Ka Hoku o ka Pakipika*, 26 Sept. 1861.

68 Ibid.

69 Ibid. ʻUlaʻula is usually translated as "red"; however, it is the word used to describe the skin color of Kanaka Maoli, so I am translating it here as "brown."

70 Lawrence W. Levine, *Black Culture and Black Consciousness* (New York: Oxford University Press, 1977), 11.

71 *Ka Hoku o ka Pakipika*, 7 Nov. 1861. The inconsistency in the capitalization of "Ilikeokeo" (Whiteskin) and "iliulaula" (brownskin) is in the original, and telling: it is consistent with capitalization practice in the English press, which capitalizes "Caucasian" but not "native."

72 *Ka Hoku o ka Pakipika*, 26 Sept. 1861.

73 Mary Kawena Pukui, E. W. Haertig, and Catherine A. Lee, *Nānā i ke Kumu (Look to the Source)*, vol. 1 (Honolulu: Queen Liliʻuokani Children's Center, 1972), 75–104.

74 Kameʻeleihiwa, *Native Land*, 47.

75 See Walter Benjamin, "The Task of the Translator," trans. Harry Zohn, in *Illuminations* (New York: Schocken, 1968).

76 *Ka Hoku o ka Pakipika*, 26 Sept. 1861.

77 Ibid.

78 Ibid. The phrase "he ʻpuahiohio,ʼ nana a make nui ai i keia lahui" seems either to be ungrammatical or to contain a typographical error (the i before keia). The translation, therefore, is a bit rough.

79 *Ka Hoku o ka Pakipika*, 26 Sept. 1861. The grammatical structure in this and the previous quote for "lilo" as "become" is unusual, but the meaning "become" is the only one that seems to fit.

80 *Ka Hoku o ka Pakipika*, 3 Oct. 1861.

81 Hawaiian Mission Children's Society, *Missionary Album*, 199.
82 *Ka Hoku o ka Pakipika*, 17 Oct. 1861; translation from the *Polynesian*, 19 Oct. 1861.
83 *Polynesian*, 19 Oct. 1861.
84 *Polynesian*, 23 Nov. 1861.
85 *Ka Hoku o ka Pakipika*, 26 Sept. 1861.
86 Ibid.
87 Ibid., 28 Nov. 1861.
88 Ibid., 31 Oct. 1861.
89 Ibid.
90 Merry, *Colonizing Hawai'i*.
91 Names (as well as pronouns) in Hawaiian are not gendered, and this is a particularly gender-confounding name. I cannot translate the whole of it with any certainty, but the beginning "Kanewahine" means something like "female man" or "feminine man," or might possibly refer to a female form of the akua Kāne.
92 Translation from Pukui and Elbert, *Hawaiian Dictionary*, 370.
93 *Ka Hoku o ka Pakipika*, 26 Sept. 1861.
94 Nathaniel B. Emerson, *Pele and Hiiaka: A Myth from Hawaii* (Rutland, Vt.: Tuttle, 1978 [1915]); John Charlot, "Pele and Hi'iaka: The Hawaiian-Language Newspaper Series," *Anthropos* 93 (1998): 55–75; ku'ualoha ho'omanawanui, presentation at Bishop Museum, 18 Mar. 2003.
95 E.g., Barrow, writing in Emerson, *Pele and Hiiaka*, xviii.
96 *Ka Hoku o ka Pakipika*, 30 Oct. 1862.
97 Pukui and Elbert, *Hawaiian Dictionary*, 198.
98 Charlot, "Pele."
99 Pukui and Elbert, *Hawaiian Dictionary*, 192.
100 Kerry Laiana Wong, personal communication, 1997.
101 Charlot, "Pele," 58.
102 This is in contradiction to the common categorization of Pele as a minor goddess or demigod and thus raises a question about the category "akua nui," which is usually said to consist of four major gods (who are all male). Was there a bias favoring male gods in the early years of Hawaiian ethnology? Could that be related to the fact that it was males who were taken seriously as informants, and who were the first educated at Lahainaluna school and therefore created the first body of writing about Kanaka culture?
103 Pukui and Elbert, *Hawaiian Dictionary*, 88.
104 Charlot, "Pele," 57.
105 5 Mar. 1857, in Chapin, *Shaping History*, 57.

106 *Ka Hoku Loa*, Oct. 1861. The complete text of the version published in *Kuokoa* itself is given in appendix A. A comparison of the two is of interest, but space constraints prohibit it here. I made use of *Kuokoa*, Oct. 1861, and Rubellite Kawena Johnson, ed., *Ka Nupepa Kuokoa: A Chronicle of Entries 1861–1862* (Honolulu: Topgallant Publishing, 1975), for this translation.

107 For the content review of *Kuokoa*, I am grateful to Rubellite Kawena Johnson and her translation classes that produced *Ka Nupepa Kuokoa*.

108 Niklaus R. Schweizer, "Kahaunani: 'Snowwhite' and other German Fairy-Tales in Hawai'i," unpublished MS, 1998.

109 Johnson, *Ka Nupepa Kuokoa*, 40, 54.

110 Ibid., 57.

111 J. W. Kawainui, "He Mau Mea Hoonaauao i keia Lahui Hawaii," *Nupepa Kuokoa*, 1 January 1862.

112 *Ka Hoku o ka Pakipika*, 26 Dec. 1861.

113 Regarding "tactics," see Certeau, *Practice*, xix.

114 Ibid., 23.

115 Anderson, *Imagined Communities*, 45.

116 Paul F. Nāhoa Lucas, "Hawaiian Language Policy and the Courts," *Hawaiian Journal of History* 34 (2000): 4.

117 Chatterjee, *Nation*, 5.

118 For example, in Hoʻoulumāhiehie (Joseph M. Poepoe), "Ka moolelo o Hiiaka-i-ka-poli-o-Pele" (*Ka Naʻi Aupuni* 1906), Hiʻiaka is compared to Abraham.

119 kuʻualoha hoʻomanawanui, personal communication, 1998.

3 The Merrie Monarch: Genealogy, Cosmology, Mele, and Performance Art as Resistance

1 Anderson, *Imagined Communities*.

2 See, e.g., Kuykendall, *Hawaiian Kingdom*, vol. 2.

3 Ibid., 84.

4 Silva, "He Kanawai e Hoopau," 29–48.

5 For the importance of narratives to nationhood see Said, *Culture and Imperialism*, 272–73.

6 Osorio, *Dismembering Lāhui*, 168–69.

7 Ibid., 237–38.

8 Ibid., 146.

9 Kuykendall, *Hawaiian Kingdom*, vol. 3, 187.

10 Jennie Wilson, interview by Joann Kealiʻinohomoku, 1962, audiotape,

Bishop Museum Archives, Honolulu; Elizabeth Tatar, *Nineteenth Century Hawaiian Chant*, Pacific Anthropological Records no. 33 (Honolulu: Bishop Museum, Department of Anthropology, 1982), 29.

11 Adrienne L. Kaeppler, *Hula Pahu: Hawaiian Drum Dances. Vol. 1: Haʻa and Hula Pahu: Sacred Movements*, Bishop Museum Bulletin in Anthropology no. 3 (Honolulu: Bishop Museum, 1993), 24.

12 Kameʻeleihiwa, *Native Land*, 52.

13 Osorio, *Dismembering Lāhui*, 156.

14 Ethel M. Damon, *Sanford Ballard Dole and His Hawaii* (Palo Alto, Calif.: Pacific Books, 1957), 186–87.

15 George S. Kanahele, ed., *Hawaiian Music and Musicians: An Illustrated History* (Honolulu: University of Hawaiʻi Press, 1979), 201.

16 Osorio, *Dismembering Lāhui*, 225.

17 Martha Warren Beckwith, *The Kumulipo: A Hawaiian Creation Chant* (Honolulu: University of Hawaiʻi Press, 1951), 11.

18 Kamakau wrote only in Hawaiian; this and the following quotes are from the translated text titled *Ka Poe Kahiko: The People of Old*, trans. Mary Kawena Pukui (Honolulu: Bishop Museum Press, 1964), 4.

19 Kameʻeleihiwa, *Native Land*, 19, 20.

20 Some creation stories of the nineteenth century (e.g., Kepelino) report that Kāne alone created life, but these accounts are acknowledged to have been accommodations at that time to the overwhelming demands of Christianity.

21 This is not to assert a complete and unproblematic equality between men and women in the traditional world, but only to explain that women were not automatically excluded from the realm of the political. For examples of island rulers who were women, see chapter 1 and Kameʻeleihiwa, *Native Land*, 79–80.

22 Papa Kuauhau Alii o na Alii Hawaii, *Hoike a ka Papa Kuauhau o na Alii Hawaii* (Honolulu: Ka Papa Kuauhau Alii o na Alii Hawaii, 1884), 3.

23 John Charlot, *The Hawaiian Poetry of Religion and Politics*, monograph series, no. 5 (Lāʾie, Hawaiʻi: Institution for Polynesian Studies, 1985), 1.

24 In Kanaka epistemology, knowledge tends to have a purpose. See Manulani Aluli Meyer, "Native Hawaiian Epistemology: Contemporary Narratives" (Ph.D. diss., Harvard University, 1998).

25 My translation; the English version gives "Very Ancient."

26 The Hawaiian version gives a ditto mark under "I ka wa o" (time of) and then lists the name Kawelo, but the English version gives two ditto marks, implying "Time of Pele" rather than Kawelo; I believe this should be regarded as an error as well as an example of the confusion that can arise when only the English text is used for this kind of research. Kawelo,

in addition to being a supernatural person in the legend, is a real person in the genealogy.

27 Poepoe, in Beckwith, *The Kumulipo*, 2. Kamokuiki is the name of Ka-lākaua's paternal grandmother, but Beckwith does not say whether or not she was the genealogist whose book was used. I think it is likely that she was because hers is the source from which the *Kumulipo*, the Kalākaua genealogy, was recovered. See Lili'uokalani, *Hawaii's Story by Hawaii's Queen* (Honolulu: Mutual Publishing, 1990 [1897]), 407; Beckwith, *The Kumulipo*, 2.

28 Papa Kuauhau Alii, *Hoike a ka Papa*, 8.

29 Ibid., 9 (my translation).

30 *Pacific Commercial Advertiser*, 15 Nov. 1886, quoted in Esther K. Moo-kini, "The Hale Naua of David Kalakaua," unpublished manuscript, n.d., 12–13, Hawaiian Collection, Hamilton Library, University of Hawai'i, Mānoa.

31 Papa Kuauhau Alii, *Hoike a ka Papa*, 12; and translated version, Board of Genealogy of Hawaiian Chiefs, *Report of the Board of Genealogy of Hawaiian Chiefs* (Honolulu: Board of Genealogy of Hawaiian Chiefs, 1884), 11.

32 Papa Kuauhau Alii, *Hoike a ka Papa*, 15.

33 Charlot, *Hawaiian Poetry*, 1.

34 Valerio Valeri, *Kingship and Sacrifice: Ritual and Society in Ancient Hawaii* (Chicago: University of Chicago Press, 1985), 4.

35 Said describes ideological resistance as following the period of fighting the colonizer, and consists of efforts to reconstitute community. *Culture and Imperialism*, 209–10.

36 Kame'eleihiwa, *Native Land*, 2–3.

37 Lili'uokalani, *Kumulipo: An Hawaiian Creation Myth* (Kentfield, Calif.: Pueo Press, 1978 [1897]), ix.

38 *He Pule Hoolaa Alii: He Kumulipo no Ka I-amamao a ia Alapai Wahine* (Honolulu: Hui Pa'ipalapala Elele, 1889), 1–2 (cited hereafter as *Kumu-lipo*). My translation, with some assistance from Beckwith, *The Kumulipo*, 1951.

39 Pukui and Elbert, *Hawaiian Dictionary*, 333.

40 *Kumulipo*, 24, 58.

41 *Ka Leo o ka Lahui*, 5 Jan. to 12 July 1893.

42 Pukui and Elbert, *Hawaiian Dictionary*, 340.

43 Beckwith, *The Kumulipo*, 80, 82.

44 Kame'eleihiwa, *Native Land*, 23–33.

45 Beckwith, *The Kumulipo*, 119.

46 *Kumulipo*, 51.

47 See, for example, J. M. Poepoe, "Ka Moolelo Hawaii Kahiko," *Ka Naʻi Aupuni*, 17–18 May 1906.

48 *Kumulipo*, 62.

49 Beckwith, *The Kumulipo*, 99.

50 Ibid.

51 Hale Nauā, *Annual Report, 1887*, Hale Nauā File, Hawaiʻi State Archives, Honolulu. The figure of thirty years may have been chosen as an average or mid-point in progeny-generating years, favoring the male, because male aliʻi fathered children from early adulthood until old age. It is obviously arbitrary, and so the dates based on it should be viewed accordingly.

52 Beckwith, *The Kumulipo*, 117.

53 Ibid., 128.

54 McClintock, *Imperial Leather*, 11.

55 Mookini, "Hale Nauā," 2. I am indebted to Esther Mookini because much of the information in this section draws on this manuscript.

56 Hale Nauā record book, in Mookini, "Hale Nauā," 6 (her translation).

57 Ibid.

58 Liliʻuokalani, *Hawaii's Story*, 114.

59 Because Hawaiian names are not specifically male or female, I am unable to determine from the list of names the sex of every member.

60 *Pacific Commercial Advertiser*, 15 Nov. 1886, quoted in Mookini, "Hale Nauā," 12–13.

61 McClintock, *Imperial Leather*, 40.

62 Baker, *Savage*; McClintock, *Imperial Leather*, 36–39.

63 Quoted in Mookini, "Hale Nauā," 14.

64 Hale Nauā, *Annual Report*.

65 *Constitution and By-Laws of the Hale Naua, or Temple of Science* (San Francisco: Bancroft Co., 1890).

66 Mookini, "Hale Nauā," 1.

67 Hale Nauā, *Annual Report*.

68 Ibid. *The Annual Report* never gives the name of the "reverend historian," but the references to Kanaka Maoli as half-man, half-beast are made in Bingham, *Residence*.

69 Mary Kawena Pukui, *ʻŌlelo Noʻeau: Hawaiian Proverbs and Poetical Sayings* (Honolulu: Bishop Museum, 1983), 125.

70 Liliʻuokalani, *Hawaii's Story*, 104–5.

71 Amy K. Stillman, "History Reinterpreted in Song: The Case of the Hawaiian Counterrevolution," *Hawaiian Journal of History* 23 (1989): 20.

72 *Pacific Commercial Advertiser*, 12 Mar. 1883.

73 First Circuit Court Criminal File, Hawaiʻi State Archives, Honolulu.

74 Ibid.

75 *Papa Kuhikuhi o na Hula Poni Moi*, 1883, 4 and 6, Paul Kahn Collection, Hawai'i State Archives, Honolulu.

76 Pukui and Elbert, *Hawaiian Dictionary*, 221.

77 Samuel H. Elbert and Noelani Mahoe, eds., *Nā Mele o Hawai'i Nei: 101 Hawaiian Songs* (Honolulu: University of Hawai'i Press, 1970), 67.

78 Ibid.

79 *Papa Kuhikuhi o Na Hula Poni Moi.*

80 Kamakau, quoted in Helen H. Roberts, *Ancient Hawaiian Music*, Bernice P. Bishop Museum Bulletin 29 (Honolulu: Bishop Museum, 1926; Reprint, New York: Kraus Reprint Co., 1971), page references are to the reprint edition.

81 Chatterjee, *Nation*, 7.

82 E.g., *Ko Hawaii Pae Aina*, 16 June 1883.

83 *Nupepa Kuokoa*, 27 Nov. 1886.

84 Lili'uokalani, *Hawaii's Story*, 407.

85 *Daily Bulletin*, 20 Nov. 1886.

86 *Pacific Commercial Advertiser*, 22 Nov. 1886.

87 *Daily Bulletin*, 23 Nov. 1886.

88 Ibid.

89 "Ka Aha Aina Luau ma ka Pa Alii," *Ko Hawaii Pae Aina*, 27 Nov. 1886.

90 *Nupepa Kuokoa*, 27 Nov. 1886.

91 *Pacific Commercial Advertiser*, 24 Nov. 1886.

92 *Pacific Commercial Advertiser*, 29 Nov. 1886.

93 *Nupepa Kuokoa*, 4 Dec. 1886.

94 *Na Mele Aimoku, na Mele Kupuna, a me na Mele Pono o Ka Moi Kalakaua I*, 1886, 1, Bishop Museum Archives.

95 Mary Kawena Pukui, "Hawaiian Poetry and Music," unpublished transcript of lecture given at Kamehameha Schools, 1945, Hawaiian Collection, Hamilton Library, University of Hawai'i, Mānoa.

96 Ibid.; Kaeppler, *Hula Pahu*, 225–26.

97 Ibid., 213–14.

98 Tatar, *Nineteenth Century*, 179–80.

99 Valeri, *Kingship*, 7.

100 Kame'eleihiwa, *Native Land*, 48.

101 Kamakau, *Ke Kumu Aupuni*, 212.

102 Ngugi, *Decolonising the Mind*, 16.

103 Albert Memmi, *The Colonizer and the Colonized* (Boston: Beacon Press, 1991 [1965]), 91.

104 Reinecke, *Language*, 71.

105 Murray Edelman, *From Art to Politics: How Artistic Creations Shape Political Conceptions* (Chicago: University of Chicago Press, 1995), 2.

106 Ibid., 3.
107 Osorio, *Dismembering Lāhui*, 240–41.

4 The Antiannexation Struggle

1 See Coffman, *Nation Within*; Michael Dougherty, *To Steal a Kingdom* (Waimānalo, Hawai'i: Island Style Press, 1992); Russ, *Hawaiian Revolution*; William Adam Russ Jr., *The Hawaiian Republic (1894–98) and Its Struggle to Win Annexation* (Selinsgrove, Pa.: Susquehanna University Press, 1992 [1961]); Ralph S. Kuykendall, *Hawaiian Kingdom*, vol. 3; Albertine Loomis, *For Whom Are the Stars? Revolution and Counterrevolution in Hawai'i, 1893–1895* (Honolulu: University of Hawai'i Press, 1976); Merze Tate, *The United States and the Hawaiian Kingdom: A Political History* (Westport, Conn.: Greenwood Press, 1965); Lorrin A. Thurston, *Memoirs of the Hawaiian Revolution* (Honolulu: Advertising Publishing, 1936); and Sanford B. Dole, *Memoirs of the Hawaiian Revolution* (Honolulu: Pacific Commercial Advertiser, 1936).
2 Davianna McGregor-Alegado, "Hawaiian Resistance: 1887–1889" (master's thesis, University of Hawai'i, 1979); Loomis, *For Whom.*
3 Tate, *United States*, 284.
4 Kuykendall, *Hawaiian Kingdom*, vol. 3, 448, 627.
5 Ibid., 532–42, 560–66, 586–605.
6 Russ, *Hawaiian Republic*, 50, 108, 198, 207, 364.
7 Lili'uokalani, *Hawaii's Story*; John G. M. Sheldon (Kahikina Kelekona), *Ka Buke Moolelo o Hon. Joseph K. Nawahi* (Honolulu: Bulletin Pub. Co., 1908); John G. M. Sheldon, *The Biography of Joseph K. Nāwahī*, trans. Marvin Puakea Nogelmeier (Honolulu: Hawaiian Historical Society, 1988).
8 Coffman, *Nation Within.*
9 Gyan Prakash, "Writing Post-Orientalist Histories of the Third World: Indian Historiography Is Good to Think," in *Colonialism and Culture*, ed. Nicholas B. Dirks (Ann Arbor: University of Michigan Press, 1992), 353.
10 Ngugi, *Decolonising the Mind*, 16.
11 Osorio, *Dismembering Lāhui*, 210.
12 Clarence Ashford, quoted in ibid., 240.
13 Osorio, *Dismembering Lāhui*, 243.
14 Ibid., 244.
15 McGregor-Alegado, "Hawaiian Resistance," 48.
16 David William Earle, "Coalition Politics in Hawai'i, 1887–90: Hui Kā-

lai'āina and the Mechanics and Workingmen's Political Protective Union" (master's thesis, University of Hawai'i, 1993), 64–65.

17 Ibid., 67. Lyons's desire to control the organization later became problematic.

18 Ibid., 70.

19 Gina Sobrero, *An Italian Baroness in Hawaii: The Travel Diary of Gina Sobrero, Bride of Robert Wilcox, 1887*, trans. Edgar C. Knowlton (Honolulu: Hawaiian Historical Society, 1991), 118–22.

20 Earle, "Coalition," 88.

21 Grimshaw, *Paths of Duty*.

22 Earle, "Coalition," 96.

23 McGregor-Alegado, "Hawaiian Resistance," 108.

24 Earle, "Coalition," 161.

25 Ibid., 163.

26 Kuykendall, *Hawaiian Kingdom*, vol. 3, 463.

27 Earle, "Coalition," 167–69.

28 Lili'uokalani Collection, M93, Box 18, Folder 145. 1892, Hawai'i State Archives, Honolulu.

29 Lili'uokalani, *Hawaii's Story*, 234.

30 Coffman, *Nation Within*; Dougherty, *To Steal a Kingdom*; Kuykendall, *Hawaiian Kingdom*, vol. 3, 582–650; Russ, *Hawaiian Revolution*; James H. Blount, *Foreign Relations of the U.S., 1894: Affairs in Hawaii. Report of U.S. Special Commissioner James H. Blount to U.S. Secretary of State Walter Q. Gresham Concerning the Hawaiian Kingdom Investigation*, 53rd Cong. 3rd sess., 1894 (hereafter cited as Blount report).

31 Blount report, 492, 911.

32 Noenoe K. Silva, "Kū'ē! Hawaiian Women's Resistance to the Annexation," in *Women in Hawai'i: Sites, Identities, and Voices*, ed. Joyce N. Chinen, Kathleen O. Kane, and Ida M. Yoshinaga, special issue of *Social Process in Hawai'i* 38 (1997): 8.

33 Blount report, 929–30.

34 Ibid., 911–13.

35 Ibid., 914.

36 Ibid., 492.

37 Līlia Aholo, second wife of Luther Aholo, should not be confused with the well-known Lydia Aholo. Lydia Aholo was Luther's daughter by his first wife, who died in childbirth; Queen Lili'uokalani then took Lydia as her hānai within weeks of her birth. Lydia was also the major source of information for Helena G. Allen's biography of the queen, *The Betrayal of Liliuokalani: Last Queen of Hawaii, 1838–1917* (Honolulu: Mutual Publishing, 1982).

38 *Ka Leo o ka Lahui*, 27 Mar. 1893.

39 Blount report, 445–58.

40 Coffman, *Nation Within*; William Appleman Williams, *Empire as a Way of Life* (New York: Oxford University Press, 1980).

41 *Hawaii Holomua*, 7 July 1893.

42 Joyce D. Hammond, "Hawaiian Flag Quilts: Multivalent Symbols of a Hawaiian Quilt Tradition," *Hawaiian Journal of History* 27 (1993): 19.

43 Eleanor C. Nordyke and Martha H. Noyes. " 'Kaulana Nā Pua': A Voice for Sovereignty," *Hawaiian Journal of History* 27 (1993): 27–42.

44 Elbert and Mahoe, *Nā Mele*, 63–64.

45 *Ke Aloha Aina*, 1895–1897; *Ka Leo o ka Lahui*, 1893–1895.

46 See series of letters in *Ka Leo o ka Lahui*, 1893, and *Ke Aloha Aina*, 1895–1897.

47 Russ, *Hawaiian Republic*, 20, 26.

48 Henriques Manuscript Collection, Bishop Museum, Honolulu.

49 Alfred L. Castle, "Advice for Hawaii: The Dole-Burgess Letters," *Hawaiian Journal of History* 15 (1981): 24–30.

50 *Ka Leo o ka Lahui*, 3 July 1894; the translation is from *Hawaii Holomua*, 3 July 1894.

51 *Ka Leo o ka Lahui*, 3 July 1894. Laiana Wong has pointed out that "hale kaulei" can be translated two ways: "kaulei" can mean insecure or infirm, thus the phrase could read something like "unstable house," as well as the more figurative translation given above, "lei stand." Both translations express an instability that Nāwahī is contrasting to the stable government of the Kamehameha dynasty, and because in Hawaiian multiple meanings are highly valued Nāwahī likely intended the ambiguity.

52 Loomis, *For Whom*, 123–26.

53 Ibid., 113–14.

54 Chapin, *Shaping History*, 103.

55 Loomis, *For Whom*, 124–50.

56 Ibid., 153–66.

57 Loomis reports this as fact (*For Whom*, 183), but Liliʻuokalani does not mention it in her account in *Hawaiʻi's Story*.

58 Russ, *Hawaiian Republic*, 59–61.

59 Loomis, *For Whom*, 197, 203.

60 *Ke Aloha Aina* 1895.

61 Nancy Jane Morris, "Rebels of 1895," in *Trial of a Queen: 1895 Military Tribunal* (Honolulu: Judiciary History Center, 1995).

62 *Ke Aloha Aina* 1895.

63 Osorio, *Dismembering Lāhui*, 160, 161.

64 See Arista, "Davida Malo."

65 *Ke Aloha Aina*, 8 June 1895; my translation.

66 It is often said that Kanaka Maoli have the most dismal life statistics of

any ethnic group in Hawai'i nei: that is, the shortest projected lifespan; greatest per capita amount of diabetes, heart disease, various cancers; highest rates of imprisonment and substance abuse, etc.

67 *Independent*, 24 Sept. 1896.

68 *Ke Aloha Aina*; Sheldon, *Biography*.

69 Lili'uokalani, *Hawaii's Story*, 300, 302.

70 *Ke Aloha Aina*, 14 Nov. 1896.

71 Ibid., 21 Nov. 1896.

72 According to his grandson, Moses Kalauokalani, his full name is David Kalauokalani Keawe, but he is always referred to in the documents and newspapers as Kalauokalani.

73 Republic of Hawaii, *Session Laws 1896*, 189.

74 *Ke Aloha Aina*, 20 July 1895.

75 Reinecke, *Language*, 71–72.

76 Republic of Hawai'i, *Report of the Minister of Public Instruction* (Honolulu: Hawaiian Star Printing, 1898), 6–7.

77 The current public school system in Hawai'i still reflects this history. Kailua (O'ahu) High School, for example, with its large Hawaiian and lower socioeconomic student population, specializes in teaching the building trades, while Kaiser High School, with its wealthier and whiter population, specializes in college prep classes (Leslie Stewart [Teacher], personal communication, 1996).

78 For example, Sarah Keli'ilolena Nākoa recalled that while she was forbidden to speak Hawaiian at school, Hawaiian was her home language. See Sarah Keli'ilolena Nākoa, *Lei Momi o 'Ewa* (Honolulu: Tongg Publishing, 1979), 19.

79 Russ, *Hawaiian Republic*, 178–227.

80 U.S. Senate, Committee on Foreign Relations, file 55A-J11.2, RG 46, National Archives, Washington, D.C.

81 Kaulia, in *Ke Aloha Aina*, 11 Sept. 1897.

82 Ibid.

83 Kalauokalani, in ibid.

84 *Ke Aloha Aina*, 11 Sept. 1897.

85 Coffman, *Nation Within*, 275–76.

86 Helena G. Allen, *Kalakaua: Renaissance King* (Honolulu: Mutual Publishing, 1994), 26.

87 Lorrin A. Thurston, "The American League: Minister Thurston's Speech Friday Night," *Hawaiian Star*, 15 June 1894.

88 *Ke Aloha Aina*, 23 Oct. 1897.

89 The government called their confinement "quarantine," but the people confined called themselves "prisoners." People with leprosy were arrested, and the patients were called inmates. It was nearly impossible, as well, to

escape the quarantine area, which was bounded by rough seas and sheer cliffs. Prisoners were sent there for life; most would never see any family member again. Furthermore, the prisoners were not given adequate food or medical care, which added to their sense of being punished.

90 *Ke Aloha Aina*, 18 Sept. 1897.

91 Ibid., 25 Sept. 1897.

92 *San Francisco Call*, 24 Sept. and 30 Sept. 1897; *Ke Aloha Aina*, 25 Sept. 1897.

93 *San Francisco Call*, 30 Sept. 1897.

94 *Ke Aloha Aina*, 2 Oct. 1897.

95 Ibid.

96 *Ka Loea Kalaiaina* 14 Feb. 1898.

97 *Ke Aloha Aina*, 2 Oct. 1897; *Independent*, 6 Oct. 1897.

98 Department of State, "Memorial to the President, the Congress, and the People of the United States," October 8, 1897, in *Despatches from United States Ministers in Hawaii, 1843–1900* (Washington, D.C., 1954), National Archives and Records Administration microfilm, roll 29, vol. 29.

99 Nandy, *Intimate Enemy*, 100.

100 Because these events predate Gandhi, one wonders whether he knew of them.

101 Lorrin A. Thurston, *A Hand-Book on the Annexation of Hawaii* (St. Joseph, Mich.: A. B. Morse, n.d.), 37.

102 *Ka Leo o ka Lahui*, 5 Jan. to 12 July 1893.

103 *Ke Aloha Aina*, 3 July 1897.

104 E.g., in *Ke Aloha Aina*, 2 Oct. 1897.

105 *Ke Aloha Aina*, 23 Oct. 1897 (my translation, assisted by the translation by Keao Kamalani and Noelani Arista in *ʻŌiwi*, 1999).

106 *Ke Aloha Aina*, 3 July 1897.

107 Nālani Minton, personal communication, 1999.

108 *Ke Aloha Aina*, 23 Oct. 1897.

109 *Ke Aloha Aina*, 26 Mar. and 2 Apr. 1898.

110 This handshake seemed to be an important detail in the reports of their meeting with Senator Hoar. It may be because the delegates were subjected to race prejudice in Washington; some white men may have refused to shake their hands. They do not complain of this directly, however.

111 *Ke Aloha Aina*, 2 Apr. 1898. The whereabouts of the Hui Kālaiʻāina petitions are still unknown. I have looked for them without success at the U.S. National Archives and at the Pettigrew Museum in South Dakota.

112 U.S. Senate, *Senate Report 681*, 55th Cong., 2nd sess., 1898.

113 *Ke Aloha Aina*, 23 Mar. and 2 Apr. 1898.

114 Coffman, *Nation Within*, 295.

115 Department of State, "Memorial to the President."

116 Pukui and Elbert, *Hawaiian Dictionary*, 180, 177.

117 *Ke Aloha Aina*, 6 Aug. 1898.

118 Coffman, *Nation Within*, 315.

119 Kekoa, "E Hoomau i ke kupaa i ke Aloha."

120 *Ke Aloha Aina*, 26 Apr. 1902.

121 Russ, *Hawaiian Republic*.

122 In Anna Keala Kelly, "How Do We Move Forward?" *Honolulu Weekly*, 8–14 Jan. 2003, 6.

5 The Queen of Hawai'i Raises Her Solemn Note of Protest

1 Ke Ali'i 'Ai Moku was how the queen was referred to most often in the Hawaiian press; she was addressed as Ke Ali'i or Kalani. Also, she was sometimes referred to as Mō'īwahine, her formal title; almost never as kuini (queen); and as Mrs. Dominis only in the annexationist paper *Kuokoa*.

2 Lili'uokalani, *Hawaii's Story*, 387.

3 J. J. Leilani Basham, "He Puke Mele Lāhui: Nā Mele Kūpa'a, Nā Mele Kū'ē a Me Nā Mele Aloha o Nā Kānaka Maoli" (master's thesis, University of Hawai'i, 2002), 17.

4 Said, *Culture and Imperialism*, 66.

5 Fuchs, *Hawaii Pono*; Daws, *Shoal of Time*; and Russ, *Hawaiian Revolution* and *Hawaiian Republic*.

6 Fuchs, *Hawaii Pono*, 31, 34–35.

7 Daws, *Shoal*, 264, 266, 268.

8 Russ, *Hawaiian Revolution*, 28, 29.

9 Russ, *Hawaiian Republic*, 240.

10 Russ, *Hawaiian Revolution*, 351.

11 Ibid., 348.

12 "Draft of Constitution of January 14, 1893," Blount report, 1047–55. This document is followed by a statement signed by three of the queen's ministers attesting that the draft they had seen did *not* contain a property requirement for voters.

13 Lili'uokalani to Dole et al., January 1893, Blount report, 397, 866.

14 "Statement of Liliuokalani," Blount report, 865.

15 Osorio, *Dismembering Lāhui*, 242–43.

16 Kimura, "Native Hawaiian Culture," 176.

17 See chapter 1. For more complete accounts, see Kuykendall, *Hawaiian Kingdom*, vol. 1, 206–26; and Kamakau, *Ke Aupuni Mōʻī*, 149–57.

18 "Ex-Queen Liliuokalani to the President," Blount report, 219.

19 "Statement of Liliuokalani," Blount report, 868–69.

20 I am grateful to Keanu Sai for emphasizing this point to me and many others. The text of the treaties between the Kingdom of Hawaiʻi and the United States may be found at www.hawaiiankingdom.org/treaties. shtml.

21 "President's Message Relating to the Hawaiian Islands," Blount report, 443–58.

22 Blount report, 1276; quoted in Basham, "He Puke Mele Lāhui," 108.

23 "Liliuokalani to Albert Willis," 20 June 1894, State Department RG 59, U.S. National Archives, Washington, D.C.

24 Copy of letter from Grover Cleveland to H. A. Widemann, J. A. Cummins, and Samuel Parker, 15 Aug. 1894, Cleghorn collection (M164), Hawaiʻi State Archives, Honolulu.

25 Liliʻuokalani, *Hawaii's Story*, 259.

26 Ibid., 263.

27 Liliʻuokalani to McKinley, 17 June 1897, State Department RG 59, U.S. National Archives, Washington, D.C.

28 Ibid.

29 "Petition of the Hawaiian Patriotic League to President Cleveland," Blount report, 1295.

30 Bishop, quoted in Dougherty, *To Steal a Kingdom*, 166.

31 Joseph Heleluhe, "Huakai a Ke Alii," *Ka Makaainana*, 18 Jan. 1897, 1, 5.

32 Rev. Sereno E. Bishop, "A Royal Palace Democratized," *Independent* 45 no. 2327 (1893): 905, quoted in Lydia Kualapai, "Cast in Print: The Nineteenth-Century Hawaiian Imaginary" (Ph.D. diss., University of Nebraska, 2001), 166, 167.

33 Stuart Hall, "The Spectacle of the 'Other,'" in *Representation: Cultural Representations and Signifying Practices* (London: Saga, 1997), 249.

34 Jan Nederveen Pieterse, *White on Black: Images of Africa and Blacks in Western Popular Culture* (New Haven: Yale University Press, 1992), 80.

35 Liliʻuokalani, "A Queen's Appeal" *San Francisco Examiner*, 9 March 1893.

36 Kualapai, "Cast in Print," 145–83.

37 Hall, "Spectacle," 253.

38 Heleluhe, "Huakai," 5.

39 Sara Lee, quoted in Liliʻuokalani, *Hawaii's Story*, 316.

40 Liliʻuokalani, *Hawaii's Story*, 341, 347–48.

41 *New York Times*, 26 Dec. 1896 and 26 Jan. 1897.

42 Jonathan K. Kamakawiwoʻole Osorio, "A Hawaiian Nationalist Commentary on the Trial of the *Mōʻīwahine*," in *Trial of a Queen: 1895 Military Tribunal* (Honolulu: Judiciary History Center, 1996), 30.

43 Liliʻuokalani, *Pacific Commercial Advertiser*, 8 February 1895.

44 Jon M. Van Dyke, "The Trial of Liliʻuokalani," in *Trial of a Queen: 1895 Military Tribunal* (Honolulu: Judiciary History Center, 1996), 7.

45 *Pacific Commercial Advertiser*, 16 January 1895.

46 Ibid., 25 January 1895.

47 *Nupepa Kuokoa*, 2 February 1895.

48 Stillman, "Of the People Who Love the Land." See also Stillman's "History Reinterpreted in Song: The Case of the Hawaiian Counterrevolution," *Hawaiian Journal of History* 23 (1989), 1–30. I am indebted to Dr. Stillman for sharing her research on the songs composed by Queen Liliʻuokalani, which made this section possible.

49 Kamakau, *Ke Kumu*, 237.

50 Ibid., 238.

51 Ibid., 237.

52 Ibid., 238.

53 See Basham, "He Puke Mele Lāhui."

54 Recent research as yet unpublished by Rubellite Kawena Johnson and Denise Noelani Arista.

55 I term Emerson and Thrum "orientalist" because they both studied and published on Hawaiian culture, translating moʻolelo into "legends" and so forth, and both had some contempt for the lāhui Hawaiʻi at the same time. Further both men supported the provisional government and then the U.S. takeover of Hawaiʻi. This combination is analogous to what Edward Said describes in *Orientalism* (New York: Pantheon, 1978).

56 Lilikalā K. Kameʻeleihiwa, *He Moʻolelo Kaʻao o Kamapuaʻa: A Legendary Tradition of Kamapuaʻa, the Hawaiian Pig-God* (Honolulu: Bishop Museum Press, 1996), ix.

57 Liliʻuokalani, *The Queen's Songbook* (Honolulu: Hui Hānai, 1999) 119; translation by Hui Hānai.

58 Ibid.

59 Ibid., 127.

60 "Na Kahoaka a ka Po i na Alii i Hala," *Ka Leo o ka Lahui*, 3 February 1891.

61 Tatar, *Nineteenth Century*, 33.

62 Pukui, "Hawaiian Poetry and Music."

63 Basham, "He Puke Mele Lāhui."

64 Ibid., iv.

65 Stillman, "Of the People Who Love the Land," 94.

66 Basham, "He Puke Mele Lāhui," 2.

67 [Liliʻuokalani], *Ka Makaainana*, 1 Apr. 1895 (my translation, informed by that of Amy Kuʻuleialoha Stillman).

68 Van Dyke, "Trial," 3.

69 Coffman, *Nation Within*, 75–83.

70 Van Dyke, "Trial," 4.

71 [Liliʻuokalani], "Lokahi ka Manao Me ka Lahui," *Ka Makaainana*, 8 Apr. 1895. Also published as Liliuokalani [Haimoeipo, pseud.] "Aha-koa Keikei o ke Kulana," in F. J. Testa, ed., *Buke Mele Lahui* (Honolulu: Halepai Makaainana, 1895), 11.

72 Minutes of a meeting of Wood, Tenney, Bolt, Ena, Castle, Smith et al., 19 Feb. 1895, in W. D. Alexander document collection, MS B A1 1a no. 2, 6, Hawaiian Historical Society Library, Honolulu.

73 [Liliʻuokalani], "Umia ke Aloha i Paa Iloko," *Ka Makaainana*, 15 Apr. 1895. Also published as Liliʻuokalani [Haimoeipo, pseud.], "Inoa Wehi No ka Oiwi Pokii," in Testa, *Buke*, 10–11; and as Liliʻuokalani "He Inoa Wehi No Kalanianaole" in "He Buke Mele Hawaii," unpublished manuscript, Hawaiʻi State Archives, Honolulu, 127.

74 [Liliʻuokalani], "Ike Hou Ana I ka Nani," *Ka Makaainana*, 22 Apr. 1895. Also printed in Liliuokalani, "He Buke Mele Hawaii," 128; and a slightly different version is published as third verse or third song by Liliʻuokalani [Haimoeipo, pseud.], "Hoonanea A Hookuene Liliu," in Testa, *Buke*, 5.

75 Kekoaohiwaikalani, "Mele Aloha Aina," in Testa, *Buke*, 2; "He Lei No ka Poe Aloha Aina," *Ka Leo o ka Lahui*, 10 May 1893.

76 H. J. Kapu and J. K. Kaulia, "Na Paia Laumania o Kawa," in Testa, *Buke*, 3.

77 [Haimoeipo], Liliʻuokalani "Hoonanea," 5.

78 Kapu and Kaulia, "Na Paia," 2–3.

79 J. Heleluhe, and D. K. Koa, "Hua Kau i ka Umauma," in Testa, *Buke*, 7–8.

80 These were not the only songs Ke Aliʻi ʻAi Moku composed while imprisoned. For a complete list, see appendix B.

81 Emma ʻAʻima Nāwahī to Queen Liliʻuokalani, 25 Dec. 1896, Liliʻuokalani manuscript collection, Hawaiʻi State Archives, Honolulu (hereafter cited as LMC).

82 The letter translations were done by Jason Achiu of the Hawaiʻi State Archives.

83 E. A. Nāwahī to Liliʻuokalani, 16 Dec. 1896, in LMC. Loloku and Walania are among Liliʻu's names.

84 "Death of a Patriot," *Independent* (Honolulu), 24 September 1896.

85 Liliʻuokalani, *Hawaii's Story*, 305, 307.

86 Ibid., 288.

87 Kualapai, "Cast in Print," 178–79.

88 It is difficult to verify because the language Mrs. Nāwahī and the queen

use in the letters is coded (they refer to the documents as "fans" being woven by the women, for example), but it is likely these are the protest documents addressed to McKinley (women's dated Dec. 30, 1896 and the men's dated February 1897) and finally successfully delivered to the president's office, accompanied by letters from the queen and Joseph Heleluhe on 24 July 1897. See Nāwahī to Liliʻuokalani, 16 Dec. 1896, in LMC; and State Department records, U.S. National Archives, Washington, D.C.

89   E. A. Nāwahī to Queen Liliʻuokalani, 16 Dec. 1896, in LMC.

90   Ibid.

91   E. A. Nāwahī to Queen Liliʻuokalani, 22 Mar. 1897 and 2 Apr. 1897, in LMC.

92   E. A. Nāwahī to Queen Liliʻuokalani, 25 Dec. 1896, in LMC.

93   Ibid. (translation by Jason Achiu of the Hawaiʻi State Archives, with my modifications in brackets).

94   Ibid., 23 Feb. 1897 (translation mine, informed by that of Jason Achiu of the Hawaiʻi State Archives).

95   Ibid. (translation by Jason Achiu of the Hawaiʻi State Archives, with my modifications in brackets).

96   *Ka Makaainana*, 21 Dec. 1896; 28 Dec. 1896; 18 Jan. 1897, etc.; Letter apparently from Liliʻuokalani, *Ke Aloha Aina*, 6 Feb. 1897, 2; Letter from Heleluhe, *Ke Aloha Aina*, 20 Feb. 1897.

97   Nāwahī to Liliʻuokalani, 22 Mar. 1897 (translation by Jason Achiu of the Hawaiʻi State Archives).

98   Ibid., 23 Mar. 1897 (my translation).

99   Ibid., n.d. (but clearly late August or early September 1897).

100 Hui Aloha ʻĀina o Nā Wāhine to McKinley, 30 Dec. 1896, transmitted to McKinley 17 June 1897 by Joseph Heleluhe; both Hawaiian and English versions sent. U.S. State Department files, RG 59, U.S. National Archives, Washington, D.C.

101 Thurston, *Hand-Book*.

102 Ibid., 18 Aug. 1897.

103 *Ke Aloha Aina*, 18 Sept. 1897.

104 Ibid. (my translation).

105 Mahalo nui to H. James Bartels, director of Washington Place, for bringing this diary entry to my attention. Liliʻuokalani manuscript collection, M93, Box 12, Folder 127, Hawaiʻi State Archives.

106 *Ke Aloha Aina*, 11 June 1898, 4; 18 June 1898.

107 Ibid., 6 Aug. 1898.

108 *Ke Aloha Aina*, 6 Aug. 1898.

109 Liliʻuokalani, "A Queen's Appeal."

110 See cases at www.hawaiiankingdom.org.

111 Siba N'Zatioula Grovogui, *Sovereigns, Quasi Sovereigns, and Africans: Race and Self-Determination in International Law* Borderlines (Minneapolis: University of Minnesota Press, 1996), 42.

112 Mrs. Kawohikapulani, "Hooheno No Liliu," *Hawaii Holomua*, 9 Feb. 1893, quoted in Basham, "He Puke Mele Lāhni."

113 Lili'uokalani, in an unsigned letter from San Francisco, *Ke Aloha Aina*, 2 Oct. 1897, 4.

Glossary

Note: Information in quotes is from Mary Kawena Pukui and Samuel H. Elbert, *Hawaiian Dictionary*, rev. ed. (Honolulu: University of Hawai'i Press, 1986).

'aha. A religious ritual

'ahahui. Organization, association

ahupua'a. "Land division usually extending from the uplands to the sea"

aikāne. Friend, also lover of the same sex

'ai kapu. Eating taboos; the system of eating taboos; to observe the eating taboos

'āina. Land

'ai noa. Free eating

akua. Deity, also spirit, ghost

akua wahine. Female akua

ali'i. Belonging to the class of rulers as determined by genealogy

ali'i 'ai moku. Island-ruling ali'i; in the monarchy era, the monarch

ali'i nui. High-ranking ali'i; in the nineteenth century, monarchy, members of the royal family, as well as other high-ranking ali'i

ali'i wahine. female ali'i

alo ali'i. Those surrounding the ali'i; royal court

aloha 'āina. Love of the land; love of country

ao. Daylight; eras of human beings in the *Kumulipo*

auē! Exclamation of dismay, sorrow, surprise

aupuni. "Government, kingdom, dominion, nation . . . national"

haku mele. Composer, poet

hālau hula. Hula school, troupe

hālāwai maka'āinana nui. Mass meeting or rally

hānai. To raise or adopt; to feed. The adoptive parent or child

haole. Originally, any foreigner;

from nineteenth century on, specifically white foreigner

heiau. "Pre-Christian place of worship; shrine; some heiau were elaborately constructed stone platforms, others simple earth terraces"

hīmeni. Hymn or any hymnlike song

hoaʻāina. Tenant

hōʻailona. "Sign, symbol . . . omen, portent"

hoʻokupu. Ceremonial gift-giving; church offering

hui. Organization, association

ipu hula. Gourd used as drum in hula

iwikuamʻo. Spine, backbone; also "near and trusted relative of a chief who attended to his personal needs and possessions"

kahiki. The East, and by extension all foreign lands; also, but not exclusively, Tahiti

kāhili. Feather standard

kahu. "Honored attendant, guardian, nurse . . . regent, keeper, administrator, caretaker"

kahuna. Adviser to aliʻi on religion and politics, conductor of religious ceremonies; also experts in various fields, such as waʻa construction

kahuna lapaʻau. Medical kahuna

kahuna nui. "High priest and councilor to a high chief"

kaikuaʻana. Older sibling of the same sex

kalana. "Division of land smaller than a . . . district"

kalo. Taro; staple food of the Kanaka Maoli

kamāliʻi, kamāliʻiwahine. Aliʻi child; glossed as prince or princess in the monarchy era

Kanaka. Person, people, but also Hawaiian; Kānaka is plural form, Kanaka is singular and the category

Kanaka Maoli. Real person or people, i.e., native

Kanaka ʻŌiwi. Native

kānāwai. Law, rule, edict

kāne. Man, husband, boyfriend, male. Also an akua nui

kanikau. Chant or song of mourning

kaona. Hidden meaning or concealed reference, double meanings

kapu. "Taboo, prohibition; special privilege or exemption from ordinary taboo; sacredness . . . sacred, holy, consecrated"

kaua. Battle, war

kaukau aliʻi. Lower-ranking aliʻi relative to aliʻi nui

kauoha. Order, command, will

kiʻi. Image; puppet

kino lau. Many bodies, or "the many forms taken by a supernatural body"

konohiki. Aliʻi under an aliʻi ʻai moku who managed a land area such as an ahupuaʻa, kalana, or smaller area such as an ʻili

kuhina nui. Co-ruler with mōʻī

kula. "Plain, field, open country, pasture"

kuleana. Sphere of right, responsibility, and authority; blood relative

Kumu hula. Hula master

kupuna; kūpuna (plural). Grandparents, elders, ancestors

Lā Hoʻihoʻi Ea. Restoration Day

Lā Kūʻokoʻa. Independence Day

lāʻau lapaʻau. Native herbal medicine

lāhui. People, nation. Often (problematically) glossed as race

lāhui Hawaiʻi. People / nation of Hawaiʻi

lāhui kanaka. A specific people / nation; most often the Kanaka Maoli

lehua. "The flower of the ʻōhiʻa tree (*Metrosideros macropus*) . . . *Fig.* a warrior, a beloved friend or relative . . . expert"

lei. Garland of flowers, feathers, or other material. Metaphor for a beloved

limu. Seaweed

loʻi. Irrigated terrace, especially for taro

luna. On plantations, foreman. Otherwise, commissioner, cabinet minister, supervisor of any sort

mā. A particle attached to names to indicate the other people usually accompanying that person

mahaʻoi. Intrusive

māhele. Division. Term for the change of land tenure to private property

maʻi. Disease, illness. Genitals

maʻi ahulau. Epidemic

maʻi ʻokuʻu. Crouching disease, probably dysentery

maile. "A native twining shrub . . . believed to be sisters with human and plant forms. . . . The maile vine has shiny fragrant leaves and is used for decorations and leis, especially on important occasions"

makaʻāinana. Ordinary people of the land who farm, fish, etc., as opposed to aliʻi and kahuna

makuahine. Mother

mālama ʻāina. Care for the land

malu. Protection, safety

mana. Power, authority, privilege, derived from genealogy / the divine

mele. Song, chant, poetry

mele inoa. Name song or chant

mele koʻihonua. Genealogical chant

mele lāhui. National songs, including national anthems and protest songs

mele maʻi. Song in honor of genitals, as of a chief, as composed on his or her birth

mōʻī. Highest aliʻi, i.e., island ruler, or ruler over the archipelago; in the monarchy era, monarch

mōʻīwahine. Female monarch, queen

moʻokūʻauhau. Genealogy

moʻolelo. History, legend, story, literature, narrative of any kind

moʻolelo kahiko. Moʻolelo about the ancient eras of precolonial history

moʻopuna. Grandchild; descendant

naʻauao. Educated, wise, enlightened, civilized

ʻōiwi. Native

ʻōlelo noʻeau. Wise saying; proverb; figurative saying

oli. Chant that is not accompanied by dance

one hānau. Birthplace

ʻopihi. Limpet

palapala. Reading and writing; document; text

Papa; Papahānaumoku. Akua

wahine said to have given birth to the islands

pō. Night; time before human beings; realm of the ancestors who have passed on

poʻe. People

poʻe aloha ʻāina. The people who love the land; i.e., the people who worked for the independence of the country

poʻe paʻahao kālaiʻāina. Political prisoners

poni mōʻī. Coronation

pono. "Goodness, uprightness, morality . . . correct or proper procedure, excellence, well-being, prosperity, welfare, benefit, sake . . . just, virtuous, fair"

pule. Pray, prayer

ulua. "Certain species of crevalle, jack, or pompano . . . This fish was substituted for human sacrifices . . . probably because of word magic . . . Since an ulua replaces a man, *ulua* also means 'man, sweetheart'"

wā. Period of time, era

wā kahiko. Ancient times

wahine. Woman; wife; girlfriend; female

waʻa. Native sailing vessel

Bibliography

Alexander, Arthur C. *Koloa Plantation, 1835–1935: A History of the Oldest Hawaiian Sugar Plantation*. Līhu'e, Hawai'i: Kaua'i Historical Society, 1937.

Alexander, Mary C. *William Patterson Alexander in Kentucky, the Marquesas, Hawaii*. Honolulu: privately printed, 1934.

Alexander, W. D. "A Brief History of Land Titles in the Hawaiian Kingdom." In *Hawaiian Almanac and Annual for 1891*. Honolulu: Press Publishing Co., 1890.

Allen, Helena G. *The Betrayal of Liliuokalani: Last Queen of Hawaii, 1838–1917*. Honolulu: Mutual Publishing, 1982.

———. *Kalakaua: Renaissance King*. Honolulu: Mutual Publishing, 1994.

Anderson, Benedict. *Imagined Communities: Reflections on the Origin and Spread of Nationalism*. Rev. ed. New York: Verso, 1991.

Arista, Denise Noelani Manuela. "Davida Malo: Ke Kanaka o ka Huliau / David Malo: A Hawaiian of the Time of Change." Master's thesis, University of Hawai'i, 1998.

Baker, Lee D. *From Savage to Negro: Anthropology and the Construction of Race, 1896–1954*. Berkeley: University of California Press, 1998.

Baldwin, James. "A Talk to Teachers." In *The Graywolf Annual Five: Multi-Cultural Literacy*, ed. Rick Simonson and Scott Walker. Saint Paul: Graywolf Press, 1988 [1963].

Basham, J. J. Leilani. "He Puke Mele Lāhui: Nā Mele Kūpa'a, Nā Mele Kū'ē A Me Nā Mele Aloha O Nā Kānaka Maoli." Master's thesis, University of Hawai'i, 2002.

Beckwith, Martha Warren. *The Kumulipo: A Hawaiian Creation Chant*. Honolulu: University of Hawai'i Press, 1951.

Beechert, Edward D. *Working in Hawai'i: A Labor History*. Honolulu: University of Hawai'i Press, 1985.

Benjamin, Walter. "The Task of the Translator." In *Illuminations*, trans. Harry Zohn. New York: Schocken, 1968.

Bicknell, James. "Hawaiian Kahunas and Their Practices." *Friend* (September 1890).

———. "A Plea for Hawaiians." *Friend* (August 1892).

———. "A Quickening of Hawaiian Consciousness." *Friend* (July 1892).

Bingham, Hiram. *O Ke Kumumua na na Kamalii; He Palapala e Ao aku i na Kamalii Ike Ole i ka Heluhelu Palapala*. Honolulu: Mea Pai Palapala Na Na Misionari, 1835.

———. *A Residence of Twenty-One Years in the Sandwich Islands*. Rutland, Vt.: Tuttle, 1981 [1847].

Blount, James H. *Foreign Relations of the U.S., 1894: Affairs in Hawaii. Report of U.S. Special Commissioner James H. Blount to U.S. Secretary of State Walter Q. Gresham Concerning the Hawaiian Kingdom Investigation*. 53rd Cong., 3rd sess., 1894.

Board of Genealogy of Hawaiian Chiefs. *Report of the Board of Genealogy of Hawaiian Chiefs*. Honolulu: Board of Genealogy of Hawaiian Chiefs, 1884.

Britsch, R. Lanier. *Moramona: The Mormons in Hawaii*. Lā'ie, Hawai'i: Institute for Polynesian Studies, 1989.

Buck, Elizabeth. *Paradise Remade: The Politics of Culture and History in Hawai'i*. Philadelphia: Temple University Press, 1993.

Castle, Alfred L. "Advice for Hawaii: The Dole-Burgess letters." *Hawaiian Journal of History* 15 (1981): 24–30.

Certeau, Michel de. *The Capture of Speech and Other Political Writings*. Trans. Tom Conley. Minneapolis: University of Minnesota Press, 1997.

———. *The Practice of Everyday Life*. Trans. Steven Rendall. Berkeley: University of California Press, 1984.

Chakrabarty, Dipesh. *Provincializing Europe: Postcolonial Thought and Historical Difference*. Princeton: Princeton University Press, 2000.

Chapin, Helen Geracimos. "Newspapers of Hawai'i, 1834 to 1903: From 'He Liona' to the 'Pacific Cable.'" *Hawaiian Journal of History* 18 (1984): 47–86.

———. *Shaping History: The Role of Newspapers in Hawai'i*. Honolulu: University of Hawai'i Press, 1996.

Charlot, John. *The Hawaiian Poetry of Religion and Politics*. Monograph series, no. 5. Lā'ie, Hawai'i: Institute for Polynesian Studies, 1985.

———. "Pele and Hiʻiaka: The Hawaiian-Language Newspaper Series." *Anthropos* 93 (1998): 55–75.

Chatterjee, Partha. *The Nation and Its Fragments: Colonial and Postcolonial Histories*. Princeton: Princeton University Press, 1993.

Chinen, Joyce N., Kathleen O. Kane, and Ida M. Yoshinaga, eds. *Women in Hawaiʻi: Sites, Identities, and Voices*. Special issue of *Social Process in Hawaiʻi* 38 (1997).

Chun, Malcolm Nāea. *Must We Wait in Despair: The 1867 Report of the ʻAhahui Lāʻau Lapaʻau of Wailuku Maui on Native Hawaiian Health*. Honolulu: First People's Productions, 1994.

Constitution and By-Laws of the Hale Naua, or Temple of Science. San Francisco: Bancroft Co., 1890.

Coffman, Tom. *Nation Within*. Kāneʻohe, Hawaiʻi: EpiCenter Press, 1998.

Crosby, A. W. "Hawaiian Depopulation as a Model for the Amerindian Experience." In *Epidemics and Ideas: Essays on the Historical Perception of Pestilence*, ed. Terence Ranger and Paul Slack. New York: Cambridge University Press, 1992.

Daily Bulletin. 1886.

Damon, Ethel M. *Sanford Ballard Dole and His Hawaii*. Palo Alto, Calif.: Pacific Books, 1957.

Daws, Gavan. *Shoal of Time: A History of the Hawaiian Islands*. Honolulu: University of Hawaiʻi Press, 1968.

Deloria, Vine Jr. *God Is Red: A Native View of Religion, the Classic Work Updated*. Golden, Colo.: Fulcrum Publishing, 1994.

Dening, Greg. *The Death of William Gooch: A History's Anthropology*. Rev. ed. Honolulu: University of Hawaiʻi Press, 1995.

Dole, Sanford B. *Memoirs of the Hawaiian Revolution*. Honolulu: Pacific Commercial Advertiser, 1936.

Dougherty, Michael. *To Steal a Kingdom*. Waimānalo, Hawaiʻi: Island Style Press, 1992.

Earle, David William. "Coalition Politics in Hawaiʻi 1887–90: Hui Kālaiʻāina and the Mechanics and Workingmen's Political Protective Union." Master's thesis, University of Hawaiʻi, 1993.

Edelman, Murray. *From Art to Politics: How Artistic Creations Shape Political Conceptions*. Chicago: University of Chicago Press, 1995.

Elbert, Samuel H., and Noelani Mahoe, eds. *Nā Mele o Hawaiʻi Nei: 101 Hawaiian Songs*. Honolulu: University of Hawaiʻi Press, 1970.

Ellis, William. *Polynesian Researches: Hawaii*. Rutland, Vt.: Tuttle, 1969.

Emerson, Joseph S. "The Lesser Hawaiian Gods." *Hawaiian Historical Society Papers* 2 (1892): 6–15.

Emerson, Nathaniel B. *Pele and Hiiaka: A Myth from Hawaii*. Rutland, Vt.: Tuttle, 1978 [1915].

——. *Unwritten Literature of Hawaii: The Sacred Songs of the Hula*. Rutland, Vt.: Tuttle, 1965 [1909].

Farmer, David C. "The Trial of the Queen: A Valid Exercise of Judicial Power or a Travesty of Justice?" *Hawaiʻi Bar Journal* (March 1997): 30–34.

Foucault, Michel. *Discipline and Punish: The Birth of the Prison*. Trans. Alan Sheridan. New York: Vintage, 1995.

——. *The History of Sexuality* Vol. 1, *An Introduction*. Translated by Robert Hurley. New York: Vintage, 1990.

——. *Power/Knowledge: Selected Interviews and Other Writings, 1972–1977*. New York: Pantheon, 1980.

——. "The Subject and Power." In *Michel Foucault: Beyond Structuralism and Hermeneutics*, ed. Hubert L. Dreyfus and Paul Rabinow. 2nd ed. Chicago: University of Chicago Press, 1983.

Friend. 1845.

Fuchs, Lawrence E. *Hawaii Pono "Hawaii the Excellent": An Ethnic and Political History*. Honolulu: Bess Press, 1961.

Gossett, Thomas F. *Race: The History of an Idea in America*. Dallas: Southern Methodist University Press, 1963.

Grimshaw, Patricia. *Paths of Duty: American Missionary Wives in Nineteenth-Century Hawaii*. Honolulu: University of Hawaiʻi Press, 1989.

Grovogui, Siba NʻZatioula. *Sovereigns, Quasi Sovereigns, and Africans: Race and Self-Determination in International Law*. Borderlines. Minneapolis: University of Minnesota Press, 1996.

Hale Nauā. *Annual Report*. 1887. Hale Nauā File. Hawaiʻi State Archives, Honolulu.

Hall, Stuart. "The Spectacle of the Other." In *Representation: Cultural Representations and Signifying Practices*. London: Sage Publications, 1997.

Hammond, Joyce D. "Hawaiian Flag Quilts: Multivalent Symbols of a Hawaiian Quilt Tradition." *Hawaiian Journal of History* 27 (1993): 1–26.

Handy, E. S. Craighill, and Elizabeth Green Handy. *Native Planters in Old Hawaiʻi: Their Life, Lore, and Environment*. Honolulu: Bishop Museum Press, 1972.

Hawaii Holomua. 1893–1896.

Hawaiian Mission Children's Society. *Missionary Album: Portraits and Biographical Sketches of the American Protestant Missionaries to the Hawaiian Islands*. Enlarged, sesquicentennial ed. Honolulu: Hawaiian Mission Children's Society, 1969 [1937].

He Pule Hoolaa Alii: He Kumulipo no Ka I-amamao a ia Alapai Wahine. Honolulu: Hui Paʻipalapala Elele, 1889.

Hereniko, Vilsoni. "Indigenous Knowledge and Academic Imperialism." In

Remembrance of Pacific Pasts: An Invitation to Remake History, ed. Robert Borofsky. Honolulu: University of Hawaiʻi Press, 2000.

Herman, R. D. K. "The Dread Taboo, Human Sacrifice, and Pearl Harbor." *Contemporary Pacific* 8, no. 1 (spring 1996): 81–126.

Holt, John Dominis. *On Being Hawaiian*. Honolulu: Ku Paʻa Publishing, 1995 [1964].

Hoʻoulumāhiehie [Joseph M. Poepoe?]. "Ka Moolelo o Hiiaka-i-ka-poli-o-Pele." *Ka Naʻi Aupuni*, November 30, 1905–November 29, 1906.

Hui Hawaii Aloha Aina o na Wahine. "Statement of Protest." Henriques Manuscript File, Bishop Museum Archives, Honolulu.

Hutchison, William R. *Errand to the World: American Protestant Thought and Foreign Missions*. Chicago: University of Chicago Press, 1987.

Independent. 1896–1897.

Johnson, Rubellite Kawena, ed. *"Ka Nupepa Kuokoa": A Chronicle of Entries, 1861–1862*. Honolulu: Topgallant Publishing, 1975.

——. *Kumulipo: The Hawaiian Hymn of Creation*. Honolulu: Topgallant Publishing, 1981.

Jordan, Winthrop D. *The White Man's Burden: Historical Origins of Racism in the United States*. New York: Oxford University Press, 1974.

Ka Elele. 1845.

Ka Hae Hawaii. 1856–1861.

Ka Hoku Loa. 1859–1861.

Ka Hoku Loa o Hawaii. 1856.

Ka Hoku o ka Pakipika. 1861–1863.

Ka Leo o ka Lahui. 1889–1896.

Ka Loea Kalaiaina. 1897–1898.

Kaeppler, Adrienne L. *Hula Pahu: Hawaiian Drum Dances. Vol. 1: Haʻa and Hula Pahu: Sacred Movements*. Bishop Museum Bulletin in Anthropology no. 3. Honolulu: Bishop Museum Press, 1993.

Kahiolo, G. W. "He Moolelo no Kamapuaa." *Ka Hae Hawaii*, June 26, 1861–September 25, 1861.

——. *He Moolelo no Kamapuaa*. Trans. Esther T. Mookini and Erin C. Neizman, with David Tom. Honolulu: Hawaiian Studies Program, University of Hawaiʻi, Mānoa, 1978.

Kamakau, Samuel Mānaiakalani. "Ka Moolelo o na Kamehameha." *Nupepa Kuokoa*, December 20, 1867.

——. *Ka Poʻe Kahiko: The People of Old*. Trans. Mary Kawena Pukui. Honolulu: Bishop Museum Press, 1964.

——. *Ke Aupuni Mōʻī*. Honolulu: Kamehameha Schools Press, 2001.

——. *Ke Kumu Aupuni: Ka Moʻolelo Hawaiʻi no Kamehameha Ka Naʻi Aupuni a me Kāna Aupuni i Hoʻokumu ai*. Honolulu: Ke Kumu Lama, ʻAhahui ʻŌlelo Hawaiʻi, 1996.

——. *Ruling Chiefs of Hawaii*. Rev. ed. Honolulu: Kamehameha Schools Press, 1992.

Kameʻeleihiwa, Lilikalā. *He Moʻolelo Kaʻao o Kamapuaʻa: A Legendary Tradition of Kamapuaʻa, the Hawaiian Pig-God*. Honolulu: Bishop Museum Press, 1996.

——. *Native Land and Foreign Desires: Pehea lā e Pono ai?* Honolulu: Bishop Museum Press, 1992.

Kanahele, George S., ed. *Hawaiian Music and Musicians: An Illustrated History*. Honolulu: University of Hawaiʻi Press, 1979.

Kane, Herb Kawainui. "Forum on Robert Borofsky: Cook, Lono, Obeyesekere, and Sahlins." *Current Anthropology* 38, no. 4 (April 1997): 265.

Kānepuʻu, J. H. "Mooolelo no ka Hookumu ana o ka Hoku o ka Pakipika." *Ka Hoku o ka Pakipika*, November 14, 21, and 28, 1861.

Kapihenui, M. J. "He Mooolelo no Hiiakaikapoliopele." *Ka Hoku o ka Pakipika*, December 26, 1861 to July 17, 1862.

Kawailiʻulā, S. K. "Mooolelo no Kawelo." *Ka Hoku o ka Pakipika*, September 26 to October 10, 1861.

Ke Aloha Aina. 1895–1897.

Kealiʻinohomoku, Joann. Interview with Jennie Wilson, audiotape, 1962. Bishop Museum Archives, Honolulu.

Ke Au Okoa. 1870.

Kekoa, Edward. "E Hoomau i ke Kupaa i ke Aloha i ka Aina." *Ke Aloha Aina*, January 20, March 3, April 28, 1900.

Kelly, Anne Keala. "How Do We Move Forward?" *Honolulu Weekly*, January 8–14, 2003.

Kelly, Marion. *Loko Iʻa o Heʻeia: Heʻeia Fishpond*. Honolulu: Department of Anthropology, Bishop Museum, 1975.

Kent, Noel J. *Hawaii: Islands under the Influence*. Honolulu: University of Hawaiʻi Press, 1993.

Kimura, Larry. "Native Hawaiian Culture." In *Report on the Culture, Needs, and Concerns of Native Hawaiians*. Vol. 1. Washington, D.C.: Native Hawaiians Study Commission, 1983.

Ko Hawaii Pae Aina. 1883.

Kualapai, Lydia. "Cast in Print: The Nineteenth-Century Hawaiian Imaginary." Ph.D. diss., University of Nebraska, 2001.

Kūkahi, Joseph L. "Ke Kumulipo." *Nupepa Kuokoa*, May 16, 1902.

Kuykendall, Ralph S. *The Hawaiian Kingdom*. Vol. 1: *1778–1854, Foundation and Transformation*. Honolulu: University of Hawaiʻi Press, 1938.

——. *The Hawaiian Kingdom*. Vol. 2: *1854–1874, Twenty Critical Years*. Honolulu: University of Hawaiʻi Press, 1953.

———. *The Hawaiian Kingdom. Vol. 3: 1874–1893, The Kalakaua Dynasty*. Honolulu: University of Hawai'i Press, 1967.

Levine, Lawrence W. *Black Culture and Black Consciousness*. New York: Oxford University Press, 1977.

———. *The Unpredictable Past: Explorations in American Cultural History*. New York: Oxford University Press, 1993.

Lili'uokalani. "He Buke Mele Hawaii." Unpublished manuscript, Hawai'i State Archives, Honolulu.

———. *Hawaii's Story by Hawaii's Queen*. Honolulu: Mutual Publishing, 1990 [1897].

———. *The Kumulipo: An Hawaiian Creation Myth*. Kentfield, Calif.: Pueo Press, 1978 [1897].

———. "A Queen's Appeal." San Francisco *Examiner*, March 9, 1893.

———. *The Queen's Songbook*. Honolulu: Hui Hānai, 1999.

Loomis, Albertine. *For Whom Are the Stars? Revolution and Counterrevolution in Hawai'i, 1893–1895*. Honolulu: University of Hawai'i Press, 1976.

Lucas, Paul F. Nāhoa. "Hawaiian Language Policy and the Courts." *Hawaiian Journal of History* 34 (2000): 4.

Mabanglo, Ruth Elynia. "Metaphors of Protest: Anti-Colonial Themes in Tagalog Poetry." Paper presented at the conference "Multi-Ethnic Literatures of the United States," University of Hawai'i, Honolulu, 1997.

Makaainana. 1894–1898.

Malo, David. "On the Decrease of Population in the Hawaiian Islands." Trans. Lorrin Andrews. *Hawaiian Spectator* 11, no. 2 (April 1839): 122–24.

McClennan, Carol A. "Hawai'i Turns to Sugar: The Rise of Plantation Centers, 1860–1880." *Hawaiian Journal of History* 31 (1997): 111.

McClintock, Anne. *Imperial Leather: Race, Gender, and Sexuality in the Colonial Contest*. New York: Routledge, 1995.

McGregor-Alegado, Davianna. "Hawaiian Resistance: 1887–1889." Master's thesis, University of Hawai'i, 1979.

Memmi, Albert. *The Colonizer and the Colonized*. Boston: Beacon Press, 1991 [1965].

Merry, Sally Engle. *Colonizing Hawai'i: The Cultural Power of Law*. Princeton University Press, 2000.

Meyer, Manulani Aluli. "Native Hawaiian Epistemology: Contemporary Narratives." Ed.D. diss., Harvard University, 1998.

Mignolo, Walter D. *The Darker Side of the Renaissance: Literacy, Territoriality, and Colonization*. Ann Arbor: University of Michigan Press, 1995.

Mohanty, Chandra. "Under Western Eyes: Feminist Scholarship and Colonial Discourses." In *Third World Women and the Politics of Feminism*, ed.

Chandra Talpade Mohanty, Ann Russo, and Lourdes Torres. Bloom-
ington: Indiana University Press, 1991.
Mookini, Esther K. "The Hale Naua of David Kalakaua." Unpublished
manuscript, n.d. Hawaiian Collection, Hamilton Library, University of
Hawaiʻi, Mānoa.
——. *The Hawaiian Newspapers*. Honolulu: Topgallant Publishing, 1974.
Morris, Nancy Jane. "Ka Loea Kalaiaina, 1898: A Study of a Hawaiian Lan-
guage Newspaper as a Historical Reference Source." Master's thesis, Uni-
versity of Hawaiʻi, 1975.
——. "Rebels of 1895." In *Trial of a Queen: 1895 Military Tribunal*.
Honolulu: Judiciary History Center, 1995.
Nākoa, Sarah Keliʻilolena. *Lei Momi o ʻEwa*. Honolulu: Tongg Publishing,
1979.
Nakuina, Moses K. *Moolelo Hawaii o Pakaa a me Ku-a-Pakaa*. Honolulu:
Kalamakū Press, 1991 [1902]. Translated as *The Wind Gourd of
Laʻamaomao* by Esther T. Mookini and Sarah Nakoa. Honolulu: Ka-
lamakū Press, 1990.
Na Mele Aimoku, na Mele Kupuna, a me na Mele Pono o ka Moi Kalakaua I.
1886. Bishop Museum Archives, Honolulu.
Nandy, Ashis. *The Intimate Enemy: Loss and Recovery of Self Under Colonial-
ism*. New York: Oxford University Press, 1988.
Napoleon, Harold. *Yuuyaraq: The Way of the Human Being*. Fairbanks: Cen-
ter for Cross-Cultural Studies, College of Rural Alaska, 1991.
Ngugi Wa Thiongʻo. *Decolonising the Mind: The Politics of Language in Afri-
can Literature*. Portsmouth, N.H.: Heinemann, 1986.
Nordyke, Eleanor C., and Martha H. Noyes. "ʻKaulana Nā Puaʼ: A Voice
for Sovereignty." *Hawaiian Journal of History* 27 (1993): 27–42.
Nupepa Elele Poakolu. 1883.
Nupepa Kuoka. 1861–1862, 1895.
Obeyesekere, Gananath. *The Apotheosis of Captain Cook: European Mythmak-
ing in the Pacific*. Princeton: Princeton University Press, 1997.
Osorio, Jonathan K. Kamakawiwoʻole. "Determining Self: Identity, Nation-
hood, and Constitutional Government in Hawaiʻi, 1842–1887." Ph.D
diss., University of Hawaiʻi, 1996.
——. *Dismembering Lāhui: A History of the Hawaiian Nation to 1887*.
Honolulu: University of Hawaiʻi Press, 2002.
——. "A Hawaiian Nationalist Commentary on the Trial of the
Mōʻīwahine." In *Trial of a Queen: 1895 Military Tribunal*. Honolulu: Judi-
ciary History Center, 1996.
Pacific Commercial Advertiser. 1856–1861.
Papa Kuauhau Alii o na Alii Hawaii. *Hoike a ka Papa Kuauhau o na Alii
Hawaii*. Honolulu: Ka Papa Kuauhau Alii o na Alii Hawaii, 1884.

Papa Kuhikuhi o na Hula Poni Moi (with N. B. Emerson's handwritten nota-
tions). 1883. Paul Kahn Collection. Hawaiʻi State Archives, Honolulu.

Piercy, LaRue W. *Hawaii's Missionary Saga: Sacrifice and Godliness in Paradise.*
Honolulu: Mutual Publishing, 1992.

Pieterse, Jan Nederveen. *White on Black: Images of Africa and Blacks in Western Popular Culture.* New Haven: Yale University Press, 1992.

Poepoe, Joseph M. "He Moolelo no Kamehameha Ka Naʻi: Aupuni o
Hawaii," *Ka Naʻi Aupuni*, November 27, 1905–November 16, 1906.

——. "Ka Moolelo Hawaii Kahiko." *Ka Naʻi Aupuni*. February 1 to
November 29, 1906.

Polynesian. 1858, 1861.

Prakash, Gyan. "Writing Post-Orientalist Histories of the Third World:
Indian Historiography Is Good to Think." In *Colonialism and Culture*, ed.
Nicholas B. Dirks. Ann Arbor: University of Michigan Press, 1992.

Pukui, Mary Kawena. "Hawaiian Poetry and Music." Unpublished transcript
of lecture given at Kamehameha Schools, 1945. Hawaiian Collection,
Hamilton Library, University of Hawaiʻi, Mānoa.

Pukui, Mary Kawena, and Samuel H. Elbert. *Hawaiian Dictionary.* Rev. ed.
Honolulu: University of Hawaiʻi Press, 1986.

Pukui, Mary Kawena, E. W. Haertig, and Catherine A. Lee. *Nānā i ke Kumu
(Look to the Source).* Vol. 1. Honolulu: Queen Liliʻuokalani Children's
Center, 1972.

Ralston, Caroline. "Hawaii 1778–1854: Some Aspects of *Makaʻāinana*
Response to Rapid Cultural Change." *Journal of Pacific History* 19, no 1
(1984): 21–40.

Reed, Ishmael. "America: The Multinational Society." In *The Graywolf
Annual Five: Multi-Cultural Literacy*, ed. Rick Simonson and Scott
Walker. Saint Paul: Graywolf Press, 1988.

Reinecke, John E. *Language and Dialect in Hawaii: A Sociolinguistic History to
1935.* Honolulu: University of Hawaiʻi Press, 1969.

Republic of Hawaii, Department of Public Instruction. *Report of the Minister
of Public Instruction.* Honolulu: Hawaiian Star Printing, 1898.

Roberts, Helen H. *Ancient Hawaiian Music.* Bernice P. Bishop Museum Bulletin 29. Honolulu: Bishop Museum, 1926 Reprint, New York: Kraus
Reprint Co., 1971.

Rollins, Judith. "Invisibility, Consciousness of the Other, and *Ressentiment*
among Black Domestic Workers." In *Working in the Service Society*, ed.
Cameron Lynne MacDonald and Carmen Sirianni. Philadelphia: Temple
University Press, 1996.

Russ, William Adam, Jr. *The Hawaiian Republic (1894–98) and Its Struggle to
Win Annexation.* Selinsgrove, Pa.: Susquehanna University Press, 1992
[1961].

———. *The Hawaiian Revolution (1893–1894)*. Selinsgrove, Pa.: Susquehanna University Press, 1992 [1959].

Sahlins, Marshall. *Historical Ethnography. Vol. 1, Anahulu: The Anthropology of History in the Kingdom of Hawai'i*, edited by Patrick Kirch and Marshall Sahlins. Chicago: University of Chicago Press, 1992.

Said, Edward. *Culture and Imperialism*. New York: Vintage, 1993.

———. *Orientalism*. New York: Pantheon, 1978.

San Francisco Call. 1897.

Schütz, Albert J. *The Voices of Eden: A History of Hawaiian Language Studies*. Honolulu: University of Hawai'i Press, 1994.

Schweizer, Niklaus R. "Kahaunani: 'Snowwhite' and Other German Fairy-Tales in Hawai'i." Unpublished manuscript, 1998.

Sheldon, John G. M. (Kahikina Kelekona). *The Biography of Joseph K. Nāwahī*. Trans. Marvin Puakea Nogelmeier. Honolulu: Hawaiian Historical Society, 1988.

———. *Ka Buke Moolelo o Hon. Joseph K. Nawahi*. Honolulu: Bulletin Pub. Co., 1908.

Silva, Noenoe K. "He Kanawai e Hoopau i na Hula Kuolo Hawaii: The Political Economy of the Banning of Hula." *Hawaiian Journal of History* 34 (2000): 29–48.

———. "Kū'ē! Hawaiian Women's Resistance to the Annexation." In *Women in Hawai'i: Sites, Identities, and Voices*, ed. Joyce N. Chinen, Kathleen O. Kane, and Ida M. Yoshinaga, special issue of *Social Process in Hawai'i* 38 (1997): 2–15.

Sinclair, Marjorie. *Nāhi'ena'ena: Sacred Daughter of Hawai'i*. Honolulu: University of Hawai'i Press, 1976.

Sobrero, Gina. *An Italian Baroness in Hawaii: The Travel Diary of Gina Sobrero, Bride of Robert Wilcox, 1887*. Trans. Edgar C. Knowlton. Honolulu: Hawaiian Historical Society, 1991.

Spivak, Gayatri Chakravorty. "Can the Subaltern Speak?" In *Colonial Discourse and Post-Colonial Theory*, ed. Patrick Williams and Laura Chrisman. New York: Columbia University Press, 1994.

———, ed. *In Other Worlds: Essays in Cultural Politics*. New York: Routledge, 1988.

Stillman, Amy Ku'uleialoha. "History Reinterpreted in Song: The Case of the Hawaiian Counterrevolution." *Hawaiian Journal of History* 23 (1989): 1–30.

———. "The Hula Ku'i: A Tradition in Hawaiian Music and Dance." Master's thesis, University of Hawai'i, 1982.

———. "Of the People Who Love the Land: Vernacular History in the Poetry of Modern Hawaiian Hula." *Amerasia Journal* 28, no. 3 (2002): 85–108.

———. *Sacred Hula: The Historical Hula ʻĀlaʻapapa*. Bishop Museum Bulletin in Anthropology 8. Honolulu: Bishop Museum Press, 1998.

Tatar, Elizabeth. *Hula Pahu: Hawaiian Drum Dances. Vol. 2, The Pahu: Sounds of Power*. Bishop Museum Bulletin in Anthropology no. 3. Honolulu: Bishop Museum, 1993.

———. *Nineteenth Century Hawaiian Chant*. Pacific Anthropological Records no. 33. Honolulu: Bishop Museum, Department of Anthropology, 1982.

Tate, Merze. *The United States and the Hawaiian Kingdom: A Political History*. Westport, Conn.: Greenwood Press, 1965.

Testa, F. J. (Hoke [Jose]), ed. *Buke Mele Lahui*. Honolulu: Makaainana Publishing House, 1895.

Thrum, Thomas G. "Brief Sketch of the Life and Labors of S. M. Kamakau, Hawaiian Historian." In *Twenty-Sixth Annual Report of the Hawaiian Historical Society*. Honolulu: Paradise of the Pacific Press, 1918.

Thurston, Lorrin A. "The American League: Minister Thurston's Speech Friday Night." *Hawaiian Star*, June 15, 1894.

———. *A Hand-Book on the Annexation of Hawaii*. St. Joseph, Mich.: A. B. Morse, n.d.

———. *Memoirs of the Hawaiian Revolution*. Honolulu: Advertising Publishing, 1936.

Tillman, Benjamin R. "The Race Question." *Van Norden's Magazine* (April 1907): 19–28.

Trask, Haunani-Kay. *From a Native Daughter: Colonialism and Sovereignty in Hawaiʻi*. Monroe, Maine: Common Courage Press, 1993.

U.S. Congress. Senate. Committee on Foreign Relations. File 55A-J11.2 RG 46. National Archives, Washington, D.C., 1897.

U.S. Congress. Senate. *Senate Report 681*. 55th Cong., 2nd sess., 1898.

Valeri, Valerio. *Kingship and Sacrifice: Ritual and Society in Ancient Hawaii*. Chicago: University of Chicago Press, 1985.

Van Dyke, Jon M. "The Trial of Liliʻuokalani." In *Trial of a Queen: 1895 Military Tribunal*. Honolulu: Judiciary History Center, 1995.

Weber, Max. *The Protestant Ethic and the Spirit of Capitalism*. Trans. Talcott Parsons. New York: Scribner, 1958.

Williams, William Appleman. *Empire as a Way of Life*. New York: Oxford University Press, 1980.

Index

Advertiser, Pacific Commercial, 55, 56, 109, 181, 182

African Americans, 54, 66, 136, 176

Africans, 54, 66, 176

ʻAhahui Hoʻopuka Nūpepa Kūikawā o Honolulu, 63–64, 68, 71, 109. See also *Hoku o ka Pakipika*

ʻAi kapu, 27–28; ending of, 29–32

Akua, 78; aloha ʻāina and, 140–41; Cook and, 23; importance of ability to rule, 75, 119–20; Kamehameha and, 24, 28; loss of mana of, 29–30; relationship to kanaka, 41; as voyagers, 19; worship of, 9, 58–59, 62

Albert, Ka Haku o Hawaiʻi (Prince of Hawaiʻi), 48

Alexander, W. D., 39

Alexander, William P., 50, 51, 70

Alexander Liholiho (Kamehameha IV), 46–48, 60, 88, 91, 122

Aliʻi, 107; attaining ʻai moku status, 73, 75, 93; ʻauhau (tribute) and, 40; bones of, 95–96; blamed for depopulation, 24–27; featherwork and, 177; lack of, 18; land tenure and, 40–43; leadership of hui, 162; and makaʻāinana, 18, 39–42, 104, 156; mele (songs) for, 118–20, 182–85; monarchy and, 10; palapala (literacy) and, 32–33; pono and, 26, 40–43, 120; resistance to American ways, 47; system, 98; wars between, 18, 25, 26, 121; adoption of Western ways, 16, 37. See also Genealogy; Hōʻailona

Aliʻi wahine: domestication of, 54–55, 60–61; genealogy and, 93, 102–3; in government, 38, 43–44, 94, 162; Hale Nauā and, 104–5; as long-distance voyagers, 19, 21. See also Women

Aloha ʻāina, 11, 101–2, 130, 139–42, 147, 155, 161, 189–91. See also Nationalism

Aloha ʻĀina (newspaper), 139, 142, 143, 148, 155, 195–97

American Board of Commissioners for Foreign Missions, 31, 48, 57, 70, 90, 115

Anderson, Benedict, 49, 88

Andrews, Lorrin, 25, 33

Anglican Church, 48, 88

Annexation treaty, 130, 136, 146–47, 160, 169; Lili'uokalani's protest of, 172–73; memorial of protest against, 151–54. *See also* Hui Aloha 'Āina; Hui Kālai'āina; Petitions, antiannexation

Armstrong, Richard, 47, 50, 56, 59, 82, 84, 85

'Auhau, 40, 42

Auld, William, 109–10, 112, 158–59

Bailey, Edward, 50, 72

Baker, Lee D., 53, 54

Bana Lāhui Hawai'i. *See* Royal Hawaiian Band

Basham, J. J. Leilani, 164, 186, 187

Bayonet Constitution. *See* Constitution; Kalākaua, King

Beckwith, Martha, 93, 101, 102, 103

Bertelmann, Henry, 138–39

Bingham, Hiram, 30, 31, 34

Bishop, Sereno E., 166, 173, 176

Blount, James, 124, 130–32, 134, 169–70

Board of Commissioners to Quiet Land Titles, 41

Board of Genealogy of Hawaiian Chiefs. *See* Genealogy

Boki, 34

Bush, John Ailuene (Edwin), 127, 132, 138, 155, 186, 193

Calvinism, 16–17, 51–54, 62

Campbell, Abigail Kuaihelani Maipinepine, 130, 133, 161, 194; antian-

nexation petition and, 148, 150, 197; as leader of nation, 144, 158

Castle, William R., 109–10

Certeau, Michel de, 5, 6, 9, 10, 84

Chakrabarty, Dipesh, 20

Chapin, Helen Geracimos, 55, 56, 80, 84, 125

Charleton, Richard, 36

Charlot, John, 78, 94, 97

Chatterjee, Partha, 7, 105

Christianity, conversion to, 26, 31–33, 44. *See also* Calvinism; Colonialism; Missionaries

Civil War (United States), 47

Cleveland, Grover, 130, 134, 136, 138, 169, 170–72

Colonialism, 2–3, 4–6, 121; capitalism and, 49–51; genealogy and, 104; as moral issue, 154; resistance to, 6–11, 125, 163. *See also* Sugar

Constitution: adoption of, 36–38; Bayonet, 122–29, 152, 168; of Lili'uokalani, 166, 167, 170, 178; resistance to first, 38; of Republic, 136–37, 166. *See also* Kalākaua, King

Cook, Captain James, 16–23, 99

Cornwall School, 31

Countercoup (1895), attempted, 138–139; Lili'uokalani and, 180

Daily Bulletin, 114, 115

Daws, Gavan, 1, 165–67

Death, mass, 3, 24–27, 58, 93, 101, 110, 142, 165; discursive use of, 69; relationship to Māhele, 29–30, 39, 41–43

Depopulation. *See* Death, mass

Discourses: of civilization, 53–54, 59, 73, 90, 100–101, 105, 115; of work, 51–53, 72

Dole, Sanford B., 136, 165–66, 167, 170

Emerson, John S., 58–59, 63
Emerson, Joseph, 63
Emerson, Nathaniel B., 47, 76, 110, 184
Emma, Queen, 1, 48, 88, 111–12; death of, 122; election campaign of, 90–92
Epidemics. *See* Death, mass

Fornander, Abraham, 56, 71–72, 97
Foucault, Michel, 5, 6, 50
Fuchs, Lawrence, 165–67
Fuller, J., 56, 59

Genealogy, 93–95, 104; battle between Emma and Kalākaua, 111–12; Board of, 94–97; *Kumulipo* and, 95, 97
Genocide. *See* Death, mass
Gibson, Walter Murray, 89, 109, 111, 114–15, 117
Greive, Robert, 109

Haʻalilio, Timoteo, 36–37
Hae Hawaii, 35, 56, 59–63, 66, 73, 81, 82, 84
Hale ʻAha ʻŌlelo Aliʻi. *See* House of Nobles
Hale Nauā, 87, 98, 102, 103, 104–7
Hāloa, 101–2, 111
Haole, 12, 23–24; ascension to power of, 45–46; desire for control and, 67–72; first arrival of, contested, 18–20; protest of appointment of, 38–39; support of *Ka Hoku o ka Pakipika*, 71–72. *See also* Colonialism
Haumea, 41, 102–3. *See also* Papahānaumoku
Hawaiian Evangelical Association, 52, 57, 80, 82

Hawaiian language , 2–5, 7, 10, 12–13, 155–56, 163; loss of, 144–45; missionary opposition to, 64–71; poetics, 65–67, 183–86, 190–91; power of, 169, 186; schools, 46, 144–45; as threat to colonialism, 84–85; writing of, 32–33. *See also* Kaona; Newspapers, Hawaiian-language; Translation issues
Hawaiian people, terms for, 12–13
Heleluhe, Joseph, 159, 173, 179, 198; imprisoned, 191; letters to *Ka Makaainana*, 192, 196; travel with Liliʻuokalani, 193
Hereniko, Vilsoni, 5, 13
Hiʻiakaikapoliopele, 76–79, 111, 155
Hilo Boarding School, 139
Historians, Kanaka Maoli. *See* Basham, J. J. Leilani; Kameʻeleihiwa, Lilikalā; McGregor-Alegado, Davianna; Osorio, Jonathan Kay Kamakawiwoʻole; Stillman, Amy Kuʻuleialoha
Historiography, 1–3, 125, 155, 163; colonial, 5, 9–10; Cook and, 16–23; Hale Nauā and, 107; Kamakau and, 20–21; women in, 7–8
Hōʻailona (cosmic signs), 185–86, 193
Hoar, George, 158–59
Hoku Loa, 55–59
Hoku Loa o Hawaii, 55
Hoku o ka Pakipika, 10, 55, 56, 64–79, 82–86
Homosexuality, 61, 67, 76–77
Hoʻohōkūkalani, 11, 27–28, 101
Hopu, Thomas, 30–31
House of Nobles, 38, 47, 94, 122, 126, 127; women in, 44, 162
House of Representatives, 47

Hui Aloha'Āina, 124, 137; convention, 143–44, 194; establishment of, 130; Kalaupapa branch of, 148; men's branch, 131; protest of Newlands resolution, 160–61; role in antiannexation petitions, 146, 150–51, 157–59, 161–62, 197–99; women's branch, 132–34, 136, 139, 143, 146, 192–99

Hui Kālai'āina, 124, 127, 128, 146, 161; antiannexation petitions and, 151, 157–59, 195, 198–99; convention, 143–44, 194

Hula, 7, 76–77; Kalākaua and, 89, 90, 108–10, 113, 116–19

'Ī'ī, John Papa, 39

Independence Day. See Lā Kū'oko'a

'Iolani Palace, 108; Lili'uokalani imprisoned at, 139, 180, 182

Ka'ahumanu, 29–30, 32, 33–35, 38, 61

Kaeppler, Adrienne, 91, 119

Ka Hae Hawaii. See Hae Hawaii

Kahiki, 18, 19, 20

Ka Hoku o ka Pakipika. See Hoku o ka Pakipika

Kahuna, 25, 28, 30, 95

Ka'iulani, 165, 185–86, 200, 202

Kaiwi, J. W., 65

Kalākaua, King, 1, 10, 56, 88–93, 97, 98, 103, 106, 120, 126; Bayonet Constitution and, 122, 125–28; funeral of, 186; jubilee of, 112–20; mele for, 118–20, 184; mo'olelo and, 121; pono mō'ī (coronation) of, 108–12; racism and, 173, 176. See also Hula

Ka Lama Hawaii. See Lama Hawaii

Kalaniana'ole, Jonah Kūhiō, 139, 189–90

Kalani'ōpu'u, 18, 21, 28, 121

Kalauokalani, David: antiannexation petitions and, 157–59, 192, 197–99; election as president of Hui Kālai'āina, 144; Emma Nāwahī and, 195; memorial against annexation and, 151; protest of Newlands Resolution and, 161; speech against annexation, 147

Kalaupapa, 148–50, 157

Ka Leo o ka Lahui. See Leo o ka Lahui

Kaliuwa'a, 58, 63

Kalo, 26, 50–51, 62, 101–2, 103

Ka Makaainana. See Makaainana

Kamakau, Samuel Mānaiakalani, 26, 29, 183; mo'olelo of Cook and, 16–23. See also Historiography

Kamāmalu, 38

Kamapua'a, 63, 101

Kame'eleihiwa, Lilikalā: on 'ai kapu, 29–30; on ali'i pono 120; on genealogy, 93, 98; on kaona, 184; on land tenure, 39–40, 43

Kāmeha'ikana, 102

Kamehameha I, 17–18, 24, 28, 29, 91, 103, 117, 121

Kamehameha II, 28–29, 33–34

Kamehameha III, 28, 33–34, 35; Kaomi and, 61; legacy of, 43–44; loss and recovery of sovereignty and, 36–37

Kamehamela IV, 46–48, 60, 88, 91, 122

Kamehameha V, 46, 88–89, 122

Kānepu'u, J. H., 114, 184; and 'Ahahui Ho'opuka Nūpepa Kūikawā o Honolulu, 63–64; defense of hula program, 109; and desire for chants, 76; Hoku o ka Pakipika and, 67–68; and petitions for Hawaiian-language paper, 55

Ka Nonanona. See *Nonanona*
Kaomi, 61–62
Kaona, 5, 8, 66, 183, 184, 186
Kapihenui, M. J., 76, 79
Kapiʻolani (wahine of Kalākaua), 94,
    104, 108, 177
Kapiʻolani (wahine of Kamehameha),
    32
Kaua kūloko. *See* Countercoup
    (1895), attempted
Kaulana Nā Pua. *See* Mele ʻAi Pōhaku
Kaulia, James Keauiluna, 128, 132,
    191, 200; antiannexation petitions
    and, 157–59, 192, 195, 197–99;
    election as president of Hui Aloha
    ʻĀina, 144, 194; *Ke Aloha Aina* and,
    196; memorial protesting annexa-
    tion treaty and, 151; protest of
    Newlands Resolution, 161; speech
    against annexation, 146–47
Kaʻulu, 18
Kaumakapili Church, 134, 157
Kaumualiʻi, 24, 31
Kauwahi, J. W. H., 56, 71
Kawaiahaʻo Church, 55, 148, 155
Kawainui, Joseph U., 111, 116–17
Kawananakoa, David, 169, 200
Kawelo, 73–75, 95, 103, 114, 119–20
Ke Aliʻi ʻAi Moku. *See* Liliʻuokalani
Keaweaheulu, 91, 114
Keʻelikōlani, 38, 122
Kekauluohi, 35, 38
Kekuaokalani, 28–29
Ke Kumu Hawaii. See Kumu Hawaii
Kelekona, Kahikina, 124, 193
Keoni Ana, 38, 39
Keōpūolani, 28, 32
Kīnaʻu, 35, 38
Kinney, William, 146, 188–89
Kiwalaʻō, 28, 121
Ko Hawaii Pae Aina, 111–12, 116

Konohiki, 40–42
Kūaliʻi, 20
Kuamoʻo, 29
Kuhina nui (regent, premier), 28–29,
    32, 35, 38
Kūhiō. *See* Kalanianaʻole, Jonah
    Kūhiō
Kūkāʻilimoku, 28–30, 121
Kumu Hawaii, 34–35
Kumulipo, 10, 89, 92, 93, 95, 97–104,
    157, 184
Kuykendall, Ralph, 1, 23, 48, 124

Laʻamaomao, 96
Lāʻau lapaʻau, 25, 58, 61, 78–79
Lahainaluna, 16, 27, 34, 139
Lā Hoʻihoʻi Ea, 36–37
Laʻilaʻi, 87, 102–3
Lā Kūʻokoʻa, 37, 113, 117, 143, 158
Lama Hawaii, 34, 40
Land: māhele, 41–43; rights of ten-
    ants preserved, 42–43; sale of, to
    foreigners, 39, 42–43; traditional,
    tenure, 39–41. See also *Aloha ʻĀina*
Language. *See* Hawaiian language
LaPlace, Cyrille, 35
Leo o ka Lahui, 100, 133, 155, 178
Levine, Lawrence, 5–6
Liholiho, 28–29, 33–34
Liliha, 34, 38
Liliʻuokalani, 11, 98, 99, 201–3; anti-
    annexation petitions and, 192, 197–
    99; arrest and imprisonment of,
    180–82, 187–89, 194; formal pro-
    tests of, 167–73; *Hawaii's Story by
    Hawaii's Queen*, 178–79; called Ke
    Aliʻi ʻAi Moku, 155, 164; mele
    (songs) of, 182–91; overthrow of,
    130; racist representations of, 173–
    80; as represented in history, 165–
    67; takes office, 129; trial of, 180–81

Literacy, 13, 30, 32–35, 44, 55
Lonoikamakahiki, 19, 97, 98, 103
Lota Kapuāiwa, 46, 88–89, 122

Māhele. See Land
Mahelona, Laura, 151
Maine (U.S. ship), 160
Makaʻāinana, 1, 9, 11, 18, 33, 39–43,
    85, 107, 162; petitions of, 38–39
Makaainana, 182, 187, 190, 192, 193,
    196
Malo, Davida, 25, 95, 103, 140
Masonic societies, 104–5, 109
Māui (akua), 103, 114
McClintock, Anne, 7, 104, 105
McGregor-Alegado, Davianna, 123,
    127, 128
McKinley, William, 145–46, 157, 172,
    194, 197
Medicine. See Lāʻau lapaʻau
Mele: in antiannexation struggle, 135;
    epistemology and, 18–21, 97;
    importance of composers of, 182–
    86; for Kalākaua, 118–20, 184; of
    Liliʻuokalani, 182–91, 201–2, 207–
    8; national identity and, 85, 88, 95,
    111, 118–20; for Pele, 78, 111;
    struggles over, 64–66, 82, 108–11;
    women and, 79, 83
Mele ʻAi Pōhaku, 135, 190
Metcalf, Simon, 23
Michelson, Miriam, 150
Military, U.S., 122, 126, 128;
    Liliʻuokalani's imprisonment and,
    194; role in annexation, 160, 161,
    166; role in 1893 coup, 167–68,
    170, 173
Mills, G. W. (Mila), 63, 68, 71
Missionaries: arrival, 30–32; attempts
    to silence Kanaka Maoli, 66, 68–71,
    72–73; discourses of work and civi-

lization and, 51–54; newspapers
    and, 54–63; palapala (literacy) and,
    32–35; racism and, 53–54; resis-
    tance to, 32–34, 61–62, 66, 73, 83–
    85, 107; role in plantation capital-
    ism, 49–51. See also Christianity,
    conversion to; Colonialism
Mookini, Esther, 104, 105, 106
Moʻolelo: epistemology and, 96–97,
    103; in Kalākaua's jubilee, 113–16,
    120; kaona in, 184; in print, 10, 35,
    62–63, 73–79, 81; resistance to dis-
    course of savagery, 89, 107; strug-
    gle over, 58–59, 63; of voyages,
    19; women and, 83–84. See also
    Kawelo; Hiʻiakaikapoliopele
Morgan, John T., 147, 148, 151, 155,
    159

Nāhiʻenaʻena, 34
Nationalism, 7, 9, 11, 90; genealogy
    and, 103–4; Kalākaua's coronation
    and, 108; newspapers and, 13, 55,
    84–85, 88; songs and, 182. See also
    Aloha ʻĀina
Nāwahī, Emma ʻAʻima, 133, 142, 143,
    157; antiannexation petitions and,
    148, 150; Ke Aloha Aina and, 139,
    144, 155, 195–96; letters to
    Liliʻuokalani, 192–99
Nāwahī, Joseph K., 90, 128; arrest of,
    138; biography of, 124; death of,
    142; Hui Aloha ʻĀina and, 130,
    132, 133; Ke Aloha Aina and, 139–
    41; Liliʻuokalani and, 142–43; re-
    sistance to Republic, 137–42, 144
Neilson, Henry A., 48
Neutrality (of Hawaiian state), 47
Newlands Resolution, 160–61
Newspapers, Hawaiian-language:
    colonizing role of, 54–63, 81–83;

genealogical battle in, 111–12; impact on historiography, 1–2; language loss and, 145; Liliʻuokalani and, 182, 187–91, 195–96, 201; nationalism and, 13, 55, 84–85, 88; political mele in, 182; resistance to annexation and, 165, 181–82, 186, 187–91, 196, 201; resistance to colonialism and, 9, 54–55, 63–79, 83–85; table of, 56. *See also* ʻAhahui Hoʻopuka Nūpepa Kūikawā o Honolulu; *Aloha ʻĀina; Hae Hawaii; Hoku o ka Pakipika; Hoku Loa; Kumu Hawaii; Lama Hawaii; Leo o ka Lahui; Makaainana; Nonanona; Nupepa Elele Poakolu, Nupepa Kuokoa*

Nonanona, 35

Nowlein, Samuel, 138

Nupepa Elele Poakolu, 111–12

Nupepa Kuokoa, 62, 80–82, 114, 116–18, 181–82, 205

Obeyesekere, Gananath, 16–17

Olowalu massacre, 23

ʻŌpūkahaʻia, 30–31

Osorio, Jonathan Kay Kamakawiwoʻole, 41, 42, 90, 92, 126, 139, 168, 180

Pacific Commercial Advertiser. See Advertiser, Pacific Commercial

Pahikaua, 34

Pākī, 34

Papahānaumoku (Papa), 11, 28, 93, 101–3, 141

Papa Kūʻauhau Aliʻi o Nā Aliʻi Hawaiʻi. *See* Genealogy

Parker, Henry, 55–56

Parker, Robert Waipā, 194

Paulet, George, 36–37, 169

Pele, 19, 62, 76–79, 84, 95, 111, 155

Petitions, antiannexation, 3, 4, 124, 145–59, 163, 192, 195, 197–99; to Blount, 132; of makaʻāinana to Kamehameha III, 38–39; to overturn Bayonet Constitution, 128–29

Pettigrew, Richard, 158, 159

Philippines, 160, 175, 178, 200

Pilipo, G. W., 90, 109

Plantation economy. *See* Sugar

Poepoe, Joseph Mokuohai, 41, 98

Poetry. *See* Mele

Polynesian, 35, 71

Poni Mōʻī. *See* Kalākaua, King

Pono: aliʻi and, 25–26, 28, 29, 43, 48, 120; idea of, in government, 37–39, 101; in *Kumulipo*, 100; meanings of, 12, 16, 93; transformation of 33, 40

Poʻomaikelani, 94, 104

Provisional government, 130, 136, 137, 152, 167–70; Cleveland's denouncing of, 134

Pukui, Mary Kawena, 17, 100, 119, 186

Puni Maʻemaʻe and Puni Nūpepa, 64–66

Queen Liliʻuokalani. *See* Liliʻuokalani

Quilts, flag, 134

Racism, 11; in Bayonet Constitution, 126; discourse of civilization and, 53–54; in government newspaper, 60, 73; in government survey, 49–50; interpretation of resistance as, 90; against Liliʻuokalani, 173–79; public discussion of American, 148

Reciprocity treaty, 47, 89, 90, 125–26, 128

Republic of Hawaiʻi: establishment of, 136–38; resistance to, 136–45, 170–71

Restoration Day. *See* Lā Hoʻihoʻi Ea

Richards, William, 34, 36, 37
Richardson, John, 157, 158, 159
Royal Hawaiian Band, 134–35, 200
Russ, William Adam, 124, 163, 165–67

Sacred Falls. *See* Kaliuwa'a
Sai, David Keanu, 4, 42
Said, Edward, 2, 5, 15
Sandalwood, 26
Schools, 3; English-language, 44, 85,
 121, 163; Hawaiian-language, 55,
 144–45; mission, 32–35; select and
 common, 46, 52, 144–45
Sheldon, J. G. M. *See* Kelekona,
 Kahikina
Simpson, George, 36
Songs. *See* Mele
Sovereignty: genealogy and, 112;
 quest for, 4, 135; recognition of, 16,
 37, 43; threats to, 35–36, 47, 84,
 89–90, 169
Spanish-American War, 160
Spivak, Gayatri Chakravorty, 7–8
Stevens, John L., 130, 134, 166, 167,
 168, 170, 171
Stillman, Amy Ku'uleialoha, 1, 108, 182
Stories, European, 81
Stories, Hawaiian. *See* Mo'olelo
Sugar: duty-free sale of, 47, 125; plan-
 tations, 48–50, 53. *See also* Colo-
 nialism; Reciprocity treaty
Survey of population, 49

Taro. *See* Kalo
Tatar, Elizabeth, 90, 186
Tax, 26
Testa, F. J., 151, 182, 191, 192, 196
Thiong'o, Ngugi wa, 2, 125
Thomas, Richard, 36
Thrum, Thomas, 16, 17, 111, 114,
 116–17, 184; attempt to shut down
 Ke Aloha Aina and, 197

Thurston, Lorrin, 90, 145, 154, 165,
 166, 171, 188
Translation issues, 11, 12, 59, 67, 161,
 185; Kamakau and, 17–23; of
 pono, 16, 30, 33, 37
Trask, Haunani-Kay, 1, 2
Treaties. *See* Annexation treaty; Reciprocity treaty

'Umi, 28, 29, 81, 103
United States. *See* Military, U.S.

Valeri, Valerio, 97, 120
Vancouver, 23–24
Victoria, Queen, 36, 179
Victoria Kamāmalu Ka'ahumanu. *See*
 Kamāmalu
Voyagers (long-distance), 18–20, 107

Wākea, 11, 28, 93, 101, 103, 141
Wars. *See* Ali'i
Weber, Max, 51–53
Whitney, Henry, 55, 56, 67–70, 80–
 83, 111
Wilcox, Robert W. Kalanihiapo, 127–
 28, 139
Willis, Albert, 138, 167, 170–71
Wilson, Charles B., 194
Wilson, Jennie, 90
Women: "civilizing" of, 60–61; dis-
 empowerment of, 54; in mo'olelo,
 75–79, 83–84; and petitions to
 Blount, 132; and petitions for con-
 stitution, 129; protest of Republic,
 136; publication of mele, 79, 184.
 See also Ali'i wahine; Hui Aloha
 'Āina: women's branch
Writing system. *See* Hawaiian
 language
Wyllie, Robert, 49

Young, John Jr. *See* Keoni Ana

NOENOE K. SILVA

is an Assistant Professor of Political Science
and Hawaiian Language at the University
of Hawai'i at Mānoa.

Library of Congress Cataloging-in-Publication Data
Silva, Noenoe K.
Aloha betrayed : native Hawaiian resistance to American colonialism /
Noenoe K. Silva.
p. cm. — (American encounters/global interactions)
Includes bibliographical references and index.
ISBN 0-8223-3350-3 (cloth : alk. paper)
ISBN 0-8223-3349-X (pbk. : alk. paper)
1. Hawaiians — Colonization. 2. Hawaiians — Government relations.
3. Hawaiians — Politics and government. 4. Imperialism — History.
5. Hawaii — Annexation to the United States. 6. Hawaii — History —
Overthrow of the Monarchy, 1893. 7. Hawaii — Foreign relations —
United States. 8. United States — Foreign relations — Hawaii. 9. Hawaii —
Historiography. 10. Hawaii — History — Sources. I. Title. II. Series.
DU625.S49 2004
996.9'02 — dc22